The Essential Guide to Buddhism

THE ESSENTIAL GUIDES TO RELIGION

This series introduces students to world religions in various contexts, from their origins and scriptures, through to contemporary issues such as religion and sexuality, economics, and politics. Experts in the field explore religious traditions such as Christianity, Buddhism, and Islam. Each book comes illustrated throughout and includes suggestions for further reading. Students benefit from a glossary of key terms and concepts to guide learning about the world religions.

Also available:

The Essential Guide to Christianity, edited by Dyron B. Daughrity

The chapters in this book were first published in the digital collection *Bloomsbury Religion in North America*. Covering North America's diverse religious traditions, this digital collection provides reliable and peer-reviewed chapters and eBooks for students and instructors of religious studies, anthropology of religion, sociology of religion, and history. Learn more and get access for your library at www.theologyandreligiononline.com/bloomsbury-religion-in-north-america

BLOOMSBURY
RELIGION IN
NORTH AMERICA

The Essential Guide to Buddhism

EDITED BY GWENDOLYN GILLSON

BLOOMSBURY ACADEMIC
LONDON • NEW YORK • OXFORD • NEW DELHI • SYDNEY

BLOOMSBURY ACADEMIC
Bloomsbury Publishing Plc
50 Bedford Square, London, WC1B 3DP, UK
1385 Broadway, New York, NY 10018, USA
29 Earlsfort Terrace, Dublin 2, Ireland

BLOOMSBURY, BLOOMSBURY ACADEMIC and the Diana logo are
trademarks of Bloomsbury Publishing Plc

First published online 2021
This print edition published 2024

A catalogue record for this book is available from the British Library.

Library of Congress Cataloging-in-Publication Data
Names: Gillson, Gwendolyn, editor.
Title: The essential guide to Buddhism / edited by Gwendolyn Gillson.
Description: 1. | New York : Bloomsbury Academic, 2024. | Series: The essential guides
to religion ; vol. 1 | Includes bibliographical references and index.
Identifiers: LCCN 2023057172 | ISBN 9781350385030 (paperback) |
ISBN 9781350385023 (hardback)
Subjects: LCSH: Buddhism.
Classification: LCC BQ4012 .E875 2024 | DDC 294.3–dc23/eng/20240104
LC record available at https://lccn.loc.gov/2023057172

ISBN: HB: 978-1-3503-8502-3
PB: 978-1-3503-8503-0

Series: The Essential Guides to Religion

Typeset by Integra Software Services Pvt. Ltd.
Printed and bound in Great Britain

To find out more about our authors and books visit www.bloomsbury.com
and sign up for our newsletters.

Contents

Illustrations

List of Contributors

A.W. Barber, Director of East Asian Studies at the University of Calgary, is an internationally recognized Buddhist scholar, the Editor-in-Chief of *The Tibetan Tripitaka: Taipei Edition* (72 vols), author of two monographs, thirty-five articles, forty-six professional papers, and consultant for three documentaries.

Courtney Bruntz earned her PhD in Buddhist Studies from the Graduate Theological Union in 2014 and is currently Associate Dean of Arts and Sciences at Southeast Community College in Lincoln, NE. Her research focuses on the intersections of Religion and Economics in Contemporary Chinese Buddhism. Recent publications include *Buddhist Tourism in Asia, Buddhist Technoscapes: Interrogating "Skillful Means" in East Asian Monasteries*, and *Buddhism, Consumerism, and the Chinese Millennial.* Her forthcoming work is the *Oxford Handbook of Lived Buddhism.*

Jim Deitrick is Professor of Comparative Philosophy and Religion at the University of Central Arkansas. He holds a PhD in Religion and Social Ethics from the University of Southern California.

David M. DiValerio is Associate Professor of Religious Studies and History at the University of Wisconsin-Milwaukee. His research focuses on the contemplative and ascetic traditions of Tibetan Buddhism.

Gwendolyn Gillson is Associate Professor of Asian Studies at Illinois College. She researches at the intersection of anthropology of religion, Buddhist studies, and gender studies with a focus on contemporary Japanese women's Buddhism.

Ronald S. Green is Professor of Asian Religions, Department Chair, and Director of Asian Studies at Coastal Carolina University. He is a textual scholar specializing in the history of Japanese religions.

Matthew Hayes is the Librarian for Japanese Studies and Asian American Studies at Duke University. He is an active researcher in Japanese Buddhism and is currently focused on lay-oriented ritual practices in the Shingon school during the Meiji era (1868–1912).

Gurmeet Kaur holds a PhD from Panjab University, specializing in exploring the socio-economic dynamics of Tibetan women. Her research sheds light on the hurdles faced by women, providing valuable insights into the societal structures of the exile community. Committed to gender studies, Dr. Kaur's work significantly enriches discussions on women's empowerment in Buddhist and Tibetan Studies.

Napakadol Kittisenee is a historian and anthropologist of Theravāda Buddhism of Mainland Southeast Asia and its diasporas. He is a PhD candidate in history at the University of Wisconsin-Madison, currently working on the history of magical monks at the borderlands of Cambodia, Thailand, and Laos.

Alyson Prude is an Associate Professor in the Department of Philosophy and Religious Studies at Georgia Southern University. Her research focuses on issues of power and gender in Himalayan Buddhism, especially as they relate to the Tibetan delog (return from death) tradition.

1

Introduction to Buddhism

Gwendolyn Gillson

Buddhism is a religion that arose out of northern India more than two millennia ago. As it has grown and spread around the world, it has become extremely diverse, drawing on traditional ideas but adapting and transforming them for new times, places, and peoples. Sometimes, the sheer variety of religious practices and ideas that are considered Buddhist can be overwhelming and may not seem to have much in common. Nevertheless, their identification as Buddhists and their concern with *buddha*(s) draws them together.

Today, Buddhism is the fourth largest religion in the world, after Christianity, Islam, and Hinduism. The exact number of followers is difficult to calculate but the Pew Research Center (2017: 8–10) estimates that there were about 500 million Buddhists, or about 7 percent of the global population, in 2015, although they predict that number to fall to 426 million by 2060 due to low birth rates in some of the most-populous Buddhist countries. Buddhism is strongest in Sri Lanka, Thailand, Cambodia, and Myanmar, as well as China, Tibet, Japan, and both Koreas. In addition, there are thriving communities of Buddhists in India and Western countries even though they make up a small percentage of the religious population.

The images that come to the West of Buddhism are often quite jumbled because of Buddhism's inherent diversity. Many are familiar with the Dalai Lama as an international Buddhist figure who promotes peace and mindful living. Others are acquainted with the idea of Zen meditation or the concept of karma. At the same time, Buddhism also appears in the news in ways that do not always square with the common perception of it such as the persecution of Rohingya Muslims at the hands of Buddhists in Myanmar ("Myanmar Rohingya: What You Need to Know about the Crisis" 2018). The goal of this overview will be to help sort through what is known as "Buddhism," outlining its emergence, development, and flowering into the religion existing today.

The Historical Buddha

Buddhism was founded in what is now northern India and Nepal between the sixth and fourth century BCE by a man who left traditional family life for spiritual teaching to a group of followers. This is all that scholars know with certainty about the historical Buddha. (His name was not "Buddha" but rather the term **buddha** is a title meaning "awakened one" or one who has achieved enlightenment.) However, this rather bare-bones biography of the historical Buddha, also known as Gautama Buddha, does not do justice to the rich variety of traditions associated with his life.

Tradition asserts that Gautama Buddha was born in 560 BCE as Siddhartha Gautama. Queen Māyā, his mother, had a dream where the buddha-to-be, in the form of a six-tusked white elephant, pierced her right side and entered her womb. After ten lunar months, she sets out because it was the custom at the time for an expectant mother to give birth in the houses of their father. She stops at Lumbini Grove for a brief break, places her hand upon a tree branch, and Siddhartha comes as a fully formed child out of her right side (see Figure 1.1). He then takes seven steps upon which bloom seven lotus blossoms, points one finger to earth and one to heaven and declares:

> I am chief of the world,
> Eldest am I in the world,
> Foremost am I in the world.
> This is the last birth.
> There is now no more coming to be.
>
> (BuddhaNet 2008)

He, his mother, and their retinue return to Kapilavastu near Nepal to his father King Śuddhodana of the Śākya clan. Māyā dies seven days after giving birth, and Siddhartha is then raised by his mother's sister Mahāprajāpatī, who is also married to—or subsequently marries, depending on the source—King Śuddhodana.

Shortly after the birth, an ascetic named Asita who lived near the kingdom went to visit the king. Upon seeing the child, Asita proclaimed Siddhartha would either become a great wheel-turning king (*cakravartin*) or a great religious leader (buddha). The king, who preferred that his son take up the crown, limited his son's access to the outside world and showed him all the pleasures of palace life. The prince grew up in the luxury of the palace and never appeared interested in the outside world. He got married and had a son.

At the age of twenty-nine he decides that he should see his kingdom. Thus, the king designates days where the prince can go out into Kapilavastu and orders that all people not in the prime of health or happiness be removed from the city. The appointed days arrive, and prince Siddhartha rides out in a chariot. All goes well until he sees an old man who has remained in the city. Because of his sheltered life, Siddhartha has never seen an elderly person before. He asks his chariot-driver Chandaka about it who

FIGURE 1.1 *Tenth-century Indian statue of Queen Māyā giving birth to Siddhartha Gautama.* Source: *Cleveland Museum of Art, John L. Severance Fund.*

responds that it is what happens to all people. Troubled, Siddhartha returns to the palace. He then sets out to the city three more times: seeing a diseased person, then a dead person, and on his final outing, he sees a religious ascetic, someone who had left regular life to pursue liberation and study religious truth. The prince then realizes that this is the path he must take to understand the suffering and dissatisfaction inherent in life. These experiences are known as the Four Sights and set Siddhartha on his path to becoming the Buddha. He leaves his wife and newborn son to search for truth.

For the next six years, his life is a series of attempts at understanding truth. First, he studies with two very famous and well-respected ascetics: Ārāḍa Kālāma and Udraka Rāmaputra. They specialize in meditational techniques that Siddhartha masters but does not think will ultimately lead to enlightenment. He leaves them and then joins a group of five ascetics who specialize in fasting and diet restriction; it is said that he was so accomplished at this that it was possible to see his spine through his stomach (see Figure 1.2). But he understands this also will not bring him closer to the realization of truth and decides to sit under a tree to rest. A woman named Sujātā gives him a bowl of rice porridge that invigorates him but disgusts his five companions to the point that they depart. Siddhartha remains under the tree and decides to contemplate truth.

Under this tree, known as the "Bodhi tree" or tree of awakening/enlightenment, Siddhartha becomes Gautama Buddha at the age of thirty-five (see Figure 1.3). Afraid that this would happen, the demon Māra tries to tempt him with beautiful women but Siddhartha is not swayed. Over three watches of the night, he understands first his own past lives, then the past lives of all others, and finally comes to insight in the causal conditions of existence. This is his enlightenment, which is also known as *nirvana*. According to the *Ariyapariyesana Sutta*, Gautama Buddha was so content with his awakening that he felt he would stay there forever and never teach. This worried the great god Brahmā so much that Brahmā descends to Earth and tries to convince Gautama Buddha to go out and teach. The Buddha finally assents and rises to spread his newfound knowledge, which comes to be known as the Buddhist teachings.

When the Buddha sets out to teach, he decides that the most appropriate students would be his first two teachers but hears of their recent deaths. Undiscouraged, he seeks out his former five ascetic companions who, after some resistance, decide to listen and seat themselves in the Deer Park in Sarnath. Thus, the Buddha gives his first sermon, which has seventeen versions in four different languages (Batchelor 2017: 82), although one that is commonly referenced is the *Dharmacakrapravartana Sutra* or "The Sutra of Turning of the Wheel of Dharma."

This sermon is centered on two primary ideas. The first is that Buddhism is the "Middle Path" between indulgence and ascetism. Siddhartha's life is set as an example of one who experienced extreme indulgence (as a prince) and extreme asceticism (as a renunciant) but that neither could bring him to enlightenment. Rather, he had to find balance between the two and so should others who seek to follow him.

FIGURE 1.2 *Statue of the ascetic bodhisattva Siddhartha at Wat Umong, Thailand.* Source: *Cleveland Museum of Art, Leonard C. Hanna, Jr. Fund.*

FIGURE 1.3 *Ming Dynasty Chinese depiction of the historical Buddha under the Bodhi tree.* Source: *Cleveland Museum of Art, Purchase from the J. H. Wade Fund.*

The second is what is known as the Four Noble Truths (*catvāri āryasatyāni*). These are:

1 **Duhkha**, which can perhaps best be translated as unsatisfactoriness although it is often translated as suffering. It is what characterizes life within the realm of rebirth.
2 *Samudaya*, which is the origin or cause of *duhkha*. The Buddha associates this with cravings and desires. Beings try to satisfy themselves with things, or people, or ideas but that satisfaction never lasts.
3 **Nirodha**, which is the fact that duhkha can cease; this state is better known as nirvana. It is often interpreted as snuffing out the things that keep pushing sentient beings through the cycle of rebirth.
4 *Marga*, which is the path to the cessation of suffering. This is known as the Eightfold Path, which "represents a ladder of perfection" (Radhakrishnan 1996: 19). In order, the path consists of right understanding, right thought, right speech, right action, right livelihood, right effort, right mindfulness, right concentration. A practitioner moves progressively up the path until accomplishing right concentration, attaining enlightenment.

One of the most common metaphors for the Four Noble Truths is that of medicine. The Buddha as doctor diagnoses an illness (first Truth), recognizes its cause (second Truth), gives the patient hope for a cure (third Truth), and then prescribes medicine (Fourth Truth). Despite some questions about the historical importance of the Truths (Anderson 2015), most practitioners and scholars understand them as the basis of much Buddhist thought and practice.

Gautama Buddha then dives into his second sermon, which is recorded in the *Anātmalakṣaṇa Sutra*, about another fundamental principle of Buddhism: *anātman* or no-self. Rather than a permanent, unchanging self, sentient beings are made up of five *skandhas* (aggregates): form, sensation, perception, mental formations, and consciousness. When these are taken away, there is nothing permanent left. Thus, the self is impermanent (*anitya*). To try to hold onto a permanent, unchanging self just brings a person further into *duhkha*. In the *Dhammapada*, these three characteristics—duhkha, impermanence, and no-self—are called the "three marks of existence" (*trilakṣaṇa*), which describe the fundamental nature of delusion that the Four Noble Truths seek to address. At the end of this sermon (or sometimes the first sermon), the five ascetics decide to become monks and found the Buddhist monastic order. According to some versions, they achieve enlightenment at this point and become **arhats** or those who become enlightened by hearing the Buddhist teachings, known as the Dharma.

For the next forty-five years, Gautama Buddha travels around northern and central India, spreading his teachings and bringing people into his nascent religious movement. He ordains monks and nuns and encourages the participation of laypeople. It is almost universally agreed that at the age of eighty, the Buddha ends his teachings. The *Mahāparinirvāṇa Sutra* from the Theravada tradition tells of the metalworker Cunda who offered the Buddha a dish of pork. Gautama Buddha eats the food and then commands Cunda to bury the rest because no other being could eat it. It turns out that although the Buddha could eat it, he contracted dysentery; he lay down on his side in preparation for death (see Figure 1.4). His followers were distraught, particularly one of his closest followers known as Ananda to whom the Buddha said,

> But, Ananda, whatever bhikṣu or bhikṣuni [monk or nun], layman or laywoman, abides by the Dharma, lives uprightly in the Dharma, walks in the way of the Dharma, it is by such a one that the Tathagata is respected, venerated, esteemed, worshipped, and honored in the highest degree. Therefore, Ananda, thus should you train yourselves: "We shall abide by the Dharma, live uprightly in the Dharma, walk in the way of the Dharma."
>
> (Sister Vajira and Story 1998)

Thus, the Buddha instructed his followers to not mourn the loss of him but instead focus on the Buddhist teachings and use them to guide their way. After teaching a little longer, Gautama Buddha passed away, entering *parinirvana* (the final nirvana). His followers cremated his body and distributed the eight remaining pieces of bone to eight different followers. They in turn created eight stupas or reliquaries in which to place the relics of the Buddha.

The amount of detail contained in the various stories of Gautama Buddha that we have today varies wildly. In some stories, his wife does not give birth to his son until after the Buddha attains enlightenment, managing to stop her pregnancy for the six years of asceticism that the Buddha endured. Other stories say that Siddhartha was always enlightened, merely pretending to attain nirvana under the Bodhi tree to inspire others. Regardless, stories of Gautama Buddha have always been part of Buddhism and have often been used to illustrate Buddhist doctrine so that others can learn from his example and teachings.

The Spread of Buddhism

Without the historical Buddha to guide them, the first followers of Buddhism started a long process of codifying and developing his teachings. Buddhism was an almost exclusively oral tradition for at least 300 years following its founding (Harrison and Hartmann 2014: viii). Almost all Buddhist traditions agree that about three months following Gautama Buddha's parinirvana, 500 arhats gathered in Rājagṛha. Ananda, known for his acute memory, recited the entirety of the Dharma for the assembly. After Ananda, another arhat named Upāli recited the rules for monastics, known as the Vinaya. These oral teachings form the foundation of Buddhist scriptures, teachings, and practices although they underwent continual transformation and adaption for at least another millennium.

FIGURE 1.4 *Relief of* parinirvana *(death) of the historical Buddha from the Gandhara region.* Source: *Wellcome Collection.*

As happens with many developing religions, differing ideas began to emerge as Buddhism spread throughout India. According to the *Cullavagga*, there was a second council in Vesālī about 100 years after the first where 700 monks gathered to address an issue with the monastic rules. Their disagreement stemmed from ten practices that had arisen among some monks that were seen to be incompatible with the traditional vinaya (Pandit 2005: 225). Some monks agreed that these practices should be banned while others argued that they were acceptable, which led to the first major split in the Buddhist order: the more conservative Sthaviravāda school and the more liberal Mahāsāṅghika. Whether this account is true or not (Hirakawa 1990: 82), it is indicative of the emerging divisions within Buddhism.

The first solid evidence for the spread of Buddhism comes from the stone inscriptions of King Aśoka. As leader of the Maurya empire from *c.* 268 BCE to 232 BCE, Aśoka spread his influence across much of the Indian subcontinent and united varying clans and regions under his reign. Buddhists remember him as one of the earliest and most powerful proponents of Buddhism, and while he seemed to have a personal appreciation for Buddhism, the inscriptions emphasize the spread of religious tolerance within his nation. Rather than focusing on the Buddhist Dharma, he appears to have been a proponent of righteousness and sent missionaries to the kings of Syria, Egypt, and Macedonia (Hirakawa 1990: 95–100). He is also said to have taken the original eight relics of the Buddha and divided them, along with other artifacts of Buddhist significance, among 84,000 stupas throughout his kingdom. According to the Theravada strain of Buddhism, Aśoka sent his son and daughter to Sri Lanka to establish monastic lineages there but historical evidence points to a later date (Assavavirulhakarn 2010). Regardless, Aśoka was instrumental in the spread of Buddhism beyond northern and central India and helped to establish it as a permanent religion.

Following this period, Buddhism spread further and further from India, to both east and west, due in large part to vast trading networks, particularly the Silk Road. Buddhism likely entered China in the first half of the first century BCE through merchants and missionaries along the Silk Road (Wood 2002: 93) and from there, it spread to Malaysia, Indonesia, and further parts of China in the first few centuries CE (Bareau 2013: 42). Some of the greatest monuments to Buddhism west of India were the gigantic Bamiyan buddhas in the Afghan valley that were likely built in the fifth century CE (Liu 2011: 56–7). By the seventh century CE, it had spread across all of India and Central Asia, as evidenced by two Chinese pilgrims who wanted to see the land of the Buddha for themselves (Bareau 2013: 32–5).

There are many possible reasons for its success. One of the primary reasons given for the spread of Buddhism was its association with medicine. Buddhist missionaries and merchants carried medicine with them along the Silk Road, which not only helped local populations but was effective in showing the worth of Buddhism through its ability to heal those in need (Neelis 2003; Salguero 2014; Zysk 2003). On a more philosophical note, scholar Xinru Liu argues that the increasing focus on and number of **bodhisattvas**—buddhas-to-be who dedicate themselves to helping others achieve liberation—secured it a spot in the Chinese religious imagination (1998: 13). Whatever the reasons, Buddhism spread further and further across Asia and became entrenched in numerous cultures and civilizations. What is perhaps surprising is its death in the land of its birth, India. Although there was a brief resurgence of Buddhism in India in the twentieth century, it has gained little widespread traction. Buddhism has become a largely non-Indian religion grounded in Indian philosophy and culture.

The Three Jewels

When greeted by the diversity that characterizes Buddhism, it can be difficult to articulate what it means to be Buddhist. One of the only aspects of Buddhism that almost all practitioners can agree on is the Three Jewels. Buddhists "take refuge" in the Three Jewels; thus, they are also known as the Three Refuges. They are: the Buddha, the Dharma, and the Sangha.

The Buddha often refers to Gautama Buddha and accepting that he achieved enlightenment and came to the world to teach the truth, namely, Buddhism. It is not a profession of faith per se, but rather an acknowledgment of the profound impact he had on human knowledge. Sometimes other buddhas are added to or supersede Gautama Buddha as the center of the refuge. At other times, the idea of a buddha, as one who has attained enlightenment, is more central.

The Dharma is the teachings of Buddhism. These are vast and refer to the truths Gautama Buddha revealed, in addition to subsequent oral and written teachings. The most codified versions of the Dharma come from numerous Buddhist religious texts passed down as the *Tripiṭaka* (Three Baskets). There are various versions of the Tripiṭaka associated with different groups and viewpoints.

Vinaya, or the rules of monastic order, is the first of the three baskets. These refer to the lists of rules for male and female monastics and cover things such as proper clothing and sexual relations. The Theravada Vinaya, used today in Sri Lanka and Southeast Asia, contains 227 rules for monks and 311 for nuns. Mahayana Buddhists, centered in East Asia, traditionally followed 250 rules for monks and 350 for nuns although today this varies greatly. Sutras comprise the second basket and are the Buddha's sermons. They contain a bewildering variety of teachings and stories about Buddhism. Lastly is the Abhidharma or "study of the dharma," which consist of numerous commentarial traditions on the sutras by various monastics and scholars. Early Buddhist schools in India were often divided not by which sutras they considered authoritative but upon which abhidharma they followed (Hirakawa 1990: 127).

The final of the three Jewels is the sangha, or the community of Buddhists. Most visible in the sangha are *bhikṣu* (male monastics). Easily recognizable by their robes (*kāṣāya*), they also shave their heads as a sign of dedication to pursuing the Buddhist path. Monks typically leave lay life to live in a monastery or temple. Traditionally, scholars differentiated between monastics who specialized in learning the Dharma and ones who focused on insight but in reality most monks participated in both (Clough 2018). *Bhikṣuṇī* (nuns) also reach back to Gautama Buddha but there are few official nuns today due to the disappearance of most official ordination lineages. Throughout much of the Buddhist world, there are a variety of unofficial female monastic orders that range from strict adherence to the vinaya to adopting some parts of monastic regulation.

Often when people and texts use the word "sangha" they refer exclusively to the monastic orders but, in fact, it refers to all Buddhists, monastic and layperson alike. Laymen (*upāsaka*) and laywomen (*upāsikā*) vastly outnumber monastics as they do not require ordination. Although *upāsaka* appears historically to have been a narrower term (Nattier 2003: 78–9), today the term is broadly applied to all laymen.

Relations between monastics and laypeople are often quite close because monastics are "fields of merit" or those who accrue copious good karma. Monks have the time and ability to dedicate themselves to the development of good karma while often laypeople simply do not, largely due to the demands of everyday life. Therefore, laypeople donate goods, food, time, and services to monastics who have renounced the pursuit of many of these things and in return, laypeople receive good karma. Laypeople can then keep this merit to secure a good rebirth or donate it to deceased relatives, deities, or the good of the world. This idea of the "transfer of merit" (*pariṇāmanā*) appears to have been developed late in the Buddha's lifetime (Gombrich 2018: 105) and has endured as an essential part of the relationships between Buddhists both living and dead.

Understanding the Buddhist World

Attaining nirvana is traditionally considered to be the goal of Buddhism. What exactly constitutes nirvana is the subject of much speculation because Gautama Buddha did not actually share what exactly it is; instead, he left the Four Noble Truths as the guide to attaining it. It literally means "extinguishing," so some practitioners think of this is the extinguishing of the person. This ties into the idea of the *tathāgata*, an alternate name of the Buddha, as the "thus gone one" or one who has gone out of this world. But many other Buddhists dislike this depiction, instead saying that it is the extinguishing of dukkha characterized by full tranquility and peace where one has not gone from the world but has removed its problematic influence.

Buddhism relies on a set of assumptions about the world as expressed by Gautama Buddha and expanded by the tradition. The most well known is the concept of **karma**, which can best be defined as moral causation. It is the idea that there are repercussions, either good or bad, behind every action. What is unique about Buddhist karma is the focus on intention. For example, Buddhists generally view murder negatively. But what if the murder occurred to prevent the deaths of others? According to Buddhist karma, the negative karma from the murder would be mitigated because it was done out of compassion for others. Early on, the concept of karma as intent led to the idea that action was unimportant, but this was countered by the idea that actions carried out are stronger versions of intent because they can inspire others.

There are a few things frequently misunderstood about karma. First, karma can be immediate in the sense that an action can have an immediate consequence. At the same time, Buddhism accepts the idea of reincarnation in which people are born again and again throughout eons. Therefore, karma can also have repercussions literally millions of years from now. This helps explain why some people appear to benefit from terrible actions; sometime in the future they will suffer the consequences. Second, the idea of "good karma" is somewhat complicated. Good acts, such as kindness to others, bring good karma but do not contribute to attaining nirvana. They are "good" acts but they are not the "right" acts that actually help practitioners escape duhkha. To attain nirvana, one must eliminate all karma, good or bad, and perform the right acts that lead to liberation.

Many of these acts stem from the removal of **kleśa**, often translated as "defilements" but more clearly as "negative emotions." These are bad mental qualities that in turn manifest into bad actions. There are many different kleśa such as anxiety and fear, but the most central ones are ignorance (*avidyā/moha*), attachment (*rāga*), and aversion (*dveṣa*), also often translated as stupidity, greed, and anger. Together they are known as the "Three Poisons" (*triviṣa*) or the "Three Unwholesome Roots" (*akuśala-mūla*). In Tibet, they are often depicted by a pig (ignorant enough to sleep in dirt and eat anything), a bird (one known for becoming extremely attached to its mate), and a snake (who will strike out at any who disturb it).

Beings that are bound by karma are also bound within the cycle of duhkha and rebirth, known as **samsara.** They pass through this cycle again and again, through the chain of causation, a chain of twelve links: ignorance (*avidyā*), mental formations (saṃskāra), consciousness (vijñāna), name and form (*nāmarūpa*), six sense bases (ṣaḍāyatana), contact (*sparśa*), sensations (*vedanā*), craving (*tṛṣṇā*), clinging (*upādāna*), coming into existence (*bhava*), birth (*jāti*), old age and death (*jarāmaraṇa*). Sentient beings continually circle the links, moving from one life to the next through the process of reincarnation.

Concomitant with the twelve links is Buddhist cosmology. Sources vary on the exact number of the worlds (*loka*) of rebirth. Early texts describe three worlds, that of sense-desire (*kāma*), form (*rūpa*), and formless (*arūpa*), which are then divided into thirty-one realms. However, most Buddhists focus on five or six realms, located largely in the world of sense-desire (see Figure 1.5). At the bottom are hell realms where exist demons, torture, and immense suffering. Above the hells are the realms of the hungry ghosts (*preta*), beings consumed by desire for food but unable to eat. Next is the animal realm, where one is born as an animal that must suffer from ignorance and natural drives. These three are considered bad rebirths as the result of negative karma. The human realm comes next and it is the world in which we live. The *asura* realm lies either above or below humans, depending on the source; some sources leave out the *asura* realm entirely. Often translated as the realm of the "jealous gods," jealousy fuels its inhabitants. The *deva* (godly) realm is a place of pleasure and enjoyment where inhabitants know no suffering. It is tempting to think of the deva realms as the most positive, but Buddhists argue that the best rebirth is human. As a god, the joys

FIGURE 1.5 *Tibetan depiction of the twelve links (outer), the six realms of samsara (middle), and the three poisons (inner).* Source: *Apexphotos/Getty Images.*

of godhood entice beings away from studying the Dharma, much as hell-beings are too consumed with suffering to explore doctrine. Humanity is considered the best, if briefest, rebirth because humans experience a balance of suffering and joy; it is a place where duhkha is visible and the tool to address it, Buddhism, is readily available.

Major Traditions of Buddhism

Buddhism spread and transformed throughout Asia, adopting and adapting itself to local ideas and practices, creating new traditions in the process. In fact, it might be better to speak of regional Buddhisms when trying to depict its sheer variety. However, it is traditional to speak of Buddhism according to its overarching major traditions, which is further divided into numerous schools and sects. There are largely three divisions within Buddhism: Theravada, Mahayana, and Esoteric (which is sometimes seen as a branch of Mahayana).

Theravada Buddhism

Theravada is the name most often used to describe the form of Buddhism scholars believe to be the oldest surviving; it is often translated as the "teaching of the elders" but more literally as the "doctrine of the senior monks" (Crosby 2014: 2). Theravada prides itself on ancient traditions and many of the doctrines and stories discussed thus far play an important part in Theravada today. It is somewhat unique in being simultaneously a Buddhist tradition and school.

Theravada is the last of a group of Buddhist schools labeled Hinayana, or "lesser vehicle," in the centuries surrounding 0 CE by another emerging Buddhist movement known as Mahayana, or "greater vehicle." Obviously, the term Hinayana bears negative overtones and Theravada Buddhists are not keen to embrace it. Alternate names suggested have been Śrāvakayāna (vehicle of the hearers) and Nikāya Buddhism (Buddhism of the Schools), but scholars often prefer Hinayana for its historical roots. Theravada emerged out of what is traditionally known as the eighteen Hinayana schools, although there is textual and archeological evidence for twenty to thirty Indian schools (Bareau 2013: 4). All these schools died out over the subsequent centuries, yet Theravada survived. Even so, practitioners in Sri Lanka and Southeast Asia did not begin to talk about themselves as Theravada until the nineteenth century (Skilling 2009).

According to many early Indian schools and the contemporary Theravada tradition, there are four stages of rebirth in the process of escaping the cycle of rebirth. First, one becomes a stream-enterer (*srotāpanna*) who has truly begun to understand the Dharma. She will only be reborn seven times, all of which will be favorable, before attaining nirvana. Second, she becomes a once-returner (*sakṛdāgāmin*), which usually means that the practitioner will gain fuller understanding of Buddhism and only needs to be reborn once. Third, she will be reborn as the non-returner (*anāgāmin*) and never again experience rebirth as a human; she will be reborn in the higher realms exclusively. Fourth, the practitioner is born as an arhat, a fully awakened being. Escaping the cycle of samara, she has attained enlightenment.

The goal of the arhat is the ideal for Theravada Buddhists but is one of three paths to enlightenment open to sentient beings. Buddhaghosa, the great Indian Buddhist philosopher from the fifth century, discusses the three vehicles of enlightenment (*triyāna*) in his *Visuddhimagga* (The Path of Purification). The greatest vehicle, and thus the most difficult, is that of the buddha; one who has attained enlightenment on his own and decides to teach others. Then there is the *pratyekabuddha*. He attains enlightenment on his own but decides to pass away before teaching others. Lastly is the arhat, who has heard the words of a buddha and become enlightened through them. Despite some debate about the true attainment level of arhats among early Buddhist communities and a tendency to raise Buddhahood above the other two vehicles (Crosby 2014: 34), these three are central to Theravada belief.

Although the spiritual goal of Theravada Buddhism is to become an arhat, generating good karma, known as merit-making, is the center of most Theravada practice in Asia (Holt 2017: 189–238). One of the most iconic images of Theravada Buddhism is that of monks on mendicant rounds. According to the Theravada vinaya, monks are not allowed to cook their own food; instead, they file in a procession throughout the local village with begging bowls that are filled by the laity (see Figure 1.6). The monks thus gain sustenance while the laypeople gain good karma by providing for the monks. This exchange extends to clothing, objects, and even money although money is often donated to a temple rather than to individual monks. Monks help the laity secure a good rebirth and assist with rituals for the deceased, those in need, and to make a better world.

A practice unique to Thailand involves the temporary ordination (*pabbajja*) of young men. Rather than dedicating themselves to a life of Buddhism, boys who take the temporary ordination are monks for a specific period, often a few months, and then return to lay life. One of the main reasons for this is to accrue good karma and pay back the immense debt they owe their mothers for raising them; only after paying this debt can they truly become full members of Thai society (Holt 2017: 131). There is no negative perception of the decision to step down from ordination in Thailand because the lines between laypeople and monastics are relatively fluid. This differs from Sri Lanka where reneging on ordination vows is seen as a great failure (149). After the initial ordination, men can take vows intermittently throughout their life to accrue additional good karma (or escape the demands of contemporary life). There is an official limit to the number of times men can take monastic vows but in practice, they can do it as often as they like (Hayashi 2003: 106). Women are not given this option as all Thai nuns are unofficial; they are often fully devoted to a religious life when they take vows but as unofficial or lay nuns (*mae chii*) they live between laity and full monastics (Kameniar 2009).

Theravada Buddhism is often characterized as more conservative and thus also likely to be more aligned with Gautama Buddha's historical teachings. Nevertheless, it is not a static tradition; it has evolved and transformed over the centuries. Additionally, expressions of Theravada across Asia can differ greatly depending on the cultures and communities despite technically being one school.

FIGURE 1.6 *Theravada monks on their medicant rounds, shading themselves from the sun with their fans, one of their only official possessions.* Source: *Frans Lemmens/Getty Images.*

Mahayana Buddhism

The second of the mainstream Buddhist traditions to be discussed is Mahayana. It did not emerge fully formed from any existing Buddhist schools; rather, the ideas that come to be associated with Mahayana arose over time and in a variety of places. Mahayana likely developed between the first century BCE and the first century CE but could have been as late as the fifth or sixth centuries (Schopen 2005: 12). Indeed, it is difficult to discuss the early actions of Mahayanists because there is little evidence of their actions; what remain are writings containing Mahayana ideas. These writings developed into Mahayana, although the sheer variety of teachings at times directly contradicted each other making it difficult to speak of a unified tradition (Williams 2009: 3). Nevertheless, it grew into something completely new and different that appealed largely to practitioners in East Asia.

One of the defining differences between Theravada and Mahayana Buddhism is the goal of Buddhist practice. Instead of an arhat, Mahayana Buddhists strive to become buddhas, taking vows to become bodhisattvas, or buddhas-to-be, by developing *bodhicitta* or the "enlightenment mind." According to most Mahayana texts, after awaking *bodhicitta*, practitioners pursue the six perfections (*pāramitā*): generosity (*dāna*), morality (*śīla*), patience and forbearance (*kṣānti*), vigor (*vīrya*), meditation (*Dhyāna*), and wisdom (*prajñā*). Much like the Eightfold Path, practitioners move through the perfections to attain insight and help bodhisattvas advance on the path to Buddhahood by cultivating wisdom and compassion, the two greatest Mahayana virtues.

The idea that all beings would become buddhas is accompanied by a fundamental shift in the perception of buddhas. Early Mahayana thinkers pushed back against the idea that Gautama Buddha was both unique in his attainments and departed from this world. With the goal of universal Buddhahood, it does not make sense for there to be one buddha at a time in a succession; rather, there must be many buddhas dedicated to helping others attain Buddhahood. The idea developed that buddhas, including Gautama Buddha, do not depart this world forever upon physical death; instead, they remain available to help others escape samsara.

Another point of differentiation between the preceding schools and Mahayana is the concept of emptiness (*śūnyatā*). The earliest forms of Buddhism argue for the concept of no-self, or the lack on an unchanging essence of self and emptiness extends this idea to all existence. Nothing has inherent existence (*svabhāha*), whether a table, bird, or human; instead, everything is created and destroyed (Williams 2009: 70). As a concept, emptiness is difficult to describe fully and the school with which it was originally associated, Mādhaymika, became famous in part for its attempts to explain emptiness through negation, known as the *prasaṅga* argumentation style.

One of the issues that arose in response to emptiness was how to understand the workings of karma. If nothing has inherent existence, how does karma continue working? Proponents of the early Yogācāra school in the mid-third century CE addressed this question through the "seeds" (*bījā*) of karma planted in the "storehouse consciousness" (*ālayavijñāna*). Seeds can be created or destroyed depending upon people's actions, which in turn create their world. Although the idea of the storehouse was not largely popular outside Yogācāra, thinking of karma as seeds of future deeds endured into other forms of Mahayana Buddhism. The concept of the womb/embryo of the buddha (*tathāgatagarbha*), which argues for the cultivation of an embryonic buddha inside oneself, emerged around the same time, drawing on the same image of cultivation.

Another issue encountered by early Mahayanists was that early texts did not speak of an eternal buddha, emptiness, or many ideas important to Mahayanists. Moreover, newer texts by developing Mahayanists discuss things that were sometimes in direct conflict with ideas present in other strains of Buddhism. Thus, **skillful means** (*upāyakauśalya*) begins to emerge. Although found in pre-Mahayana texts (Pye 2003), this idea flowers in Mahayana Buddhism, especially the *Lotus Sutra* (Federman 2009), an extremely popular Mahayana text. It draws on the idea that Gautama Buddha weighed the capabilities of his interlocutors and adjusted his teachings accordingly. This helps explain the differences apparent in Buddhist teachings and writings by showing that discrepancies do not demonstrate fundamental inconsistencies in Buddhism but rather differences in people's ability to comprehend Buddhist law.

Interdependence, an important aspect of Buddhism from the beginning, gained even more prominence within Mahayana. In China, the Huayan (Flower Garland) school argues for the interconnectedness of all things, illustrated through the story of Indra's

Net wherein the god Indra sets up an infinitely large net and hangs a jewel at each knot where the ropes come together. Looking into just one of the jewels reflects an infinity:

> Why is this? It is because one jewel contains all the other jewels. Since all the jewels are contained in this one jewel, you are sitting at that moment in all the jewels. The converse that all are in one follows the same line of reasoning. Through one jewel you enter all jewels without having to leave that one jewel, and in all jewels you enter one jewel without having to rise from your seat in the one jewel.
>
> (de Bary and Bloom 1999: 473)

Thus, by being in a universe with a buddha, as we all are, all sentient beings reflect that Buddhahood within themselves; this is known as "**buddha nature**."

Huayan also draws on the concept of nonduality that is central to Mahayana. Nondualism argues that although we perceive the mundane world and the buddha world as separate, they are actually interconnected. Nirvana requires samsara and to understand one is to have insight into the other. It is like the two sides of a coin: heads and tails are separate but both are necessary to make a coin. Mahayana Buddhism extends this to explanations of existence; to exist in the world is to be in a nondual state. For some, nirvana can be the state of true insight into that nonduality.

The ideas discussed thus far have been extremely popular and enduring within Mahayana Buddhism; their associated schools less so. Many schools have arisen over the past millennia since the development of Mahayana. Here, we will focus on Pure Land and Zen, two of the most commonly practiced schools of Buddhism today.

Likely drawing from a variety of devotional traditions, Pure Land Buddhism is more officially traced back to the translation of the Pure Land scriptures in the second century CE into Chinese (Mitchell 2008: 226). It draws its name from the idea of heaven-like Pure Lands where beings can reside and practice Buddhism unperturbed under the infinite compassion and wisdom of buddhas. Although there are many Pure Lands, Pure Land Buddhism centers on Amitābha Buddha (Buddha of Infinite Light) also known as Amitāyus (Infinite Life) whose Pure Land, known as Sukhāvatī (Land of Bliss) resides far in the west (see Figure 1.7). There he, Avalokiteśvara (bodhisattva of compassion), and Mahāsthāmaprāpta (bodhisattva of wisdom) assist all who *nian* ("recollect"; Jpn. *nen*) Amitābha in attaining Buddhahood. *Nian* is difficult to translate into English and is quite ambiguous in the Pure Land scriptures. In China and Korea, it encompasses many practices including meditation on Amitābha, visualizing his Pure Land, circulating statues, and chanting his name. In Japan, developments in Pure Land Buddhism from 1100 to 1300 CE focused exclusively on chanting the name of Amitābha Buddha. Contemporary Buddhists draw on these practices across East Asia and into the United States.

Another form of Buddhism long popular is that of Zen, also known as the Meditation School. Zen literally translates as "meditation" and comes from the Chinese "Chan" (or "Seon" in Korean), which is a transliteration of one of the Sanskrit words for meditation (*dhyāna*). Chan Buddhism developed in China during the Tang dynasty (618–907 CE) and gained dominance among monastics in the following Song dynasty (960–1279 CE)

FIGURE 1.7 *Amitabha Buddha (center) with Avalokiteśvara Bodhisattva (right) and Mahasthamaprapta Bodhisattva (left) in Hangzhou, Zhejiang province, China.* Source: *Metropolitan Museum of Art, Louis V. Bell, Mary Trumbell Adams, and Harris Brisbane Dick Funds, 2011.*

(Schlütter 2008: 2). As a school focused on meditation, it is often associated with monasticism; nevertheless, it was popular throughout East Asia among both monastics and laypeople.

Zen Buddhism provides a path for recognizing buddha nature and relies heavily on the guidance of experienced teachers, considered to be living buddhas. A popular form of practice is contemplation of *koan*, confusing or illogical stories of great Zen masters. Practitioners are intended to meditate and consider the meaning of *koan* until eventually their confusion and doubt push past conventional thinking into the realm of emptiness and ultimate truth. Other forms of Zen rely on the idea of "just sitting" meditation in which a practitioner meditates without any intentions and comes to realize buddha nature. Meditation in Zen and other schools does not always require sitting; the idea of "constant meditation" wherein all of life is a form of meditation requires the care and attention necessary in seated meditation to extend to all facets of life. Zen encourages the practice of meditation in the pursuit of buddha nature, whatever form that may take.

This brief overview of Mahayana Buddhism just begins to touch on its diversity. Unlike Theravada, Mahayana has little to unite itself other than its opposition to some of the basic tenets of the Hinayana schools. There is a third major tradition within Buddhism that is sometimes considered part of Mahayana and sometimes not: Esoteric Buddhism.

Esoteric Buddhism

The name "Esoteric Buddhism" points to the idea that it is something hidden, secret, and separate. It is also known as the Vajrayana (Diamond/Thunderbolt Vehicle) or Tantric Buddhism, a reference to the tradition's unique writings known as *tantra*; the name choice often depends on which branch a person studies or practices (Lü 2017). There are various narratives of its emergence (Wedemeyer 2014: 17–32) but scholars agree that it seems to have come out a disparate group known as the *siddha* in the third to tenth centuries CE. They opposed mainstream Buddhism (Davidson 2002) and lived outside mainstream society in monastic or quasi-monastic settings (Wedemeyer 2014: 187). Their wildly divergent beliefs draw on concepts of secret but powerful magic passed down from master to student in carefully guarded lineages (Sørensen 2017). Drawing on these teachings enables practitioners to achieve enlightenment immediately; it is the quick and direct path. "Vajrayana" draws on this image as "vajra" can be translated as "thunderbolt," conjuring the image of enlightenment hitting one with the surety and immediacy of a thunderbolt. Carefully performed ritual plays a particularly important part in Esoteric Buddhist practice, which attempts to harness transgressive power to help speed the path to enlightenment.

Central to esoteric Buddhism's disparate teachings are the "three mysteries" (*triguhya*, Ch. *sanmi*). These consist of body, speech, and mind that are the vehicles for the expression of Buddhist truth. Although initially separate, the three mysteries came to be associated with particular religious practices known as mudra, mantra, and mandala (Orzech and Sørensen 2011: 76). Mudra are associated with the body and are particular hand gestures associated with Buddhist values. Buddhas are often depicted with particular mudra, which helps with identification (see Figure 1.8). Mantra joins with speech to refer to vocal proclamations. Mantra, and their longer cousins *dhāranī*, consist of a set series of words that a practitioner must chant; sometimes sensical and sometimes not. The key is to chant them in Sanskrit—or as close as one can come to Sanskrit—which helps them come into contact with ultimate truth. Finally, mandala are exercises of the mind, specifically three-dimensional projections of the Buddhist universe built within the mind (see Figure 1.9). Two-dimensional versions became a common way to assist in the process of mental creation. The three mysteries, like many other aspects of Esoteric Buddhism, were adopted and adapted into Mahayana Buddhism in various ways, firmly tying the two traditions.

FIGURE 1.8 *Statue of the Bodhisattva Padmapani Lokeshvara with his raised right hand in the mudra of exposition*. Source: *Metropolitan Museum of Art*.

FIGURE 1.9 *Chakrasamvara mandala from Nepal.* Source: *Metropolitan Museum of Art, Rogers Fund, 1995.*

Tibetan Buddhism is the most visible form of Esoteric Buddhism today. According to tradition, Esoteric Buddhism came to Tibet in the fifth or sixth century CE through the ruler Songtsen Gampo, although it is likely that it trickled in over time, much as Mahayana Buddhism did throughout Asia (Bellezza 2017: 204). In the sixteenth century, the Mongol leader Altan Khan formally recognized Sonam Gyatso (1543–1588) as the Third Dalai Lama (retroactively identifying his teachers as the first and second) and established the line of Dalai Lamas as Tibetan political leaders (Williams 2009: 191). As the leader of the dominant Gelug (Yellow Hat) school, the Dalai Lama also became the de facto spiritual leader. The current Dalai Lama, the fourteenth, retains spiritual leadership but relinquished political control in 2011 (Tricycle 2011).

The Dalai Lama is one of many lamas, a title that simply refers to a Tibetan monk, usually of some experience and knowledge. However, the Dalai Lama is also a *tulku*, the reincarnation of a Buddhist master; all tulku are lamas but not all lamas are tulku. Tulku are identified often at a young age and trained to take upon their lineage as leaders. The Dalai Lama is a particularly special tulku in that he is the reincarnation of Avalokiteśvara, the bodhisattva of compassion. Tulku have become problematic in recent history due to the Chinese annexation of Tibet. The process for finding and training Dalai Lamas involves the help of the Panchen Lama. However, the tenth Panchen Lama disappeared shortly after his identification as a tulku. There are legitimate worries that the Chinese government will attempt to control the life and training of the fifteenth Dalai Lama upon the current one's death. This has led him to declare that he will likely be reincarnated outside of China or even not at all (Westcott 2019).

Issues in Contemporary Buddhism

Buddhism holds a special place within the global religious community: it is an "Eastern" religion largely accepted as both legitimate and admirable by Westerners. Through charismatic figures like the Fourteenth Dalai Lama (1935–) and Thich Nhat Hanh (1926–2022), it has enjoyed mass appeal as a religion that advocates for peace and coexistence. Practices such as mindfulness meditation have transcended Buddhism's religious boundaries to become effective forms of medical treatment for various ailments (Bojic and Becerra 2017; de Souza et al. 2015; Leyland, Rowse, and Emerson 2019). Its popularity has relied on a global sense of goodwill that draws on relatively recent transformations.

Many images of Buddhism prominent today come out of changes instigated by contact with Euro-American colonial powers. Western dominance in political and spiritual matters worked across the colonized world to transform and delegitimize traditional forms of religion; although this often focused on indigenous religions, Buddhism was no exception (Keyes, Kendall, and Hardacre 1994: 4–9). Responding to threats to their religion, Buddhists across Asia began reform movements, often focusing on practices or beliefs seen as corrupt or superstitious. Within the Theravada tradition, this resulted in the creation of "Buddhist modernism." These transformations were generated by Euro-American colonial powers but drew on both Western and Eastern ideas, emphasizing "a new form of more philosophically inclined and intellectually oriented monastic vocation" (McMahan 2009: 6) that drew largely from the written Buddhist canon. It arose in conjunction with more traditionalist reform movements focused on the extant Sangha (Teeuwen 2017: 2), which in turn often grew alongside budding nationalist movements with a deep interest in Buddhism, tying both religion and nation together (Holt 2017: 6–7). In Japan, later reform-minded Buddhists called for "critical Buddhism," which attempted to prune what they considered to be nonessential beliefs and practices that had seeped into Japanese Buddhism (Hubbard and Swanson 1997). These issues continue to evolve and transform Buddhism today.

As colonial encounters transformed Buddhism within Asia, colonialists also brought Buddhism, as they understood it, back home. Many Westerners—disenfranchised with Christianity or seeking something new, mystical, and "Oriental"—turned to Buddhism. One way it flourished even among Christians was its redefinition as a philosophy rather than a religion; Euro-American seekers saw Buddhism as a nontheistic philosophy or spirituality focused on human self-effort. They also sought a religion in line with democratic principles, compatible with a scientific explanation of the universe, and included an internal meditative practice aligned with individualism (Holt 2017: 7). In other words, a rational form of Buddhism propagated by many Buddhist modernists. This perception continues through figures such as the Dalai Lama who David McMahan (2009: 247) describes as "in many respects, the quintessential modernizer" who advocates for "world-affirming, egalitarian, and democratic reinterpretations of the path." The genial figure of the Dalai Lama has come to embody Buddhism for much of the West, but his form of Buddhism arose out of contact with Western conceptions of Buddhism.

Images of Buddhism as a completely pacifist religion are also problematic because Buddhism has often played a part in conflict. Japan is perhaps the most obvious historical example. During the imperial period (1868–1945), Japan expanded rapidly across East Asia. To protect against Western encroachment into East Asia, Japan created the Greater East-Asia Co-Prosperity Sphere, which forcefully conquered both Korea and parts of China in the name of defense; one of the claims made for the propagation of the Sphere was the protection of Buddhism (Jaffe 2004). During Japan's overseas aggressions against China, Korea, and later the United States, Buddhist monks were on the front lines, if not fighting, then actively helping Japanese colonial expansion and war efforts (Jum-Suk 2012; Victoria 2006).

Relationships between religious and racial identity within Buddhist countries in the twenty-first century are increasingly important, despite being largely unaddressed by most scholars (Borchert 2014: 595–6). Myanmar is one of the most ethnically diverse countries in the world (Chaturvedi 2012) but tensions between Buddhists and Muslims have resulted in what the United Nations have called "atrocious" human rights violations for the 1.4 million people in the Rakhine state since 2012 (Rosenthal 2019: 6–7). Much of this violence is rooted in Buddhist nationalist rhetoric and activism that followed the political reforms of 2011 (Hayward and Frydenlund 2019: 2). Recent activism in the country has focused on the powerful MaBaTha group, which is "first and foremost an expression of the popular desire to ensure that a particular understanding of 'traditional values and practices' is not undermined by the overwhelming forces of capitalism and globalization" (3). Thus, the connection between the traditional ethnic majority and their traditional religion, Buddhism, puts them at odds with the multicultural, global nature of contemporary Myanmar. Monks such as U Gambira who have attempted to speak out against the discriminatory rhetoric have been imprisoned and/or banned from the country (Yeng 2018: 316). In 2015, Nobel Peace Prize laureate Aung San Suu Kyi was democratically elected as president but has done little to curb the violence or nationalism, preferring the term "ethnic clashes" to "ethnic cleansing" and turning away UN rights-advocacy groups (Yeng 2018: 294–5). Buddhists in Myanmar continue to draw strength from their religion, which they see as supporting their treatment of the Rohingya minority (see Figure 1.10).

Alternatively, many Buddhists have felt it necessary to take a stand on social issues; they form a disparate movement known as socially engaged Buddhism, a term coined by Vietnamese activist monk Thich Nhat Hanh. Engaged Buddhists bring together social concerns with Buddhist values and see their work as expressions of Buddhism (King 2009: 1). Drawing on the idea of dukkha, engaged Buddhists attempt to help alleviate the suffering of the world. This stretches from the tree ordination movement in Thailand (Darlington 2012), to anti-war protest in Japan (Watts and Okano 2012) and social service in China (Huang 2018). Sulak Sivaraksa is one of the most prominent

FIGURE 1.10 *Rohingya refugees from the Rakhine state in Myanmar in 2012.* Source: *Paul Bronstein/Stringer.*

critics of the Thai government's discriminatory attitudes toward its Muslim minority and advocates for nonviolence as the foundation of the Buddhist teachings. He also founded the International Network of Engaged Buddhists (INEB) that works to bring together engaged Buddhists from around the world.

Conclusion

Buddhism is constantly changing. Through ever-increasing connection based in ever-evolving technology, Buddhists from around the world interact and join with others with whom they previously had little contact. These constant interactions push Buddhists into new and old territories, some becoming the faces of social movements while others participating in acts of atrocity. It would be false to say that Buddhism in the contemporary world is somehow more or less corrupt or pure than it historically has been. Throughout its long history and evolution, Buddhism has adapted through the people who practice it, for good or ill. It will continue to evolve, taking its already disparate present into a new and diverse future.

Further Reading and Online Resources

Access to Insight (n.d.), "Readings in Theravāda Buddhism." Available online: https://www.accesstoinsight.org/ (accessed September 25, 2020).

Crosby, K. (2014), *Theravada Buddhism: Continuity, Diversity, and Identity*, Malden, MA: John Wiley & Sons.

Harris, I. (2017), *The Complete Illustrated Encyclopedia of Buddhism: A Comprehensive Guide to Buddhist History, Philosophy and Practice*, London: Lorenz Books.

Mitchell, D.W. (2008), *Buddhism: Introducing the Buddhist Experience*, 2nd edn., Oxford: Oxford University Press.

Van Schaik, S. (2016), *The Spirit of Tibetan Buddhism*, New Haven, CT: Yale University Press.

Williams, P. (2009), *Mahāyāna Buddhism: The Doctrinal Foundations*, 2nd edn., London: Routledge.

References

Anderson, C.S. (2015), *Pain and Its Ending: The Four Noble Truths in the Theravada Buddhist Canon*, London: Routledge.

Assavavirulhakarn, P. (2010), *The Ascendancy of Theravāda Buddhism in Southeast Asia*, Chiang Mai: Silkworm Books.

Bareau, A. (2013), *The Buddhist Schools of the Small Vehicle*, trans. S. Boin-Webb and A. Skilton, Honolulu: University of Hawai'i.

Batchelor, S. (2017), *Secular Buddhism: Imagining the Dharma in an Uncertain World*, New Haven, CT: Yale University Press.

Bellezza, J.V. (2017), *Dawn of Tibet: The Ancient Civilization on the Roof of the World*, London: Rowman & Littlefield.

Bojic, S. and R. Becerra (2017), "Mindfulness-Based Treatment for Bipolar Disorder: A Systematic Review of the Literature," *Europe's Journal of Psychology*, 13 (3): 573–98.

Borchert, T. (2014), "The Buddha's Precepts on Respecting Other Races and Religions? Thinking about the Relationship of Ethnicity and Theravada Buddhism," *Sojourn: Journal of Social Issues in Southeast Asia*, 29 (3): 591–626.

BuddhaNet (2008), "Life of Buddha: Birth of the Prince (Part 1)." Available online: https://www.buddhanet.net/e-learning/buddhism/lifebuddha/2lbud.htm (accessed August 22, 2019).

Chaturvedi, M. (2012), "Myanmar's Ethnic Divide: The Parallel Struggle," *Institute of Peace and Conflict Studies*, August 1. Available online: http://www.ipcs.org/issue_select.php?recNo=476 (accessed September 25, 2020).

Clough, B.S. (2018), "Paths of Monastic Practice from India to Sri Lanka: Responses to L.S. Cousins' Work on Scholars and Meditators," *Buddhist Studies Review*, 35 (1): 29–45.

Crosby, K. (2014), *Theravada Buddhism: Continuity, Diversity and Identity*, Malden, MA: Wiley-Blackwell.

Darlington, S.M. (2012), *The Ordination of a Tree: The Thai Buddhist Environmental Movement*, Albany: State University of New York Press.

Davidson, R.M. (2002), *Indian Esoteric Buddhism: A Social History of the Tantric Movement*, New York: Columbia University Press.

de Bary, W.T. and I. Bloom, eds. (1999), *Sources of Chinese Tradition: From Earliest Times to 1600*, Vol. 1, 2nd edn., New York: Columbia University Press.

de Souza, I.C., V.V. de Barros, H.P. Gomide, T.C. Miranda, V.P. Menezes, E.H. Kozasa, and A.R. Noto (2015), "Mindfulness-Based Interventions for the Treatment of Smoking: A Systematic Literature Review," *Journal of Alternative & Complementary Medicine*, 21 (3): 129–40.

Federman, A. (2009), "Literal Means and Hidden Meanings: A New Analysis of Skillful Means," *Philosophy East and West*, 59 (2): 125–41.

Gombrich, R.F. (2018), "Ambiguity and Ambivalence in Buddhist Treatment of the Dead," *Buddhist Studies Review*, 35 (1): 97–110.

Harrison, P. and J. Hartmann (2014), "Introduction," in P. Harrison and J. Hartmann (eds.), *From Birch Bark to Digital Data: Recent Advances in Buddhist Manuscript Research*, vii–xxii, Vienna: Wien Verlag der österreichischen Akademie der Wissenschaften.

Hayashi, Y. (2003), *Practical Buddhism among the Thai-Lao: Religion in the Making of a Region*, Kyoto: Kyoto University Press.

Hayward, S. and I. Frydenlund (2019), *Religion, Secularism, and the Pursuit of Peace in Myanmar*, Transatlantic Policy Network on Religion and Diplomacy, June 24. Available online: https://religionanddiplomacy.org.uk/wp-content/uploads/2019/06/TPNRD-Hayward-and-Frydenlund-Myanmar.pdf (accessed September 25, 2020).

Hirakawa, A. (1990), *A History of Indian Buddhism: From Śākyamuni to Early Mahāyāna*, trans. P. Groner, Honolulu: University of Hawai'i Press.

Holt, J. (2017), *Theravada Traditions: Buddhist Ritual Cultures in Contemporary Southeast Asia and Sri Lanka*, Honolulu: University of Hawai'i Press.

Huang, W. (2018), "The Place of Socially Engaged Buddhism in China," *Journal of Buddhist Ethics*, 25. Available online: http://blogs.dickinson.edu/buddhistethics/2018/08/21/the-place-of-socially-engaged-buddhism-in-china/ (accessed August 22, 2019).

Hubbard, J. and P. Swanson, eds. (1997), *Pruning the Bodhi Tree: The Storm over Critical Buddhism*, Honolulu: University of Hawai'i Press.

Jaffe, R.M. (2004), "Seeking Sakyamuni: Travel and the Reconstruction of Japanese Buddhism," *Journal of Japanese Studies*, 30 (1): 65–96.

Jum-Suk, J. (2012), "The Modernity of Japanese Buddhism and Colonial Korea: The Jōdoshū Wakō Kyōen as a Case Study," *Eastern Buddhist*, 43 (1/2): 181–203.

Kameniar, B. (2009), "Thai Buddhist Women, 'Bare Life' and Bravery," *Journal for the Academic Study of Religion*, 22 (3): 281–94.

Keyes, C.F., L. Kendall, and H. Hardacre (1994), *Asian Visions of Authority Religion and the Modern States of East and Southeast Asia*, Honolulu: University of Hawai'i Press.

King, S.B. (2009), *Socially Engaged Buddhism*, Honolulu: University of Hawai'i Press.

Leyland, A., G. Rowse, and L. Emerson (2019), "Experimental Effects of Mindfulness Inductions on Self-Regulation: Systematic Review and Meta-Analysis," *Emotion*, 19 (1): 108–22.

Liu, X. (1998), *The Silk Road: Overland Trade and Cultural Interactions in Eurasia; Essays on Global and Comparative History*, Washington, DC: American Historical Association.

Liu, X. (2011), "A Silk Road Legacy: The Spread of Buddhism and Islam," *Journal of World History*, 22 (1): 55–81.

Lü, J. (2017), "The Terms 'Esoteric Teaching' ('Esoteric Buddhism') and 'Tantra' in Chinese Buddhist Sources," in Y. Bentor and M. Shahar (eds. and trans.), *Chinese and Tibetan Esoteric Buddhism*, 72–81, Leiden: Brill.

McMahan, D.L. (2009), *The Making of Buddhist Modernism*, Oxford: Oxford University Press.

Mitchell, D.W. (2008), *Buddhism: Introducing the Buddhist Experience*, 2nd edn., Oxford: Oxford University Press.

"Myanmar Rohingya: What You Need to Know about the Crisis" (2018), *BBC*, April 24, 2019. Available online: https://www.bbc.com/news/world-asia-41566561 (accessed August 22, 2019).

Nattier, J. (2003), *A Few Good Men: The Bodhisattva Path According to the Inquiry of Ugra (Ugrapariprcchā)*, Honolulu: University of Hawai'i Press.

Neelis, J. (2003), "Silk Road," in R.E. Busswell Jr. (ed.), *Encyclopedia of Buddhism*, New York: Macmillan.

Orzech, C.D. and H.H. Sørensen (2011), "Mudra, Mantra, Mandala," in C.D. Orzech, H.H. Sørensen, and R.K. Payne (eds.), *Esoteric Buddhism and the Tantras in East Asia*, 76–89, Leiden: Brill.

Pandit, S.A. (2005), "Late Hīnayāna Buddhism and the Transition to Mahāyāna: A Study of the Early Buddhist 'Saṃgha' and the Buddha Figures at Kanheri," *Eastern Buddhist*, 37 (1/2): 222–34.

Pew Research Center (2017), *The Changing Global Religious Landscape*, April 5. Available online: https://www.pewforum.org/wp-content/uploads/sites/7/2017/04/FULL-REPORT-WITH-APPENDIXES-A-AND-B-APRIL-3.pdf (accessed August 22, 2019).

Pye, M. (2003), *Skilful Means: A Concept in Mahayana Buddhism*, 2nd edn., London: Routledge.

Radhakrishnan, S., ed. (1996), *The Dhammapada: With Introductory Essays, Pāli Text, English Translation and Notes*, Delhi: Oxford University Press.

Rosenthal, G. (2019), *A Brief and Independent Inquiry into the Involvement of the United Nations in Myanmar from 2010 to 2018*, United Nations, May 29. Available online: https://www.un.org/sg/sites/www.un.org.sg/files/atoms/files/Myanmar%20Report%20-%20May%202019.pdf (accessed August 22, 2019).

Salguero, C.P. (2014), "Buddhism & Medicine in East Asian History," *Religion Compass*, 8 (8): 239–50.

Schlütter, M. (2008), *How Zen Became Zen: The Dispute over Enlightenment and the Formation of Chan Buddhism in Song-Dynasty China*, Honolulu: University of Hawai'i Press.

Schopen, G. (2005), *Figments and Fragments of Māhāyana Buddhism in India: More Collected Papers*, Honolulu: University of Hawai'i Press.

Sister Vajira and F. Story, trans. (1998), "Maha-Parinibbana Sutta: Last Days of the Buddha," *Access to Insight*. Available online: https://www.accesstoinsight.org/tipitaka/dn/dn.16.1-6.vaji.html (accessed August 22, 2019).

Skilling, P. (2009), "Theravāda in History," *Pacific World*, 3 (11): 61–93.

Sørensen, H.H. (2017), "Spells and Magical Practices as Reflected in the Early Chinese Buddhist Sources (c. 300–600 CE) and Their Implications for the Rise and Development of Esoteric Buddhism," in C.D. Orzech, H.H. Sørensen, and R.K. Payne (eds.), *Esoteric Buddhism and the Tantras in East Asia*, 41–71, Leiden: Brill.

Teeuwen, M. (2017), "Buddhist Modernities: Modernism and Its Limits," in H. Hanna Havnevik, U. Hüsken, M. Teeuwen, V. Tichonov, and K. Wellens (eds.), *Buddhist Modernities: Re-Inventing Tradition in the Globalizing Modern World*, 1–11, Oxford: Oxford University Press.

Tricycle (2011), "Dalai Lama Steps down from Position as Tibet's Political Leader," *Tricycle: The Buddhist Review*, March 10. Available online: https://tricycle.org/trikedaily/dalai-lama-steps-down-position-tibets-political-leader/ (accessed August 22, 2019).

Victoria, B.D. (2006), *Zen at War*, 2nd edn., Lanham, MD: Rowman & Littlefield.

Watts, J.S. and M. Okano (2012), "Reconstructing Priestly Identity and Roles and the Development of Socially Engaged Buddhism in Contemporary Japan," in I. Prohl and J. K. Nelson (eds.), *Handbook of Contemporary Japanese Religions*, 345–72, Leiden: Brill.

Wedemeyer, C.K. (2014), *Making Sense of Tantric Buddhism: History, Semiology, and Transgression in the Indian Traditions*, New York: Columbia University Press.

Westcott, B. (2019), "Dalai Lama's Reincarnation Must 'comply with Chinese Laws,' Communist Party Says," *CNN*, April 11. Available online: https://www.cnn.com/2019/04/11/asia/dalai-lama-beijing-tibet-china-intl/index.html (accessed August 22, 2019).

Williams, P. (2009), *Mahāyāna Buddhism: The Doctrinal Foundations*, 2nd edn., London: Routledge.

Wood, F. (2002), *The Silk Road: Two Thousand Years in the Heart of Asia*, Berkeley: University of California Press.

Yeng, S. (2018), "Refuge and Refugees in Myanmar: A Theravada Buddhist Response," *Soundings: An Interdisciplinary Journal*, 101 (4): 291–321.

Zysk, K.G. (2003), "Medicine," in R.E. Busswell Jr. (ed.), *Encyclopedia of Buddhism*, New York: Macmillan.

Glossary Terms

Arhat Literally "worthy one," one who has eliminated all defilements and attained nirvana according to the Theravada tradition. Different from a buddha (who comes to understand Buddhist truth on his own and decides to teach about it) or a pratyekabuddha (who comes to understand Buddhist truth on his own but passes on without ever teaching), arhat come to enlightenment through hearing the teachings of a buddha. It is the final step on the four-step path to enlightenment for advanced Theravada practitioners: stream-enterer, once-returner, non-returner, and arhat. Mahayana Buddhism tends to downplay the importance of the arhat, preferring the bodhisattva path, but arhat are revered as ones who have attained deep insight into Buddhist truth.

Bodhisattva Beings who have awakened the aspiration for enlightenment (bodhicitta) and dedicated themselves to attaining Buddhahood. In the Theravada tradition, it refers to the historical Buddha prior to his final rebirth and awakening. In Mahayana, the goal is for all sentient beings to become buddhas and thus all beings must become bodhisattvas. Mahayana Bodhisattvas commit themselves to achieving universal Buddhahood and work to help achieve that goal. Although the term is sometimes used to refer to all Mahayanists, it more regularly refers to advanced bodhisattvas who are embodiments of Buddhist values, such as Avalokiteśva, the bodhisattva of compassion.

Buddha A general term referring to beings who have achieved enlightenment through their own efforts and have decided to teach others. They can be identified by the thirty-two marks of a buddha, which include elongated earlobes, a forehead protrusion, and dark hair. In Theravada, only the historical buddha, Gautama Buddha, is generally discussed even though they do believe in a succession of buddhas that coincide with every cycle of world creation and destruction. The ultimate goal of Mahayana Buddhists is the attainment of Buddhahood for all sentient beings. Mahayana Buddhism relies on a vast system of buddhas who help others attain enlightenment; some of the more famous buddhas are Gautama, Amitābha, and Maitreya.

Buddha nature The inherent Buddhahood inside all sentient beings and often extended to all things. The concept is associated with Mahayana Buddhism and some Mahayana schools, including Zen, focus primarily on recognizing the buddha nature in oneself and others. There are numerous explanations of buddha nature itself, mostly centering on its relationship to emptiness and the interdependent relationship among all things. It is frequently associated with the "womb/embryo of the buddha" (*tathāgatagarbha*), which refers to the nascent buddha inside all beings that must be nurtured and cultivated to become a buddha. There is no consensus as to whether the terms refer to the same or different thing.

Dukkha What characterizes existence within the cycle of birth and death and is the first of the Four Noble Truths. Often translated as "suffering," it is better translated as "unsatisfactoriness." It is compared to a chariot wheel that is slightly out of alignment; it is possible to live with it, but it will continue to cause problems until addressed. Buddhism is the antidote to dukkha, particularly the Eightfold Path. Theravada, Mahayana, and Esoteric Buddhists all agree about the importance of dukkha to understanding the nature of reality but their approach to solving it differs and is often the basis for their tradition.

Karma The system of moral causation that fuels the cycle of rebirth. In Buddhism, karma is the result of intentions behind actions rather than the actions themselves; indeed, a murder done to protect others will accrue much less bad karma than a murder done without noble intentions. Actions or intentions morally perceived to be positive cultivate good karma while ones morally perceived to be negative cultivate bad karma. However, both good and bad karma fuel the cycle of samsara so to achieve nirvana, it is more appropriate to cultivate right acts that further one along the path of Buddhist understanding. In practice, however, most Buddhists focus on cultivating good karma as nirvana seems like a distant goal.

Kleśa Negative mental states that impede good judgment and actions; they help sow the seeds of karma that keep beings in the cycle of death and rebirth. Some kleśa include anxiety, fear, doubt, uncertainty, jealousy, and depression. Ignorance, craving, and aversion (also identified as greed, anger, and stupidity) are marked out for special attention as the Three Unwholesome Roots in Theravada and the Three Poisons in Mahayana. They are seen as the most basic of the kleśa from which arise the others and are also the most difficult from which to escape. There are various translations of kleśa such as defilements, negative emotions, afflictions, and destructive emotions. Scholars will often use the Sanskrit term to avoid the ambiguity in translations.

Nirvana The attainment of full insight into Buddhist truth and the nature of the universe. Literally meaning "extinguishing," it references the blowing out of a candle and is often interpreted to be the snuffing out of dukkha, or unsatisfactoriness, and escaping the cycle of death and rebirth. There are no extended descriptions of nirvana in the Buddhist texts, but it is often associated with ultimate bliss. The historical buddha experienced two kinds of nirvana. The first was his attainment under the Bodhi tree and was known as "nirvana with remainder" (*sopadhiśeṣa-nirvana*) where the "remainder" refers to the last of his karma needing to be played out. His final nirvana is known as "nirvana without remainder" (*parinirvana*) and refers to his physical death at the age of eighty; the term *parinirvana* is often used when speaking about the death of the historical Buddha.

Samsara The name for the cycle of death and rebirth. It is fueled by karma and only through enlightenment can one escape it. Attaining nirvana is to step off the wheel of samsara, whether to disappear entirely or to turn around and help others find their way off. It consists of a variety of realms of rebirth, the most prominent in discussions of samara are the realms of hell, hungry ghosts, humans, *asura* (often translated as "jealous gods"), and gods. Rebirth in the human realm is considered the most favorable although it, along with rebirth as a god and sometimes as an asura, are considered good rebirths. Rebirth as a human is also one of the briefest rebirths; aside from animals, rebirths in the other realms may last eons.

Skillful means A term most prevalent in Mahayana Buddhism that refers to the ability of buddhas, particularly the historical Buddha, to match the content of his teachings to the particular person or group with whom he spoke. It is believed that many Buddhist teachings are too complex for most people to understand unfiltered; therefore, the Buddha in his infinite wisdom and compassion, gave various teachings to match what he judged to be a person's capacity to understand them. Ideally, these teachings would set the person on the path to understanding and would enable them to move beyond the initial teachings to pursue ultimate truth. It helps to explain the sometimes directly contradictory statements apparent in the Mahayana texts, especially when compared with the Hinayana texts.

PART I

The Three Jewels

2

Buddhas and Gods

A.W. Barber

The **transmundane** and **supermundane** beings found in Buddhist traditions are a study in complexity and breadth. Buddhist texts clearly distinguish between the transmundane (e.g., buddhas, arhats) and the supermundane (e.g., gods/*devas*, *nāgas*). Drawing on the Buddhist concept of karma, for example, accumulating a vast store of positive good karma (merit) enables one to be reborn a god. However, rebirth as a god is impermanent due to the cycle of samsara, and eventually one will be reborn into another realm. Ultimately, having a store of merit is helpful in the cycle of rebirth but in itself cannot deliver one to nirvana, the ultimate goal in Buddhism.

Gods are but one example of the inherent complexities in the variety of nonhuman being that inhabit the Buddhist universe. The complexities encountered originate from disparate geographic sources, the sophistication of imagery, the multilayers of symbolism, and the extraordinary wealth presented. This chapter will examine the nature of Buddhist beings of the transmundane and supermundane through their **iconography** originating in India, China, Japan, and Tibet. It will present the most significant components of these beings, providing both their general structure and specific examples. Due to limitations of space, some artistic developments and countries are not presented.

The Indian Heritage

Buddhism in India inherited the local variation of the Indo-European people's cosmology, or ways of thinking about the development and operations of the universe. The *axis mundi* (Sk. *Meru*) at the center of the world, is the rightful home of the various divine and semi-divine beings, although they frequent other realms. The great sky god Dyauṣ Pitṛ (L. Jupiter) has various permeations (Monier-Williams 1951: 478). Just as this king of the gods has multiple legends associated with him that differ between the Greeks and Romans, in India he had his own legends including that of Indra. Indra lives in a heaven with many other gods shared by the Indo-European people as accounted in the ancient texts known as the *Vedas*. However, over time, the philosophers of India developed their understanding of cosmology in unique ways and under local influences. This complex system of gods, heavens, morality, and the world was already well developed by the time of Śākyamuni Buddha. Both major and minor Vedic deities are mentioned in Buddhist sources. These divinities act as disciples, assistants, and protectors of the Buddha's Dharma because they too need to be liberated. The god and goddesses of Indo-European divinity considered "Protectors of the Dharma" frequently encountered are (listed here with Roman approximates):

Indra Jupiter
Agni Vulcan
Yama Pluto
Varuna Neptune
Brahmā Saturn
Pṛthivī Terra
Sūrya Sol
Candra Lunus
Iśāna Bacchus
Nirṛti ? Ania
Vāyu Venti
Skanda Mars
Vināyāka Mercury

Augmenting the Vedic gods and goddesses, there is an extensive array of other divinities that populate the Indian cosmos that Buddhists have inherited. This includes **asuras** (titans) the most famous being: Vemacitrin, Rāhula, Pahārāda, and perhaps, Sujā, who married Indra to bring peace to the gods and *asuras*. Another important group are the Guardian Kings (Sk. *lokapāla*: protectors of Buddhism occupying the cardinal directions) and the semidivine beings that populate their armies. Vaiśravaṇa, the god of wealth, associated with the north, has an army of **Yakṣas** (nature spirits) while Dhṛtarāṣṭra, associated with the east, supports the kingdom in general, has an army of *Gandharvas* (male spirits of scents). Virūḍhaka, associated with the south is known as the god who increases and has an army of *Kumbhāṇḍas* (dwarf spirits) while Vīrūpākṣa, associated with the west, is the god who sees all and commands an army of **Nāgas** (semidivine serpents). Of these four, Vaiśravaṇa (north) developed a large cult following and Vīrūpākṣa (west) is mentioned in many sutras.

Furthermore, *Garuḍas* (man-eagles), *Kinnaras* (human-birds), *Apsaras* (female spirits of music), *Mahoragas* (earthquake serpents), *Rakṣas* (cannibal spirits), protectresses, ghosts, zombies, and others populate the various realms, but all can interact with humans. Mention needs to be made of Hārītī (the smallpox goddess), Gaṇapati (similar to Gaṇeśa), Lakṣmī (the goddess of wealth, merit, and prosperity), Māra (the god of the cycle of rebirth), and others who were all inherited from the pan-Indic tradition. Moreover, the knowledge of many of these gods and goddesses was exported to other Asian countries. In viewing the Buddhist iconography beyond India, we will note the assimilation but also the refinement, selection, and original generation in the spiritual traditions of each culture.

Buddhas

According to the texts, there are an infinite number of buddhas. We do have the names of many, but only a few have gained widespread popularity. Śākyamuni is considered the first buddha in our era but is also understood to be preceded by such buddhas as Dīpankara, Vipaśin, and Kāśyapa. Texts often mention from seven (Rhys Davids 1977: 189) up to more than 11,000 (Buddhas 2002: 65). Introduced here are only a few of the most eminent buddhas.

Śākyamuni Buddha

"The sage of the Śākya people," Śākyamuni Buddha was born Siddhārtha Gautama Śākya in either the sixth or fifth century BCE. The early tales do not provide a full account of his life, instead focusing on his awakening and compassionate activity up to his death at eighty years of age. Perhaps more information was handed down in the oral tradition about his early years but eventually everything about him becomes paradigmatic. That he was an extraordinary individual is indicated in art by displaying some of the Universal Emperor's thirty-two major and eighty minor physical characteristics such as wheel symbols on the soles of his feet or long fingers. Living the life of a **śramaṇa** with its renunciate lifestyle is represented in depictions through his wearing of monastic robes. That he is simultaneously beyond this status is indicated by his long hair tied in a bun in the manner of a *muni* (often represented as curls). His defeating Māra, by calling on the Earth Goddess (Pṛthivī) to bear witness, is shown in the common image of him sitting and touching the earth. His teaching is noted by holding his hands in the teaching mudra (see Figure 2.1). His lying in the lion pose on his right side represents his complete nirvana/death. These are very intentional depictions because "One who see the Buddha sees the Dharma" (Kashyap 1959: 36). That is, his presence was understood to be the actual embodiment of the teachings and of the absolute (*Dharmakāya*).

Akṣobhya Buddha

Akṣobhya Buddha was probably the most popular buddha after Śākyamuni in India based on references in multiple Mahayana texts. Akṣobhya is not a historic person but rather represents the moment in the awakening sequence of immovability when

FIGURE 2.1 *Śākyamuni Buddha.* Source: *Cleveland Museum of Art, Gift of Mr. and Mrs. J.H. Wade and Bequest of Cornelia B. Warner, by exchange.*

questioned by Māra that presages awakening. He is usually portrayed with the earth-touching mudra and his blue color represents emptiness, Mahayana wisdom in general, "mirror-like-wisdom" in particular, and the absolute. This buddha is associated with the east and sometimes wears royal jewelry. Various manifestations and affiliations of/with Akṣobhya are abundant in Vajrayana Buddhism. He is important in the Japanese Shingon School, frequently found in all branches of Tibetan Buddhism, and one of the buddhas depicted at the famous Borobudur temple complex in Indonesia (United Nations Educational, Scientific and Cultural Organization [UNESCO] 1992–2020). He has a Buddha-field (i.e., Pure Land) in the east where one can be reborn and is one of the buddhas termed Five Tathāgatas (i.e., important aspects of wisdom in the Vajrayana).

Amitābha Buddha

Amitābha Buddha has several texts providing information about him but his popularity in India was less than found in other countries. He is depicted with different mudras, representing Mahayana compassion in general and "discriminating wisdom" in particular. He can be standing or sitting cross-legged, often depicted in shades of red or gold signifying the sunset, the west, and death. The second most popular buddha in East Asia presently, rebirth in his Buddha-field is an intermediary goal for millions of people. The popularity of his Buddha-field, a perfect place to practice resembling the gods' realm, gained prominence because of a connection with the cult of the ancestors in East Asia (Tsukamoto 1979: 279–80). However, some understand his Buddha-field as a metaphor for nirvana itself (Inagaki 1998: 77). The narration of his previous life and the making of forty-eight vows garners gravity in the Pure Land Schools of East Asia. He is also considered to be one of the Five Tathāgatas.

Vairocana Buddha

Vairocana Buddha was a popular buddha in the early centuries of the current era but his popularity slowly declined, although his cult is still practiced from India to Japan (see Figure 2.2). Mentioned in many texts, he seems to be one of the first buddhas reproduced in gigantic form, which is still seen at the Dragon Grotto outside of Loyang, China, and the exquisite bronze at Tōdai-ji, Nara, Japan. Sometimes depicted as white or blue, often holding the teaching mudra (i.e., interlocking forefingers and thumbs, connected with the first teaching at Deer Park, India) his name means "Illuminator." He can represent the absolute, the union of all wisdoms or "all-encompassing wisdom," and the sun. He is sometimes counted as one of the Five Tathāgatas, but in some mandalas he is replaced by Vajrasattva, a buddha particularly associated with the Vajrayana.

Bhaiṣajyaguru Buddha

Bhaiṣajyaguru Buddha has long held a cult following even into the present. This is the Medicine Buddha, normally deep blue like the Lapis Lazuli, a healing stone, with which he is associated. He usually holds a medical plant in his right hand and a bowl of medicine in the left on his lap. According to the *Bhaiṣajyaguru vaiḍūryaprabhārāja Sūtra*, he helps with all types of medical conditions including psychological and spiritual. He also is associated with the east, made twelve vows, and helps purify negative karma. Some of the many titles of Śākyamuni are "Physician" (Pl. *bhisakka*) and "Unsurpassed Surgeon" (Pl. *anuttaro sallakata*), also indicating, perhaps unsurprisingly, that he provided medical guidance on different occasions.

FIGURE 2.2 *Buddha Vairocana.* Source: *Rubin Museum of Art, Public Domain via Wikimedia Commons.*

The Arhats

The arhats (e.g., Śāriputra, Mahāmaudgalyāyana), generally, were direct disciples of Śākyamuni Buddha, thought to have arrived at a level of awakening. There do not seem to be arguments about the listed individuals reaching awakening; rather, there were arguments on the exact nature of that level with divergence among the Buddhist sects in India. A list of 500 arhats is common but 16 are frequently encountered. That list includes Piṇḍola Bhāradvāja, Kanakavatsa, Kanaka Bhāradvāja, Subinda, Nakula, Śrībhadra, Mahākālika, Vajriputra, Gopaka, Panthaka, Rāhula, Nāgasena, Aṅgaja, Vanavāsin, Ajita, and Cūḍapanthaka. In Indian art it is often difficult to determine which arhat is indicated and we have to use the clues and contexts of the setting to aid in that determination such as the depiction of an episode in one of the narratives.

Great Bodhisattvas

Anyone who enters the bodhisattva path, the path to Buddhahood, can be considered a bodhisattva. Such an idea provides ample ground for a limitless number of bodhisattvas. There is a short list of the most important bodhisattvas that exemplify particular aspects of the nirvana project as understood within the Mahayana tradition. Mahayana places its emphasis on the twin corner stones of wisdom and compassion. Because of this, there is less emphasis on living as a monk or nun and more on the skillful means for enacting wisdom in the service of others. Examples of this would be one of the wisest bodhisattvas, the layman Vimalakīrti, or the expounder of the Buddha within (**tathāgatagarbha**) doctrine, Queen Śrīmālādevī. In this line, most bodhisattvas, male and female, are depicted wearing royal clothing and not monastic robes. In addition to indicating a more open career path for Buddhists, it also identifies them as heirs of the Dharma like a prince or princesses. In contrast to the Mahayana, the Śrāvakayāna (including the Theravada School) only recognizes two bodhisattvas; Śākyamuni before he became a buddha and Maitreya who will be the future buddha (see Figure 2.3).

Avalokiteśvara Bodhisattva is the bodhisattva of compassion. His/her (see "In China" below) wisdom is, however, not lacking. Indubitably, this is the most popular bodhisattva worldwide. One hundred and eight forms are known from Indic sources, but others appear. She/he is usually depicted in India as male while his female counterpart is Tārā Bodhisattva. Avalokiteśvara's main temple in Kathmandu has paintings of the forms around its courtyard. His/her realm is called Potala, having both an earthly presence and a presence in Amitābha's Buddha-field.

Mañjuśrī Bodhisattva is the bodhisattva of Mahayana wisdom. He is the counterpart of Avalokiteśvara but is considered to be the complement to compassion, not devoid of it. He also has many forms and appears in many texts with special connections to the Prajñāpāramitā sutras and several tantras. He has a five-peaked mountain home that may have originally been associated with the mountains around Lake Anavatapta, the lake at the center of the Buddhist cosmological world. Later, he became associated with (Mount) Wutaishan in China but also has his own Buddha-field located in the east.

Maitreya Bodhisattva is determined to be the next buddha in our world after Śākyamuni's teachings are no longer efficacious. Frequently painted yellow with hands in the teaching mudra sitting as on a chair, presently, he is teaching in Tuṣita heaven with its two courts. This is the same location that Śākyamuni abided in before his last

FIGURE 2.3 *Avalokiteśvara*. Source: *PxHere, Cco Public Domain.*

life on Earth. His name appears in a large selection of texts such as the *Cakkavatti Sīhanāda Suta* (Pali) or *Maitreyavyākaraṇa* (Sk.).

Samantabhadra Bodhisattva is considered the bodhisattva of practice or vows. As noted above, the taking of vows is important in the accounts of buddhas generating their Buddha-fields. Fulfilling those vows is the practice of the bodhisattva on the path to buddhahood. He is often depicted as white but yellow forms are mentioned also. Although his name appears in a number of texts, he seems less popular than Avalokiteśvara or Mañjuśrī. One chapter in the extensive Avataṃsaka Sutra presents the ten vows of this bodhisattva and in Sri Lanka he is considered a protector.

There are several other important bodhisattvas that have popularity within particular traditions or geographic locations. For example, Tārā, Vajrapāṇi, and Acalanātha have close affiliations with the tantric form of Buddhism and Kṣitigarbha is particularly poplar in East Asia although originating in Indian literature.

In the tantric form of Buddhism, which spread from India to Japan, all the above forms of buddhas and bodhisattvas are known. Further, this type of Buddhism also has wrathful manifestations of the buddhas and bodhisattvas. These exist in part to address the fact that negative emotional states can be very powerful and difficult to overcome. The tantras teach that these negative emotional states can be overcome by enlisting the help of the wrathful forms of buddhas and bodhisattvas. Because each person may be dominated by a particular negative emotion such as hate or envy, maintaining a lifelong practice using the appropriate form is beneficial.

FIGURE 2.4 *Chakrasaṃvara*. Source: *Tokyo National Museum, via Wikimedia Commons.*

The peaceful Buddha Akṣobhya generates the most wrathful forms noted in the literature. A few are Cakrasaṃvara (see Figure 2.4), Hevajra, Buddhakapāla, and Trailokyavijaya (Bhattacharyya 1987: 154–88). These forms of the buddha are usually detailed in blue, with cremation ground ornaments (Beer 1999: 135–320), sometimes multiple hands, legs, and faces, fanged, and with an aura of flames. These forms are seen as combating hatred. A wrathful manifestation of Amitābha is Saptaśatika Hayagrīva (Bhattacharyya 1987: 146–7) who is noted as having a miniature horse head protruding from his head in paintings along with the cremation ground ornaments. This form became very popular in Mongolia.

Wrathful manifestations of the bodhisattvas also exist. Yamāntaka, the Slayer of Death, is a manifestation of Mañjuśrī (Getty 1978: 113) and Avalokiteśvara can manifest as Māyājālakrama (69). A manifestation of Tāra is Kurukullā (127–7), an example of a semi-wrathful form who is recognized by her flowered bow and arrow, which indicates subduing in general.

There is also another class of spiritually advanced wrathful beings known as ḍāka (male) and ḍākinī (female) although much emphasis is given to the female form (Simmer-Brown 2001). Just as peaceful female bodhisattvas may act as consorts for the buddhas and peaceful male bodhisattvas, the ḍākinī can act as consorts for the wrathful buddhas and bodhisattvas. However, they are also the object of meditation within their own right and represent wisdom. Both male and female devotees are encouraged to visualize themselves as a ḍākinī in advanced practice. Vajravārāhi (Getty 1978: 132–3) the consort of Cakrasamvara, for example, is red, wears cremation ground ornaments, and of note, has a miniature sow's head protruding from her own.

In China

Before Buddhism arrived in what would eventually become China, people had already developed a complex polytheistic concept of the supermundane sphere. Indo-European gods were assimilated as additions to and not replacements of the existing system. Depictions of some of these Indo-European gods are found scattered across the landscape with a few gaining popularity. An example of a Chinese addition to the Buddhist heritage would be the red-faced, long-bearded Guan Di, a general in the Three Kingdoms era who was elevated to godhood and who became a protector of Buddhism.

Representations of the arhats are completely transformed in Chinese art. Here they are rustic types where each has one or more identifying features; they are also very eccentric. Art historians can point to notions of the Daoist Immortals influencing the artistic rendering (Sullivan 1984: 148–9), but far more influence came from the Chan/Zen School of Buddhism and its ability to artistically express aspects of awakening. Even paintings of Śākyamuni were influenced by the combination of Indian and Chinese artistic sensibilities. This, then, would be an example of the refinement of existing beings.

FIGURE 2.5 *Budai*. Source: *Gerd Eichmann via Wikimedia Commons.*

In the early centuries of the current era, Maitreya was the second most popular figure following Śākyamuni (Tshukamoto 1979: 753). He became a key figure in a widespread apocalyptic movement that lasted for a few centuries while the realm was in disunion. Unification of the country under the Sui dynasty (581–618) shifted popularity to Amitābha, particularly after his Buddha-field became associated with the Chinese cult of the ancestors, a connection that did not exist in India. In the tenth century, Maitreya's cult was reinvigorated with the manifestation of Budai (Frédéric 1995: 240), a possible tenth-century Chan/Zen monk, sometimes called "Laughing Buddha," and understood as an earthly manifestation of Maitreya (see Figure 2.5).

New forms of Avalokiteśvara (Ch. Guanyin) with no Indic precedent such as Guanyin with a Fish Basket (Ch. Yulan Guanyin) (Weidner 1994: 166–7) are found as his/her cult becomes completely sinicized. Early depictions are clearly masculine but Chinese aesthetics developed a softer look, making images of bodhisattvas more androgynous, which meant that after centuries, Guanyin became feminine in some manifestations.

Mañjuśrī's mountain realm became transposed in legend and art from the Himalayas to Wutaishan, which was eventually recognized by the Buddhist world. Avalokiteśvara's Buddha-field found a Chinese location (in Zhejiang) on a small island mountain called Putuo, off the coast of what is now called Shanghai. Samantabhadra's mountain is on the northern boarder with Tibet at Mount Emei in Sichuan. Kṣitigarbha, never very popular in India, gathered an immense following in China due to his pledge to empty the hells, as stated in the *Kṣitigarhabodhisattva pūrvapraṇidhāna Sūtra*. In East Asia, he is usually depicted as a monk, although Indic depictions have him in royal garb. His mountain home is Mount Jiuhua in Anhui. Locating the mountain homes of bodhisattvas in China demonstrates selection within Buddhism.

Tantric Buddhism spread to China before it spread to Tibet and had a following apparently among the upper classes. What would later be classified as higher and lower tantras were both transmitted but the multitude of cults, tantras, and accompanying texts were a smaller cluster than found in Tibet. Artistic examples of various tantric buddhas and bodhisattvas both peaceful and wrathful do exist and the style in general seems to not be affiliated with the two major styles that influenced Tibetan art. As with other Buddhist art forms in China, tantric images display sinicized features but the significance of the features generally holds true to their Indic origins. Chinese tantric Buddhism did not have a large following among the general population and in the later imperial periods very little survived being replaced by Tibetan forms due to the work of lamas, Tibetan religious leaders, touring in China proper.

The Chan/Zen School developed a unique artistic style well demonstrated in the painted arts starting in the Song dynastic period (960–1276). Although one finds portraits and still lifes, during this period landscapes and calligraphy come to the fore. These forms attempt to move the viewer to the awakened space of the master-artist much like the *koan* (Ch. *gong'an*) (Barber 2019: 125–45). An example would be a painting of Śākyamuni in the mountains.

In Japan

Japan inherited its Buddhist traditions from China and Korea yet refined this inheritance and developed it in a unique way. This process took centuries, but the nature of Japanese Buddhism became different from the Buddhism at its sources. The Shingon and Tendai Schools both were instrumental in introducing tantric Buddhism beginning in the early ninth century. The buddhas and bodhisattvas mentioned above, such as Vairocana, play a significant role, as does the art for meditation (Sharf and Sharf 2001: 151–97). Over time many of the Japanese native *kami* (gods) became affiliated with some buddha or bodhisattva and were understood as a manifestation of them. This is explained in the theory *honji suijaku*, or "original substance manifest traces" (Teeuwen and Rambelli 2003). With this integration, indigenization took place just as it did in China.

Mahākāla appears in a variety of forms in Sanskrit and Tibetan tantric texts. This wrathful form can function as a guardian or as the central form in meditation. The two-armed form is blue and holds a flaying knife (to destroy oath-breakers) and a skull-cup (holding Dharma enemies' blood). He wears a crown of five skulls, neckless of heads, and a snake as a sacred thread (Bhattacharyya 1987: 345–8). In Japan, he was transformed into Daikokuten a happy faced, slightly rotund man with a golden wish-granting mallet and a treasure sack (Frédéric 1995: 237). He is one of the seven gods of luck and is considered the god of wealth, the kitchen, and the household in general (see Figure 2.6).

The Japanese landscape dotted with the ubiquitous Jizō Bodhisattva (Kṣitigarbha) elevates this bodhisattva beyond his popularity in any other country. In particular, his association with children, pre- and post-birth, even to the point of being sometimes depicted as a child bodhisattva, attests to the unique process of selection in Japan (Frédéric 1995: 185–90). Shōtoku Taishi (574–622), Prince and Regent, was one of the most significant figures in Japanese Buddhist history. He is credited with composing the first Japanese constitution, which incorporated Buddhist and Confucian ideas; built temples (including Hōryū-ji, the oldest wooden building in the world); and wrote commentaries on Buddhist sutras. He is considered a manifestation of Avalokiteśvara and his image is found in both temples and nonreligious settings. These images stand as a unique Japanese development of Buddhist iconography (Kashiwahara and Sonoda 1994: 253–4).

In Tibet

By the seventh century, Tibet was surrounded by Buddhist cultures and the influences from these different traditions can still be traced in Tibetan art. For example, Tibetan paintings of clouds follow the Chinese pattern; the heavy-set wrathful forms are a copy of the style in what is today Pakistan and the graceful style of meditational forms is in the style of what today is Bengal. Although much of the wealth of Buddhism

FIGURE 2.6 *Standing Daikokuten (Mahakala) by Kaiken*. Source: *Ethnological Museum via Wikimedia Commons*.

flowed into Tibet, it was the tantric Vajrayana forms that predominated. In terms of iconography, the Vajrayana in general is less accepting of variance as other forms of Buddhism because the icons act as significant meditational tools and exacting details are important in the meditation traditions of this branch of Buddhism. Thus, an artist could not change the color of a buddha to express his/her creative idea but the face of the buddha could take on a more Tibetan appearance than an Indian one. Sometimes we find minor changes but can only speculate as to why they originated, such as the use of a Yak's head instead of a bull's head for Vajrabhairava (Getty 1978: 164). The peaceful, semi-wrathful, and wrathful manifestations of the buddhas and bodhisattvas, as exemplified above and many more, are the mainstay in Tibetan iconography and mediational practice.

In addition to buddhas and bodhisattvas, and because of the significance of the role of the guru in the Vajrayana, some of these luminaries are also depicted with much symbolism. Foremost of these is Padmasambhāva, an eighth-century master from what is now Pakistan, who is credited with the introduction of many aspects of Buddhism in Tibet. There are many historical questions surrounding this figure, but he taught Emperor Trisong Detsen (755–797[?]) and helped in the founding of the first Buddhist monastery: Samye. His depictions incorporate much Vajrayana lore. His three-pointed hat symbolizes the bodies of a buddha, he wears three sets of clothing depicting the Śrāvakayāna, Mahayana, and Vajrayana, he holds a five-wisdom vajra, a skull-cup of nectar, and a staff, etc. Machig Labdron (1055–1149), a great yogini who was a teacher of Chöd, and Jetsun Milarepa (1028–1111[?]), who was the second master in the Kagyu tradition and a great reclusive yogi and poet, as well as many others throughout the centuries find representation in Tibetan Buddhist art.

The Vajrayana in Tibet had an open ability to creatively accept the many native gods in the Tibetan pantheon. Unlike in Japan wherein the *kami* are generally beneficent if properly propitiated, the native gods of Tibet are generally malevolent by nature. A number of these are worth noting. Perhaps the most significant is the god Pehar Gyalpo, a powerful god of the native religion Bön, he was fiercely opposed to the introduction of Buddhism until subjugated by Padmasambhāva. Later this god became a protector and the oracle to His Holiness the Dalai Lama. In art, he has different depictions: sometimes white and riding a snow lion, holding weapons such as a sword, bow and arrow, and usually wearing a hat, which indicates the Buddhist refinement of a native deity. Palden Lhamo is a wrathful protectress of the Dalai Lama and Lhasa. Her identifying characteristics are associated with death, including the saddle blanket on her white mule that is made from her son's hide. In some accounts she is considered a wrathful manifestation of Śrī Devī (Lakṣmī). Finally, in Tibet, the highly controversial Dorje Shugs ldan would exemplify an original generation of a Buddhist figure. This wrathful protector of the Gelug School is thought to be the reincarnation of a Gelugpa lama—Tulku Dragpa Gyaltsen (sPrul sku Grags pa rGyal mtshan/1619–56)–whose earlier incarnation promised the founder Je Tsong kha pa to protect the order. Tulku Dragpa Gyaltsen died in mysterious circumstances and the search for his incarnation was banned. He is usually depicted riding a snow lion, wearing Tibetan-style robes and a tulku's hat, holding a wavy-blade knife to cut off defilements and a long staff crescent chopper with counter, and displaying the *kartarī* mudra, which represents discord or cutting.

Conclusion

In this brief overview we have demonstrated the complex system of transmundane and supermundane figures within Buddhism with special attention to their iconographic representations. The complexity includes an inherited system of gods originating from the Indian adaptation of the Indo-European people's cosmology, local developments, and early Buddhist expressions. Images of Śākyamuni Buddha are used to depict different aspects of the awakening experience and are important within all Buddhist-inflected countries. As the ages passed, the images of buddhas, bodhisattvas, and arhats took on more symbolic expressions reflecting increasingly complex philosophical discussions arising from Abhidharmic influences. With the transmission of Buddhism to other countries we can see a refinement, selection, and original generation of forms as three processes in the creation of each country's unique art. This chapter has focused on the artistic developments in India, China, Japan, and Tibet. Other countries such as Korea, Sri Lanka, Vietnam, and places in Central Asia also had unique developmental histories but there was not space to cover them here. There is still much research to be undertaken in the area of Buddhist depictions of the transmundane and the supermundane, and this chapter is intended to act as a brief introduction to the topic.

Further Reading and Online Resources

Beer, R. (1999), *The Encyclopedia of Tibetan Symbols and Motifs*, Boulder, CO: Shambala Publications.

Beer, R. (2003), *The Handbook of Tibetan Buddhist Symbols*, Boulder, CO: Shambala Publications.

Frédéric, L. (1995), *Buddhism Flammarion Iconographic Guides*, Paris: Flammarion.

Kleiner, F.S. (2010), *Gardner's Art through the Ages Non-Western Perspectives*, 13th edn., Boston: Wadsworth.

Lee, S.E. (1982), *A History of Far Eastern Art*, 4th edn., Englewood Cliffs, NJ: Prentice-Hall.

United Nations Educational, Scientific and Cultural Organization (UNESCO) (1992–2020), "Borobudur Temple Compounds." Available online: https://whc.unesco.org/en/list/592/ (accessed June 30, 2020).

References

Barber, A.W. (2019), *Sinicizing Buddhism: Studies in Doctrine, Practice, Fine Arts, Performing Arts*, Calgary: Vogelstein Press.
Beer, R. (1999), *The Encyclopedia of Tibetan Symbols and Motifs*, Boston: Shambhala Publications.
Bhattacharyya, B. (1987), *The Indian Buddhist Iconography*, Calcutta: Firma K.L. Mukhopadhyay.
"Buddhas' Name Sutra" (2002), *The Soka Gakkai Dictionary of Buddhism*, Tokyo: Soka Gakkai.
Buswell, R.E., ed. (2004), *Encyclopaedia of Buddhism*, New York: Macmillian.
Chandra, L. (1996), *Iconography of the Thousand Buddhas*, New Delhi: International Academy of Indian Culture and Aditya Prakashan.
Frédéric, L. (1995), *Buddhism Flammarion Iconographic Guides*, Paris: Flammarion.
Getty, A. (1978), *The Gods of Northern Buddhism*, New Delhi: Munshiram Manoharlal Publishers.
Inagaki, H. (1998), *T'an-Luan's Commentary on Vasubandhu's Discourse on the Pure Land*, Kyoto: Nagata Bunshodo.
Kashiwahara, Y. and K. Sonoda, eds. (1994), *Shapers of Japanese Buddhism*, trans. G. Sekimori, Tokyo: Kōsei Publishing.
Kashyap, B.J., ed. (1959), "Vakkali Suttaṃ," in *The Saṃyutta Nikāya* (2–3), 340–4, Bihar: Pāli Publication Board.
Monier-Williams, Sir M. (1951), *A Sanskrit-English Dictionary*, Oxford: Clarendon Press.
Rhys Davids, T.W. and C.A.F. Rhys Davids (1977), "The Ward Rune of Āṭānāṭa" in T.W. Rhys Davids (ed.), *Dialogues of the Buddha*, Part 3, 188–97, Old Woking: Unwin Brothers, Gresham Press.
Sharf, R.H. and E.H. Sharf, eds. (2001), *Living Images: Japanese Buddhist Icons in Context*, Stanford, CA: Stanford University Press.
Simmer-Brown, J. (2001), *Dakini's Warm Breath the Feminine Principle in Tibetan Buddhism*, Boston: Shambhala.
Sullivan, M. (1984), *The Arts of China*, Taiwan edn., Taipei: Southern Materials Center.
Teeuwen, M. and F. Rambelli (2003), *Buddhas and Kami in Japan: Honji Suijaku as a Combinatory Paradigm*, London: Routledge Curzon.
Tshukamoto, Z. (1979), *A History of Early Chinese Buddhism*, trans. L. Hurvitz, Tokyo: Kodansha International.
Weidner, M., ed. (1994), *Latter Days of the Law Images of Chinese Buddhism 850–1850*, Lawrence, KS: Spencer Museum of Art.

Glossary Terms

Asuras In Indian mythology, the Asuras are a class of divine beings or demigods below the gods (devas). The term is often translated as "titans." They occupy the Desire realm in the Buddhist three realm theory. In general, they are understood as being driven by jealously, anger, and pugnacity, and were frequently at war with the gods who unseated them on the top of Mount Meru. Concord was eventually reached. One is reborn into their realm due to a mix of wholesome and unwholesome merit. They can be depicted in different ways but a three-headed multiarmed form is common. There are a few commonly encountered in Buddhist literature.

Iconography The study of symbols and themes found in visual art that can be used for identification, to convey meaning, and to further a narrative. Much of Buddhist art is iconographic. Although this iconographic visual art developed originally in India and utilized symbols that were understandable within that cultural context, as Buddhism moved into other parts of Asia, aspects of the visual art changed to incorporate symbols understood in other cultures. For example, Mañjuśrī Bodhisattva is often depicted with a sword in Indian art but in Chinese art he frequently holds a Chinese sceptre. Iconography is important in the study of Buddhist art, but it is essential as a key element in certain types of meditations.

Nāgas Semi-divine serpents in Indian mythology who have magical abilities the most notable of which is shapeshifting. They can appear as a serpent, half serpent and half human, or fully human. The males are handsome, the females are beautiful, and both are powerful being beneficial or dangerous to humans. There are different clans and they are said to occupy an underground realm but frequent our world or can mount the sky. Generally, they are associated with water, wealth, and mystic knowledge. A *nāga* protected Śākyamuni Buddha from a storm and the founder of Mahayana received his knowledge of the perfection of wisdom from a *nāga*. In Indian art, they are usually depicted cobra-like but in East Asia, they appear dragon-like.

Śramaṇa General term for a religious ascetic. This term came to be associated with non-Brahmanical movements that promoted the ascetic lifestyle as the best means for achieving a religious goal. Buddhism is one of these movements but in contrast to other movements advocated a moderate form of asceticism called "the Middle Way." Commonly, a man or woman becoming a Buddhist ascetic would leave their home life to live in a monastery or to wander. Novices who keep the ten vows are called *śrāmaṇera* (m) or *śrāmaṅerī* (f). This is the first stage to becoming a fully ordained monk or nun.

Tathāgatagarbha Mahayana doctrine about the "Buddha within." This doctrine never became a Buddhist philosophical school, but it influenced different forms of Buddhist practice including Vajrayana and Zen. The concept put forth in several Mahayana sutras is that one is already a buddha but is unaware of this fact. This being true, then the way to realization is to stop producing what obscures instead of a step-by-step progress to the goal. In English this is often referred to as the "Buddha within." In the Yogācāra influenced Buddhist philosophy, *tathāgatagarbha* is understood as the potential for Buddhahood.

Transmundane/supermundane Beyond or above the world. Buddhist doctrine makes a very clear distinction between beings who are transmundane and those who are supermundane. Transmundane or beyond the world are those who have accomplished advanced levels of the Buddhist goal of liberation. This would include complete perfect buddhas, private buddhas, upper-level bodhisattvas and arhats. The element they have in common is wisdom from insight. Supermundane beings or those above the world refers to the supernatural beings who are within the three realms. This would include the gods, titans, and other semidivine beings. The element they have in common is a vast store of positive merit. Although more powerful than humans, these supermundate beings are also subject to rebirth and falling from their high status.

Yakṣas In Indian mythology, they are nature spirits associated with forests and mountains, which can be malicious or beneficial. They are associated with fruitfulness and buried treasure. Early stone depictions at Buddhist stupas of *yakṣī* (f) are beautiful young women with fruit-like breasts and full hips. Males were depicted as either warriors or rotund and dwarf-like. In Buddhism *yakṣa* generals may also be the patron spirit of particular cities and they along with their armies become protectors of Buddhism. They appear in a number of Buddhist texts but the most important is the god of the north, Vaiśravaṇa.

3

Buddhist Scripture

Ronald S. Green

There are many Buddhist traditions throughout the world, which often vary in doctrine, beliefs, and practices. Remarkably, even though there is a great diversity of Buddhist traditions worldwide, they all generally agree that the written scriptures that record and preserve the Buddha's teachings, the Dharma, may be classified into three major divisions of scriptures known as collections or baskets (Sk. *piṭaka*). These three baskets (Sk. **tripiṭaka**) are (1) the sutra collection (Sk. **Sutra Piṭaka**; Pali. Sutta Piṭaka), (2) the *vinaya* collection (Sk. **Vinaya Piṭaka**), and (3) the Abhidharma collection (Sk. **Abhidharma Piṭaka**; Pali. Abhidhamma Piṭaka).

Although this is generally agreed upon, there is sometimes disagreement about what constitutes the specific contents of one or more of these three baskets as well as which writings are more important than others. Among the collections of Buddhist scriptures in the world, the main ones used today are the **Pali canon**, the Chinese canon, and the Tibetan canon. The Pali canon is written in the Indian language Pali and is considered to be the oldest. It contains the central teachings for Theravada Buddhism, the main type of Buddhism practiced in Southeast Asia. The Chinese Buddhist canon is the main scriptural source for East Asian Mahayana Buddhists. It contains translations of Sanskrit and Pali texts, sometimes including multiple Chinese translations of the same text. The Tibetan Buddhist canon includes many of these texts as well as esoteric writings called tantras. The three divisions of Buddhist scriptures as well as some of the main differences in the three canons are considered below.

The Sutra Piṭaka

The sutra collection contains a variety of scriptures claiming to record the words of the Buddha and may include certain commentaries on the sutras by learned adherents. Just as a doctor sutures together a wound, sutra means "stitch." A sutra stitches

FIGURE 3.1 *Illustration from a twelfth-century Buddhist manuscript from Bangladesh or West Bengal, India.* Source: *Metropolitan Museum of Art.*

together ideas and it is the material these ideas are written on, just like the word "text" is related to textile. Each of the collections of Buddhist scriptures contains a huge number of sutras, making it impossible for one person to memorize any entire canon. In fact, Buddhist sects or schools typically rely on a smaller set of sutras as their primary sources for philosophy and practice (see Figure 3.1).

Sutras typically contain written stories of the Buddha's life and his words of instructions to his followers. These stories are commonly written in dialogue or discussion format. Many sutras have numerous repetitions of questions and responses.

This is likely related to the early nature of these scriptures as lessons to be learned by repetition, chanted, and transmitted orally (Norman 1997: 104). For example, a text may describe events about one person who then describes these events to another who in turn relates them to a third person (Gethin 2007). Owing to these characteristics, sutras can be extremely lengthy while the essential sayings of the Buddha therein may be relatively short. The shorter sutras often set this out in brief utterances, while the middle-length and longer sutras do so in the context of many interesting scenarios that show off the Buddha's skill in responding to people in a great variety of situations, his wit and sense of humor as well as his compassion for all humanity, even the famous mass murderer Aṅgulimāla, who is won over to the Buddha's path (*Aṅgulimāla Sutta*). While a large number of the sutras are addressed to monastics, in others he engages in talks with kings, priests, ascetics, villagers, philosophers, and those who dispute him. Some of these lessons are taught with straightforward instructions, while others involve similes and parables. Nor is the Buddha the only teacher in the sutras; his disciples are also sometimes the main speakers and teachers of the Dharma.

It is interesting to note that the Buddha did not write down any of his teachings and may have rejected the idea of translating them into Sanskrit (Horner 1963: 193–4). According to tradition, shortly after he passed away, 500 of his most learned followers gathered outside a cave in the city of Rajagaha to recite all of the teachings they had received so they could be memorized and preserved. This famous meeting is known as the **First Buddhist Council** and is traditionally dated 544 BCE or around 460 BCE by some estimates (Bechert 1991–1997). The night before the meeting, the Buddha's cousin and disciple Ananda, who was known for having an unusually good memory, achieved a higher state of insight known as arhatship. So, during the council meeting, he was able to recite the words he had heard the Buddha speak and this became the sutras. Each of the events Ananda recalled typically begin with the statement, "Thus I heard," followed by where the Buddha was when he gave the teaching and who else was there that heard it.

The monk Upali was also present for the First Buddhist Council. Upali had been a barber, which was considered to be a part of a lower caste in India that was discriminated against. However, Upali found that such discrimination did not exist within the Buddhist community and, perhaps related to this, he became very interested in the Buddhist code of behavior. For this reason, he was asked to recite all the Buddha had said about how monks and nuns should behave, that is, the vinaya, so it could be preserved and followed. At that point, the scriptures were divided into two collections: the Dharma teachings Buddha gave through discussions (the Sutra Piṭaka) and the rules for monastic conduct (the Vinaya Piṭaka). Therefore, the teachings of the Buddha came to be called the Dharma-Vinaya (Pali. Dhamma-Vinaya) before they were called "Buddhism."

The Second Buddhist Council was held about seventy years after the Buddha's passing and it is said that during it, there was a spit in the community, the sangha. Sometime after this, there is evidence that Buddhism further divided into eighteen or twenty groups, each with their own version of the teachings, which they transmitted orally. Only much later were these teachings written down in collections of scriptural texts.

The history of the formation of the Buddhist scriptural canon remains largely obscure to modern scholarship. Traditionally, this is thought to have occurred at the time of the Fourth Buddhist Council in 29 BCE (Drewes 2015: 131), about the same time that the Pali canon was written down, which is also the date Theravada Buddhism is said to have begun. It is likely that the oral traditions preserved a much larger range of the Buddha's teachings than what has survived in the various canons. For example, Emperor Asoka is said to have expelled "heretics" and reevaluated the Pali canon at the Third Buddhist Council in 250 BCE (Centāraśśēri 1998). While there exist many Buddhist texts writing in Sanskrit and in Chinese translation, the Pali canon is the only one to have survived intact in its original Indian language. The Pali canon divides the sutras into five categories based on the length of the discourse. Known as the *nikayas* (collections), these are:

- Digha Nikaya—the "long collection" (34 sutras)
- Majjhima Nikaya—the "middle-length collection" (152 sutras)
- Samyutta Nikaya—the "grouped collection" sorted by topic (2,889 sutras)
- Anguttara Nikaya—the "further-factored collection" (around 8,777 sutras)
- Khuddaka Nikaya—the "collection of little texts" (18 books plus numerous verses and fragments).

As Buddhism spread to China in the first century CE and then to Tibet in the seventh century CE, scriptures were translated into the languages of those countries (see Figure 3.3). While both the Chinese and Tibetan canons contain translations of sutras that appear in the Pali canon, they also include a unique body of literature known as the Mahayana scriptures, which reflect important shifts in thinking both in the early Indian Buddhist community and later developments. The name Mahayana means the "Greater Vehicle," which implies that Mahayana Buddhism and its scriptures represent a superior path. The ultimate aim of Mahayana practice is not the fulfillment of one's aspiration to attain the insight of arhatship as in Theravada, but the complete awakening of the Buddha. This is illustrated in Mahayana writings through the image of the ideal character know as a bodhisattva, who works for the enlightenment of both self and all others, seen as inseparably connected. In the Pali canon, only the Buddha is called the bodhisattva, meaning the "Awakening Being," the one waking up. A larger number of bodhisattvas appear in Mahayana scriptures, and the practitioner is also referred to by this designation.

In addition, some of the most important Mahayana writings, including the *Perfection of Wisdom Sutras* (Prajñāpāramitā Sutras), not found in the Pali canon, point to what is described as a more profound wisdom that can be attained through deep meditation on emptiness (*śūnyatā*). According to these writings, all things are empty of an independent self-nature, but are constantly coming into existence and passing away in interdependent relationships with all other things around them. While this is also a principle of Theravada Buddhism, these Mahayana texts stress that meditation on emptiness is central to awakening.

FIGURE 3.2 *The Tripitaka Koreana, wooden printing blocks, at the Temple of Haeinsa in South Korea. The world's most comprehensive and oldest intact version of the Buddhist scriptures in Chinese. Photograph by Joone Hur.* Source: *Wikimedia.*

The Chinese canon also contains other texts not in the Pali canon, but which are said to be in the words of the Buddha. Theravada Buddhists and others have called such texts, including the famous *Lotus Sutra*, fictitious. The oldest and most comprehensive version of the Chinese Buddhist canon is the *Tripiṭaka Koreana* (see Figure 3.2) carved onto 81,258 wooden printing blocks in the thirteenth century CE. Housed in the Temple of Haeinsa, which is a UNESCO World Heritage Site, the woodblocks are designated a National Treasure of South Korea. The current standard Chinese Buddhist canon is the *Taishō Shinshū Daizōkyō*. Generally known as the Taishō canon, it was compiled in during the Japanese Taishō period (1912–1926). The Taishō canon contains 2,920 works (3,053 including variant versions of the same texts), 11,970 fascicles, and 80,645 pages.

In addition to Mahayana scriptures, the Tibetan canon includes a distinctive group of Indian writings called tantras. These describe the yogic practices and rituals that lead directly to enlightenment. Such tantra practices typically involve meditations that use mudra hand gestures that imitate the postures of specific bodhisattvas, often while holding a ritual instrument known as a vajra and symbolizing cutting through illusions. They also involve mantra vibrational sounds associated with bodhisattvas and aimed at arousing their attainment in the practitioner, and visualizations of Buddhas and bodhisattvas that typically use mandala paintings of them. These observances are known collectively as Tantric Buddhism, which is thought of as Vajrayana, the Way of the Vajra (a symbolic weapon with properties of a diamond and thunderbolt).

The Vinaya Piṭaka

The Vinaya Piṭaka can generally be characterized as a collection of texts specifying rules of discipline or guidelines for behavior for Buddhist followers, particularly monks and nuns but sometimes including lay adherents. Beyond the regulatory directions, these scriptures have provided scholars with a wealth of additional information such as the dates, circumstances, and proceedings of monastic assemblies. In modern times, this information has been applied, for example, to understanding proper monastic behavior in 2007 during the Saffron Revolution when monks protested against the government in Myanmar (Gravers 2012). Factors such as differences in translations, interpretations, and the special circumstances of isolated communities or countries may account for slight differences in contents of vinaya scriptures. Regardless of the variety and as with the sutras, the Buddha is held to be the authority for truth of the vinaya, which Buddhists widely believe to be his direct instruction that cautions followers.

The word "vinaya" means to "lead," "remove," or "train," all of which are a part of the Buddhist interpretation of it. Although the Vinaya Piṭaka is considered to be the first of the three baskets (*tripiṭaka*) of Buddhist teachings, compared to the sutras, it receives less attention from researchers and some modern practitioners have criticized it as old fashioned, particularly outside of Asia. However, it should be remembered that the teachings of the Buddha were long called the Dharma-vinaya, implying that the sutras and the vinaya formed a unified set of teachings that came to be called Buddhism. From the perspective of those who specialize in the study of the vinaya, it is acceptance of these principles that makes one a Buddhist, not belief in the philosophy found in certain sutra favored by one sect or another. That is, it is how one lives concretely, how they are led, how they remove immorality, and how they train rather than a lofty system of beliefs that makes a Buddhist.

Some scholars have presented the vinaya as "the law" and a series of injunctions similar to that found in European legal systems rather than as a method for training (Voyce 2015). It is interesting to note that it is truly a guide for conduct rather than a set of vows as in the cases of many of the world's religions. A master officiating the reception asks the one who wishes to accept the guidelines one principle at a time if he are she is able to abide by that standard. The person receiving the principles is to respond to each with "Yes, I can."

According to tradition, at the time when the Buddha first formed the community around him, the sangha was small and devoted to his teachings. Therefore, the community lived in harmony and there was no need for warnings about behavior. The Buddha provided all of the counseling to trainees that eventually became parts of the Vinaya Piṭaka because of specific incidences that arose among the growing group of followers about behaviors that might cause disharmony within the sangha or problems for the individual's attainment. Perhaps owning to the strong physical and social desire for sex, the first rule came about because one of the Buddha's followers went home briefly and was intimate with his former wife. After the follower returned and confessed this, the Buddha made a rule that from that time onward, anyone who engaged in any type of sexual activity was "defeated" and no longer a part of the sangha. The next few rules became necessary because followers disobeyed the first in various ways that needed clarification (Stevens 1990).

Part of the guidelines deal with food restrictions. An ordained "monk" is actually called a "bhikṣu" in Buddhism and a "nun" is called a "bhikṣuṇī." Respectively, these

FIGURE 3.3 *Chinese text of the Diamond Sutra at Nung Chan Temple in Taipei, Taiwan. Photograph by Ian Chen.* Source: *Guttorm Norberg Gunderson via Wikimedia Commons.*

words literally mean male beggar and female beggar. Even though it is clear that by the time the vinaya was committed to writing, few begged for all of their meals, the officiating masters asks if the receiver is able to live the rest of their lives on alms. The vinaya also specifies that bhikṣu and bhikṣuṇī must humbly accept food and other alms from the laity so that the non-monastic community can build merit by their good deed. Further, the vinaya requires monastics to serve the laity by daily recitation of verses for their well-being.

A set of rules of behavior known as the *Pratimoksha* (Pali. *Patimokkha*) is central to the vinaya. The Buddha and his disciples passed this along orally and eventually numerous different versions arose and developed among different groups of Buddhists. While at least six different sets of vinaya texts existed in the past, three of these are used today. These are all basically the same with only minor differences. Most Buddhists in Southeast Asia follow the Theravada vinaya, which has 227 rules for bhikṣus (Pali. *bhikkhu*) and 311 for bhikṣuṇīs (Pali. *bhikkhunī*). Buddhists in East Asia mostly follow the Dharmaguptaka vinaya, which has 250 rules for bhikṣus and 348 rules for bhikṣuṇīs. Buddhists in Tibet and Mongolia follow the Mūlasarvāstivāda vinaya, which has 253 rules for the bhikṣus and 364 rules for bhikṣuṇīs. All three of these vinayas come from early Buddhist communities and none of them are Mahayana in origin. Therefore, even Mahayana Buddhist monks and nuns are ordained according to the monastic code of one of the eighteen or twenty early traditions of Buddhism.

In addition to the *Pratimoksha* section containing the main rules for behavior, the Vinaya Piṭaka also consists of other texts that explain how the rules came about, give further instructions on how to act, describe the lives of important Buddhists, and make statements about Buddhist teachings. The various sections of the Theravada Vinaya are outlined in three parts as follows:

1. *Suttavibhanga*: This includes the basic rules of conduct (*Pratimoksha*) along with the origin story for each. It is explained here that if a monk violates any one of four specific rules or if a nun violates any of eight specific rules, they are "defeated" and expelled from the order. This section of the vinaya also describes when and how one is to confess to violations before others. Rules for training and those for settling disputes are also included.
2. *Khandhaka*: The first section is about the time just after the Buddha's awakening when he gave his first talks to a group of five monks in the forest and stories about how some of his followers achieved their attainments. Procedures for observing special days of purification and services for the community are also given. The second section in this part elaborates on the conduct expected of bhikṣuṇīs. It also gives a detailed account of the First and Second Buddhist Councils, particularly in terms of the Bhikṣuṇī sangha.
3. *Parivara*: A summary of the preceding sections, with synopses of the rules reorganized in several ways.

The Abhidharma Piṭaka

The third basket of Buddhist teachings, the Abhidharma Piṭaka, formed between the third century BCE and the third century CE, and was codified between 400 CE and 450 CE (Swearer 1992: 336–42). Theravada Buddhists maintain a story in their scriptures that in the fourth week after his enlightenment, the Buddha meditated upon the contents of the Abhidharma and bright light emanated from his body as a sign of its truth. The scriptures further report that the Buddha ascended to Tuṣita heaven where he taught the truth of the Abhidharma to his mother (see Figure 3.4).

The contents of Abhidharma writings vary among traditions and are widely believed to be systematic classifications of the Buddha's teachings. Generally, Abhidharma literature lists, summarizes, expounds, and enlarges upon the essential characteristics of the Buddha's teachings found in the more elaborate and often repetitive writings of the sutras. The name Abhidharma likely gives us an indication of the intended purpose and content of these writings. "Abhi" can express such ideas as higher, best, special, etc., while "dharma" means the teachings of the Buddha. According to Buddhaghosa (early fifth century CE), who was an extremely important commentator on the Abhidharma for Theravada Buddhism, when used in conjunction, the terms abhi- and dhamma convey the feeling of supplementary and special Dharma. Owing to this meaning, some scholars feel the very word Abhidharma indicates that these writings are not a part of the Buddha's original messages but arose as teaching tools about them (Migot 1954: 537–40). However, the name may as likely express that the contents are a separate basket of essential teachings just as they are considered to be, with no indication that they are not the Buddha's words.

There are two major opinions about how the Abhidharma literature arose to become a third piṭaka. A number of Japanese scholars believe the contents of discussions and debates on the Dharma were collected, summarized, and systematized and that these became the Abhidharma Piṭaka (Nakamura 1980). A European view holds that in the Pali canon there existed three bodies of literature for study: the sutras, the vinaya, and *mātikās* (Sk. *mātikās*). An early meaning of *mātikās* is, "a list of items or words that serve as the object of debate or discussion, the technical terms of the commentarial literature" (Pruden 1988: xxxviii). It may be that the Abhidharma Piṭaka began as such a list. Over time, the bare list underwent organization to a remarkable degree. Regardless of the format as codified lists, the Abhidharma Piṭaka is more than strictly analytical documents and advice against proceeding in such a way. It contains the essentials for a philosophical and ethical basis for living and understanding reality.

There are vast amounts of materials of and about the Abhidharma Piṭaka in a number of languages, although only a small amount survive in original Indian languages compared to the sutras and vinayas. Through several chapters of the famous text *Visuddhimagga* (*The Path of Purification*), Buddhaghosa summarizes the Theravada Abhidhamma literature. Buddhaghosa systematized the writings into seven texts:

1 the *Book of the Elements of Existence* (*Dhamma-sangani*), which contains a list of both mental elements organized in relation to various meditations and material elements organized into groups;

2 the *Book of Classifications* (*Vibhanga*), which defines the aggregates (*skandha*), fields (*āyatana*), and faculties (*indriya*), and so on;

3 the *Book of Points of Controversy* (*Kathāvatthu*), which deals with 219 points of controversy significant for the history of the development of Buddhist thought;

4 the *Book of Individuals* (*Puggalapannatti*), which describes the different types of clerics and lay persons;

5 the *Book of Elements* (*Dhātukathā*), which is concerned with the elements (*dhātu*);

6 the *Book of Pairs* (*Yamaka*), which derives its name from its treatment of questions in a "doubled," namely, positive and negative, fashion; and

7 the *Book of Causality* (*Patthāna*), which describe the relations existing between individual dharmas.

FIGURE 3.4 *The Buddha teaching the Abhidhamma to his mother in Tushita heaven, at Wat Olak Madu, Kedah. Photograph by Photo Dharma from Sadao, Thailand.* Source: *Wikimedia commons.*

The first chapter dealing with the Abhidharma in the *Visuddhimagga*, chapter 14, reviews the type of information received through each sense organ and explains that which we understand as reality, consisting of sense data, is only a small part of a larger reality. That is to say, empirical reality is relative and there exists an ultimate reality beyond the scope of the senses. The three areas of analysis in the Abhidharma literature are then (1) the mind, (2) matter, and (3) ultimate reality.

The Abhidharma literature categorizes the elements of reality (dharmas) into four types: (1) mind, (2) coefficients of mind, (3) matter, and (4) ultimate reality. Of these, the first three are conditioned and impure. Accordingly, only the unconditioned can be ultimate and pure. There are three unconditioned things: space and two types of extinctions (nirvana). The two types of extinctions are "extinction due to knowledge" and "extinction not due to knowledge." We see from this that although it is stated that there are four types of reality, the first three types are clearly considered different than the fourth. Here the *Visuddhimagga* elaborately outlines the numerous categories making up each of the four types of reality. Eventually the text turns its attention back to an evaluation of the mind, which is identified as that which is at the root of our discriminated reality. Clearly, the complex divisions and categorizations have led to this most important point. The conclusion, as expounded in sutras, is that the only way to realize ultimate truth and undefiled reality is to develop and purify the mind (*citta*). From this point of view, the rationale for creating the complex analytic categories found thus far in these Abhidharma texts may stem from the assumption that individuals have no impetus for striving to understand ultimate reality until they are to the point of realizing such exists. By so methodically dealing with the nature of the senses, those committed to the teaching method of the Abhidharma now see that the mind is essentially in charge of the world and to reach further understanding, it is the mind that must be developed. After an intense treatment of the Four Noble Truths that follows, there is a detailed description of states of meditation and the specifics for the mindfulness meditation practice of Theravada Buddhism. So, the treatment of the Abhidharma flows smoothly into the prescription for practices in the text. Such practices, which are subject of some popularity today, include meditation on thirty-two parts of the body, said to lead to insight on the nature of the body without morbidity or fascination. Another of these meditations is an analysis of the body as comprised of four primary elements. This is to dispel the delusion of the body's solidity (Mendis 2006).

Buddhist Scriptures Today

There are international efforts to digitize Buddhist scriptures and to translate them into English. A nonprofit group called 84000 is committed to translating the complete Tibetan canon over the next 100 years (84000 n.d.-b). The project was started in 2009 when a group of monks became concerned that only 5 percent of Tibetan Buddhist texts had been translated into English. 84000 is the number of teachings the Buddha is said to have given (84000 n.d.-a). Meanwhile, the Buddhist Digital Resource Center headquartered in Cambridge, Massachusetts, is working to digitize the Tibetan Buddhist canon (Buddhist Digital Resource Center 2017).

The Japanese nonprofit organization Bukkyō Dendō Kyōkai (Society for Promotion of Buddhism) is also working to make a complete English translation of the modern collection of the Chinese Buddhist canon, the *Taishō Shinshū Daizōkyō* (Bukkyo Dendo Kyokai [BDK] 2020). This group also estimates that it could take 100 years to complete the project (BDK America n.d.). Translations of Buddhist texts from Chinese into English have been greatly aided by digitization projects and the creation of the Digital Dictionary of Buddhism by former University of Tokyo professor A. Charles Muller. In 2008, after fourteen years of meticulous work, a separate group of researchers led by University of Tokyo professor Masahiro Shimoda rolled out an immense digital collection of Chinese Buddhist scriptures that people around the world could access through the internet (The SAT Daizōkyō Text Database 2018) (see Figure 3.5). The digitized Chinese characters in this project, which is called SAT (short for *Saṃgaṇikīkṛtaṃ Taiśotripiṭakaṃ*, the Sanskrit phrase for the *Taishō Shinshū Daizōkyō*), are also linked to the English definitions in the Digital Dictionary of Buddhism (Muller 2020). The Taishō canon is also being digitized and distributed free on CD-ROM and the internet by the Chinese Buddhist Electronic Text Association (CBETA) in Taiwan.

In modern times, Buddhist feminists have criticized some of what is found in the Vinaya Piṭaka and related monastic practices because, for example, most Theravada Buddhist communities forbid women from entering the order, so that there is no bhikṣuṇī sangha in many countries that are majority Buddhist (Gross 1992). They have raised questions about why there should be more rules for women than men, especially in light of the fact that some of the extra rules seem to be only to give women lower status than men. For example, nuns must rise when a monk enters the room, but the opposite is not the case. The nun Dhammananda believes that Buddhism naturally implies feminism and has stated, "I became a feminist because I am a Buddhist" and "The Buddha was a feminist" (Queen et al. 1996: 269). Others are critical of the idea that Buddhism is feminism and feminism is Buddhism (Byrne 2013).

The Abhidharma Piṭaka has gained an increase in scholarly attention in recent years expressed by productions of new translations and commentaries, meditation manuals, as well as in use for guidance in meditative practice in Southeast Asia, Myanmar, and elsewhere in the world. Today, such writings are increasingly published in European languages. The American Theravada monk Bhikkhu Bodhi has offered a number of Abhidharma study sessions and some of these receive many views on YouTube (Bodhi 2018). He has also translated Abhidharma and other Theravada scriptural literature into English.

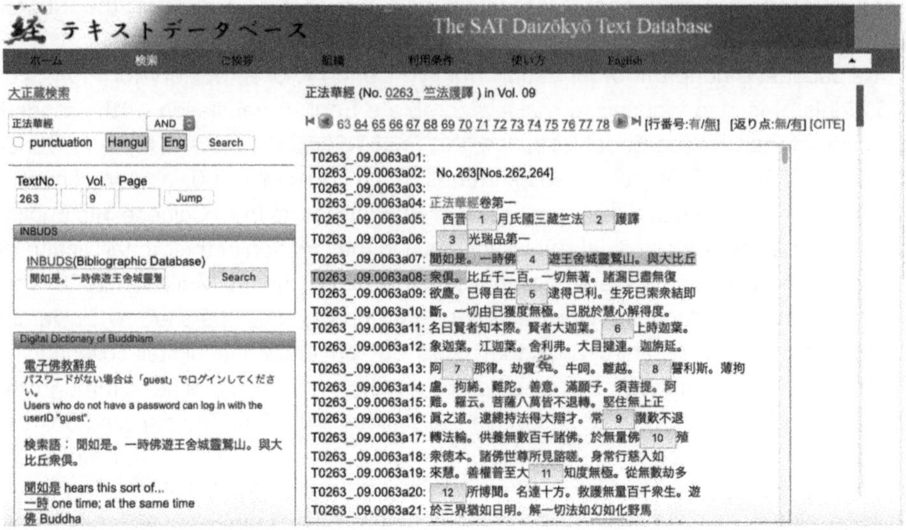

FIGURE 3.5 *Digitized version of the* Lotus Sutra *on the SAT website, showing English translations from the Digital Dictionary of Buddhism.* Source: *Ronald S. Green/University of Tokyo.*

Further Reading and Online Resources

Books

Bodhi, B., trans. (2012), *The Numerical Discourses of the Buddha: A New Translation of the Anguttara Nikaya*, Boston: Wisdom Publications.

Buddhaghosa, B.N., trans. (2010), *The Path of Purification (Visuddhimagga)*, Columbo: Buddhist Publication Society.

Emanuel, S.M., ed. (2013), *A Companion to Buddhist Philosophy*, Hoboken, NJ: Wiley-Blackwell.

Ñanamoli, B. and B. Bodhi, trans. (1995), *The Middle Length Discourses of the Buddha: A New Translation of the Majjhima Nikaya*, Boston: Wisdom Publications.

Nārada, M. and B. Bodhi, trans. (2003), *A Comprehensive Manual of Abhidhamma: The Abhidhammattha Sangaha*, Onalaska, WA: Pariyatti Publishing; Buddhist Publication Society.

Online Resources

Bhadantácariya Buddhaghosa (2010), *The Path of Purification* (*Visuddhimagga*), trans. B. Ñáóamoli. *Access to Insight.* Available online: https://www.accesstoinsight.org/lib/authors/nanamoli/PathofPurification2011.pdf (accessed September 29, 2020).

Various Translators (2005), "Tipitaka: The Pali Canon." *Access to Insight.* Available online: https://www.accesstoinsight.org/tipitaka/ (accessed September 29, 2020).

References

84000 (n.d.-a), "A Brand New Beginning." Available online: https://84000.co/brand-new-beginning/ (accessed June 28, 2020).

84000 (n.d.-b), "Home." Available online: https://84000.co/ (accessed June 28, 2020).

Aṅgulimāla Sutta (n.d.), "About Aṅgulimāla Aṅgulimāla Sutta (MN 86)." *Dhammatalks.org.* Available online: https://www.dhammatalks.org/suttas/MN/MN86.html (accessed June 28, 2020).

BDK America (n.d.), "Translation Mahayana Buddhist Canon." Available online: https://www.bdkamerica.org/translation-mahayana-buddhist-canon (accessed June 28, 2020).

Bechert, H., ed. (1991–1997), *The Dating of the Historical Buddha* (Symposium), 3 vols., Göttingen: Vandenhoeck & Ruprecht.

Bodhi, B. (2018), "The Theravada Abhidhamma with Bhikkhu Bodhi (Class #1, 5 Mar 2018)," *YouTube*, September 30. Available online: https://www.youtube.com/watch?v=mPztefkY778 (accessed June 28, 2020).

Buddhist Digital Resource Center (2017), "Home." Available online: https://www.tbrc.org/ (accessed June 28, 2020).

Bukkyo Dendo Kyokai (BDK) (2020). Available online: https://www.bdk.or.jp/english/ (accessed June 28, 2020).

Byrne, J.M. (2013), "Why I Am Not a Buddhist Feminist: A Critical Examination of 'Buddhist Feminism'," *Sociology*, 21 (2): 180–94.

Centāraśśēri, Ṭ.E.P. (1998), *History of the Indigenous Indians*, New Delhi: APH Publishing Corporation.

Drewes, D. (2015), "Oral Texts in Indian Mahayana," *Indo-Iranian Journal*, 58 (2): 117–41.

Gethin, R. (2007), "What's in a Repetition? On Counting the Suttas of the Saṃyutta-nikāya," *Journal of the Pali Text Society*, 29: 365–87.

Gravers, M. (2012), "Monks, Morality and Military: The Struggle for Moral Power in Burma—and Buddhism's Uneasy Relation with Lay Power," *Contemporary Buddhism, An Interdisciplinary Journal*, 13 (1): 1–33.

Gross, R.M. (1992), *Buddhism after Patriarchy: A Feminist History, Analysis, and Reconstruction of Buddhism*, New York: State University of New York Press.

Horner, I.B., trans. (1963), *The Book of the Discipline* (Vinaya-Piṭaka), Vol. 5, *Culla Vagga*, London: Luzac & Company.

Mendis, N.K.G. (2006), "The Abhidhamma in Practice," *Access to Insight*, BCBS edn. Available online: http://www.accesstoinsight.org/lib/authors/mendis/wheel322.html (accessed June 28, 2020).

Migot, A. (1954), "XV. Un grand disciple du Buddha: Sâriputra. Son rôle dans l'histoire du bouddhisme et dans le développement de l'Abhidharma," *Bulletin de l'École française d'Extrême-Orient*, 46 (2): 537–40.

Muller, A.C., ed. (2020), *Digital Dictionary of Buddhism*. Available online: http://www.buddhism-dict.net/ddb/ (accessed June 28, 2020).

Nakamura, H. (1980), *Indian Buddhism: A Survey with Bibliographical Notes*, Kansai University of Foreign Studies, Osaka: Motilal Banarsidass Publishers.

Norman, K.R. (1997), *A Philological Approach to Buddhism: The Bukkyo Dendo Kyokai Lectures 1994*, Vol. 5, *Buddhist Forum*, London: School of Oriental and African Studies.

Pruden, L.M. (1988), "The Abhidhamma: The Origins, Growth and Development of a Literary Tradition," in Vasubandhu, *Abhidharmakośabhāṣya*, Vol. 1, edited by L. de La Vellée Poussin, xxxviii, Berkeley, CA: Asian Humanities Press.

Queen, C.S. and S.B. King (1996), *Engaged Buddhism: Buddhist Liberation Movements in Asia*, New York: State University of New York Press.

The SAT Daizōkyō Text Database (2018), "Home." Available online: https://21dzk.l.u-tokyo.ac.jp/SAT/index_en.html (accessed June 28, 2020).

Stevens, J. (1990), *Lust for Enlightenment: Buddhism and Sex*, Boston: Shambhala Publications.

Swearer, D.K. (1992), "A Summary of the Seven Books of the Abhidhamma," in D.S. Lopez (ed.), *Buddhism in Practice*, 336–42, Princeton, NJ: Princeton University Press.

Voyce, M. (2015), "The Presentation of the Vinaya within Forms of Western Scholarship," *Journal for the Academic Study of Religion*, 28 (1): 61–90.

Glossary Terms

Abhidharma Piṭaka The third basket of Buddhist teachings, the Abhidharma Piṭaka, was compiled between the third century BCE and the third century CE, and was codified between 400 CE and 450 CE. Its contents also vary among traditions. The Abhidharma writings are widely believed to be systematic classifications of the Buddha's teachings. Generally, Abhidharma literature lists, summarizes, expounds, and enlarges upon the essential characteristics of the Buddha's teachings found in the more elaborate and often repetitive writings of the sutras. The name Abhidharma likely gives us an indication of the intended purpose and content of these writings. "Abhi" can express such ideas as higher, best, special, etc., while "dharma" means the teachings of the Buddha.

First Buddhist Council The First Buddhist Council was a gathering of senior monastics not long after the Buddha's passing or parinirvāṇa, held to agree on the contents of the Buddha's discourses and the vinaya (regulatory framework for monastics). According to tradition, 500 of the Buddha's most learned followers gathered outside a cave in the city of Rajagaha to recite all of the teachings they had received so they could be memorized and preserved. This famous meeting has been dated to 544 BCE or around 460 BCE by some estimates. The night before the meeting, the Buddha's cousin and disciple Ananda, who was known for having an unusually good memory, achieved a higher state of insight known as arhatship. So, during the council meeting, he was able to recite the words he had heard the Buddha speak and this became the sutras. The monk Upali recited the Buddhist code of behavior, which became the vinaya.

Pali canon The collection of scriptures in the Pali language and is considered to be the oldest surviving Buddhist canon. It is the primary scriptural source for Theravada Buddhism, the main type of Buddhism practiced in Southeast

Asia. The history of the formation of the Buddhist scriptural canon remains largely obscure to modern scholarship. Traditionally, this is thought to have occurred around 50 BCE, about the same time that the Pali canon was written down, which is also the date Theravada Buddhism is said to have begun. While the Chinese Buddhist canon is the main scriptural source for East Asian Mahayana Buddhists, it contains translations of Sanskrit and some texts from the Pali canon.

Sutra Piṭaka The second division of texts in the Buddhist canon. It contains a variety of scriptures claiming to record the words of the Buddha and may include certain commentaries on the sutras by learned adherents. Sutras typically contain written stories of the Buddha's life and his words of instructions to his followers. These stories are commonly written in a dialogue or discussion format. Each of the collections of Buddhist scriptures contains a huge number of sutras, making it impossible for one person to memorize any entire canon, and Buddhist sects or schools typically rely on a smaller set of sutras as their primary sources for philosophy and practice.

Tripiṭaka The three baskets (*piṭaka*), is a name for the Buddhist canon divided into three categories of writings. The three baskets are the Sutra Piṭaka, the Vinaya Piṭaka, and the Abhidharma Piṭaka. Buddhist scriptures are preserved in three main canons today: the Pali canon of Theravada Buddhism, the Chinese canon of Mahayana Buddhism, and the Tibetan canon of Vajrayana or Esoteric Buddhism. The oldest and most comprehensive version of the Chinese Buddhist canon is the *Tripiṭaka Koreana* carved onto wooden printing blocks in the thirteenth century CE. The current standard Chinese Buddhist canon is the *Taishō Shinshū Daizōkyō*. Generally known as the Taishō canon. It was compiled during the Japanese Taishō period (1912–1926) and contains 2,920 works (3,053 including variant versions of the same texts).

Vinaya Piṭaka A collection of texts specifying rules of discipline or guidelines for behavior for Buddhist followers, particularly monks and nuns but sometimes including lay adherents. Beyond the regulatory directions, these scriptures have provided scholars with a wealth of additional information such as the dates, circumstances, and proceedings of monastic assemblies. Factors such as differences in translations, interpretations, and the special circumstances of isolated communities or countries may account for slight differences in contents of vinaya scriptures. Regardless of the variety and as with the sutras, the Buddha is held to be the authority for truth of the vinaya, which Buddhists widely believe to be his direct instruction that cautions followers.

4

Buddhist Monasticism

David M. DiValerio

More so than any particular practice, scripture, or point of doctrine, it is the **sangha**—the community of monks and nuns—that has provided continuity to the Buddhist tradition for the past 2,500 years. The word sangha, which carries such meanings as association, group, or community, comes from the Sanskrit verb *saṃhan*, meaning to come together. As Buddhism spread to and became an integral part of the diverse cultures of Asia, the robed and, for the most part, celibate sangha has constituted the stable core of the religion and should continue to do so for the foreseeable future.

The centrality of the sangha is explicitly recognized by the religion, whose "Refuge Prayer" proceeds as follows: "I go for refuge to the Buddha. I go for refuge to the Dharma. I go for refuge to the sangha." If there is any single criterion that outsiders can understand as defining a person's identity as a Buddhist, it may be having faith in the Three Refuges (or the Three Jewels, as they are also commonly known). By the same token, ancient Buddhist prophecies about the eventual disappearance of Buddhism from the world declare that the sangha will outlast the scriptures, but when members of the sangha adopt the ways of worldly people, then the religion will truly be lost.

This chapter sets out to provide an introduction to Buddhist monasticism. It does so by describing the ordination process and the rules of monastic life, the symbiotic relationship between the sangha and the broader society that surrounds and supports it, some typical features of Buddhist monasteries, some key differences in the ways that monasticism has been practiced across the different regions of Asia, and lastly some important aspects of the history of Buddhist nuns.

Ordination and the Vinaya

The formal process of becoming a monk or a nun of any religious tradition is referred to as "ordination." In Buddhism, the transition from layperson to fully ordained monk or nun has typically been a two-step process. First there is what is known as "going forth," the initial ordination as a **novice**, which can be undertaken from the age of seven or eight, and which must be presided over by a monk or nun of good standing who has been in the sangha for ten years. This ritual involves, among other things, shaving the head, donning the robes, receiving a new name, and taking a set of ten vows (see Figure 4.1). Those vows have traditionally been articulated as (1) to refrain from harming living creatures; (2) to refrain from theft; (3) to refrain from all sexual activity; (4) to refrain from false speech; (5) to refrain from the consumption of intoxicants; (6) to refrain from eating after midday; (7) to refrain from attending entertainments; (8) to refrain from wearing jewelry or perfume; (9) to refrain from sleeping in lavish beds; and (10) to refrain from handling gold and silver (often interpreted as meaning to refrain from the handling of all money) (Gethin 1998: 85–111). The reader will have noticed that these vows are essentially a series of *don'ts*, a litany of restrictions on one's personal behavior. It is continued adherence to these vows, described in a body of literature called the **Vinaya**, that defines a person as a member of the sangha.

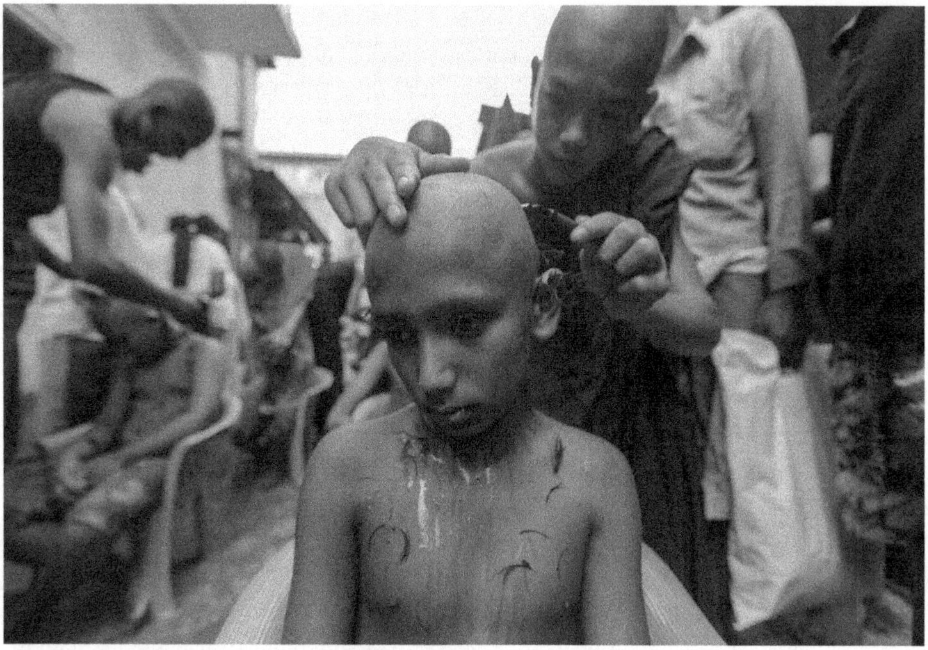

FIGURE 4.1 *A novice ordination ceremony in Sri Lanka.* Source: *Getty Images.*

The novitiate is a lesser form of monkhood, a sort of trial period or apprenticeship that ideally culminates in undertaking the ritual of full ordination once the subject has reached the age of twenty. The ceremony for full ordination, which makes a man into a **bhikṣu** and a woman into a **bhikṣuṇī**, requires the presence of ten fully ordained and legitimate monks or nuns (or only five, if conducted in a location that is far from Buddhist society). This effectively enfolds each newly made monk or nun into a lineage of monastics stretching all the way back to the Buddha himself. After this ceremony, the monk will be expected to adhere to somewhere between 227 and 253 different vows (for nuns, there are between 279 and 380 vows) (Lopez 2001: 142). The reason for the different numbers of vows results from there being different versions of the Vinaya created in ancient India, and which became normative in different parts of Asia. Monastic communities are expected to gather once every two weeks, on the days of the full and the new moon, to recite an outline of the list of rules, at which time infractions against the rules should be confessed.

In this expanded list of vows, which builds upon the basic framework of the ten vows of the novitiate, infractions are grouped into tiers, according to their importance—and the severity of the consequences for transgressing them. At the highest tier, the four most important vows are to refrain from killing a human, stealing, lying about one's own spiritual attainments, and sexual intercourse. The last of these is defined as penetration of any of the three orifices, to the depth of even a mustard seed; this applies whether one is the passive or the active participant. Committing any of these four "defeats" means the immediate, automatic, and permanent loss of one's status as a monk or a nun (His Holiness the XIV Dalai Lama 1982; Prebish 2003).

The next tier, of thirteen "remainders," includes, among others, vows against masturbation or non-penetrative sex; lustily touching a member of the opposite sex; falsely deprecating another monk or nun's conduct; and causing a rift in the sangha through some other means. When exposed at the fortnightly ceremony, an infraction against one of these vows will likely result in some form of punishment, potentially including losing certain privileges, being placed on a kind of probation, being temporarily banned from the monastery, or having to do extra work or some other kind of expiation.

The remaining tiers of 120 or so "downfalls" and 112 or so "faults" are less like vows, the transgression of which leads to some kind of punishment, but more like guidelines for how a member of the sangha should carry her- or himself. There are rules against eating after noon, going a full day without wearing the monastic robes, handling gold or silver, or giving out loans for profit. There is also a rule permitting one from knowingly killing nonhuman beings, which would traditionally be taken to mean that monks and nuns cannot engage in farming, since agricultural work is known to kill insects. There are rules against traveling with thieves, sleeping alongside a person of the opposite sex, and the consumption of alcohol. Other rules concern the sangha member's not wearing their skirts too high or too low, or bunched up at the belt; not skipping, holding hands, or swinging arms; not sitting down in a careless manner; talking with one's mouth full, and so forth.

What emerges from a comprehensive consideration of this very heterogeneous list of vows? Some of these vows directly and explicitly prevent one from performing activity that would result in the creation of bad karma (like killing or stealing). They thus ensure an individual's forward progress along the long spiritual path to eventual enlightenment. Other vows are preventative in nature, helping monks and nuns avoid finding themselves in a situation where a transgression might occur. The vows against sleeping alongside members of the opposite sex and against drinking alcohol fall into this category. (In Buddhism, the imbibing of alcohol is not seen as wrong inherently but is to be avoided because of the regrettable activities that it can lead to.) Other vows can be seen as intended to help preserve peace and stability within the sangha itself.

Another important concern addressed in the course of these many vows is to maintain the vital relationship between the sangha and lay society. This includes ensuring a degree of conformity across monks' and nuns' behavior and appearance; ensuring that their activities do not have too much in common with that of laypeople (the injunction against farming may be significant here); and ensuring that through their behavior the sangha will garner the respect of laypeople, thus preserving the elevated position of the sangha overall.

It is important to note that the extensive list of rules that a *bhikṣu* is expected to abide by, and the significantly longer list for the *bhikṣuṇī*, should in no way be taken as providing a description of how all sangha members have lived—far from it. Instead, this document should be thought of as representing an ascetic and behavioral ideal to which individual monks and nuns will strive to live up to, succeeding to varying degrees.

So what kind of ascetic ideal is expressed through this system? This is a life of renunciation, insofar as it entails living free from some of the comforts that laypeople typically take for granted (such as having a family, engaging in sexual relationships, eating whenever one likes). Nevertheless, the kind of renunciation called for by the Buddhist Vinaya must be seen as a moderate, middle-of-the-road course, considered within the broader range of ascetic lifestyles that were being enacted in South Asia around the time of the Buddha. During this period of great experimentation with ascetic livelihoods, there were individuals who, in pursuit of religious goals, engaged in fasting to the point of starvation; who went about naked and without a single possession; who never slept indoors; or who shunned all human contact (Freiberger 2006).

Siddhartha Gautama himself dabbled in these pursuits during his six years of experimentation, between renouncing his status as prince and finally achieving buddhahood. It was the discovery of a "Middle Way" between, on the one hand, the laxity of lay life and, on the other, this brand of extreme asceticism that led Siddhartha to the breakthrough that gave birth to Buddhism. For the members of the sangha, a Vinaya-based lifestyle is meant to engender a balance between the extremes of luxury and self-denial: eating every day, but in moderation; living in somewhat spartan but safe and stable conditions; covering the body, but in simple, utilitarian garb.

The basic model of robes is the same for all monks and nuns: a three-part outfit, with a skirt, an undershirt, and a shawl. Across Buddhist countries the color of these robes

FIGURE 4.2 *Tibetan monks at Tashilhünpo Monastery engaged in the daily practice of debate.* Source: *Getty Images.*

FIGURE 4.3 *South Korean monks in assembly, wearing gray robes with burnt-orange shawls.* Source: *Getty Images.*

FIGURE 4.4 *Burmese nuns entering a temple.* Source: *Getty Images.*

varies: in Tibet, all members of the sangha wear maroon, in East Asia, black, gray, or some shade of yellow. In Burma monks wear red, while nuns may wear pink. The robes serve as a uniform, making all monks or nuns within a Buddhist society look essentially the same—and clearly distinguished from the laity (see Figures 4.2, 4.3, and 4.4).

Although outsiders often assume that the Buddhist sangha is an egalitarian community, each sangha is in fact a rigidly hierarchical structure, with the fully ordained outranking all novices, and the monks or nuns within each category all strictly ranked—not according to their respective ages but based on the amount of time that has elapsed since each's respective ordination. This ranking has implications for the physical arrangement of monks within the prayer hall and other ritual functions, who gets served what food in what order, and so on. It is also the case that, while they outrank the laity, all nuns are outranked by *all* monks, as will be discussed below.

The Sangha and Society

Rather than perpetuate the ideal of living in a manner completely opposite to that of the laity (as many ascetics of the Buddha's time were attempting to do), the Buddha established a monastic order that would be a proximate, slightly elevated complement to lay society. The two would be established as mutually dependent classes within society, a basic structure that has sustained Buddhism across many generations.

Being a member of the sangha has traditionally granted individuals opportunities to do things that the majority of the laity would not typically have: the opportunity to learn to read, to memorize scriptures, to perform rituals, to learn astrology or medicine, to perform divinations, and perhaps to meditate (Ray 1994: 15–20). Being a sangha member has also meant having an opportunity to live a life of ethical purity the likes of which laypeople could never realistically aspire to, since their lives are spent mired in concerns of farming, procreating, conducting business, and sometimes even being forced to engage in acts of violence, whether against animals or people. To be a member of the sangha is thus to live a life set apart from and, in the world of Buddhist values, *above* that of the laity. Furthermore, while it is true that on an individual basis, the decision to become a monk or a nun may ideally represent a flight out of ordinary lay life—since the monk or nun is essentially deciding to cut off family relations, to preclude the possibility of ever getting married or procreating, or working in a profit-generating occupation—the sangha itself, perhaps ironically or counterintuitively, exists in symbiotic relationship with the lay society that surrounds it.

Every traditional Buddhist society has been built upon a clear division of labor. The members of the sangha are essentially professional Buddhists: it is their job to practice Buddhism. Lacking the time, the training, or the interest, the laity in contrast typically has limited involvement with the direct, personal practice of the religion. Nevertheless, they play an indispensable role in the practice of Buddhism, as supporters of the sangha. Being a community defined by their (ideally) abstaining from productive labor—including agriculture (recall the Vinaya's prohibition of killing nonhuman beings, which is interpreted as an injunction against doing agricultural work), husbandry, trade, artisanal production, and other value-producing work—the sangha is entirely dependent upon other sectors of society for food, clothing, and housing. All of this is provided by the laity. In return, what the laity gets out of materially supporting the sangha is good karma, or merit. The laity is thus given an opportunity to transform material capital into spiritual capital, which will provide them with a better future, in this and future lives.

Scholars refer to the basic dynamic of exchange between the sangha and the rest of society as the "**economy of merit**" (Borchert 2017; Gutschow 2004; Lopez 2001: 135). The act of making a donation to the sangha or one of its individual members is, in Buddhist terms, a virtuous one that creates good karma. The amount of good karma that results from this exchange is dependent upon the ethical purity of its recipient. The more virtuous the monk or nun, the greater the karmic reward accrued to the donor. If the recipient is an illegitimate monk or nun, with broken vows and poor religious practice, the donor will receive little to no return on their investment. The calculus also includes the size and the frequency of the gift: the more that is given, the more merit is received.

In the early centuries of Buddhism (and continuing today in some Theravadin Buddhist areas), this basic dynamic of exchange was played out daily, as monks and nuns walked silently through villages collecting food that provided their daily sustenance. Less directly, donations could also be made to entire monastic communities, in the form of money, building materials, cloth, paper, substances needed for performing rituals, and so forth. Donations large or small would often be made essentially as payment for the performance of a ritual by sangha members, often the recitation of scriptures to generate merit to benefit someone who had died, or for the blessing of a child.

It should be mentioned that throughout the history of the sangha, the decision to take ordination has by no means always been motivated by the highly idealized endeavor of striving to escape from *samsara*. The majority of monks historically (this may be somewhat different for nuns) have entered the monkhood not because of any fully informed, adult decision that they made on their own but on account of having been brought to the monastery in adolescence by their parents (this was particularly the case in Tibet; Goldstein and Tsarong 1985). The parents may do so to foster a better karmic or educational future for their child, to gain merit for themselves or their ancestors, or to have one less mouth to feed at home. In Tibet it was even the case that in certain areas, families were obligated to provide sons to the monastery, as a sort of tax. Monasteries have also served as de facto orphanages and homes for the elderly. History has shown adults fleeing to monasticism to avoid an undesirable marriage situation. The sangha thus attracts members for a wide range of reasons, which complicates our picture of this "religious" community and further suggests its interwovenness with lay society.

Monasteries

The majority of Buddhist monasteries will be found to have been established on the outskirts of or near to a town or a village: close enough for the sangha to be able to walk to town for their daily begging rounds, but nevertheless maintaining some distance from the distractions of village or city life (see Figure 4.5). This fact highlights the continual, symbiotic relationship between the sangha and lay society.

A Buddhist monastery typically consists of, at minimum, a temple, which provides a communal meeting space and focus of devotional activity, including the bimonthly confession ceremony, and a separate space for sleeping quarters. Rooms for the sangha would traditionally be arranged in a U-shape, surrounding an open courtyard. Most monasteries would also have stupas or pagodas, reliquaries, statues, bodhi trees, and other foci of worship utilized by the sangha and visiting laity alike. Beyond this, monasteries may also include libraries, spaces for cooking and eating, latrines, classrooms, and quarters for hosting guests (Fogelin 2015).

While most Buddhist monasteries have been quite small, serving as home to between five and ten monks or nuns, there have at times been monasteries that, because of their reputations as great centers of learning, or their proximity to a ruler or the capital city, have grown to great size. The largest monastery in the world traditionally was the Tibetan institution of Drepung, near Lhasa, which at times was home to upward of 10,000 monks (Goldstein 1998).

FIGURE 4.5 *Drepung Monastery in Lhasa, Tibet. An enormous* thanka *painting depicting a deity is on display for a celebration of the 600th anniversary of the monastery (October 2016).* Source: *Getty Images.*

Monasteries of all sizes would be under the direction of an abbot. Many monks would have jobs within the monastery, such as sweeping, working in the temple or the library, cooking, overseeing lands farmed by sharecroppers, or the maintenance of the buildings and other physical resources of the monastery. Religious life requires significant logistical support.

Regional Variations

While many features of monasticism are shared across Buddhist Asia, there are some significant differences that emerge. Attention to these differences can yield important insights into the evolution of Buddhism as it has spread from India all the way to Japan (and beyond).

The sangha is said to have started just after the Buddha's first sermon, when five of his former partners in extreme asceticism gave up their other pursuits to become his followers. Tradition maintains that during his lifetime, the Buddha simply addressed the interested party with "Come, monk" (*ehi bhikṣu*), thereby initiating the follower into the sangha. Monkhood was at first a much simpler affair, with the many rules of the Vinaya and the full-blown ordination ceremony coming into practice gradually over time (Lopez 2004: 223–9). In the earliest years, the sangha wandered continuously but soon adopted the convention of settling down during the three-month summer rainy season. The shelters where monks waited out the monsoon, donated and sponsored by wealthy patrons, evolved into the first monasteries, which would then be inhabited throughout the year. Most of the monastic population would be domesticated in this way, while a minority would continue to wander nine months out of the year. The monastic population would expand dramatically after the Buddha's time, beginning in Bihar and the other parts of northern India where Siddhartha Gautama was active, and spreading to other parts of India from there.

In the first centuries of the sangha, its members were limited to owning nothing more than a set of robes, a begging bowl, a belt, a razor for shaving the head, a needle for repairing robes, a water strainer to prevent the unintentional ingesting of insects, a walking staff, and finally a toothpick. Sandals, a pad to sit on, an umbrella for blocking the sun, and a personal fan were also allowed. These days it is not uncommon for monks to have well-furnished cells and mobile phones. In the early years of the tradition, however, it was expected that a monk's robes would be made from scraps of cloth that had been gathered, often from funerary sites. It quickly became more normal to make robes out of cloth donated by laypeople or purchased by the monks themselves.

In the Theravada Buddhist societies of Southeast Asia and Sri Lanka they adhere to the Theravādin version of the Vinaya, with 227 rules for fully ordained monks. There they maintain some key features of early monasticism that would not be continued in other parts of Asia. These practices include not eating after noon; abstaining from the handling of money; and receiving daily sustenance on silent begging rounds among the laity (see Figure 4.6). An innovation unique to Southeast Asia is the practice of temporary ordination, in which young men ordain for a year or even just a few months. (This practice has also appeared on a more limited scale in East Asia.)

In the Tibetan Buddhist parts of Asia, the Mūlasarvāstivāda version of the Vinaya is followed, with 253 rules for monks. Among the many sanghas of the Buddhist world, Tibet's stands out from all others for its sheer scale. Studies have come to the conclusion that before the radical changes brought about by the Chinese Invasion/Liberation of the 1950s, 10 to 15 percent of the male population of Tibet were monks. This may have made Tibet ten times more highly monasticized than other Buddhist societies (in Thailand, for example, only 1 or 2 percent of the male population were monks traditionally). Scholars have taken to referring to this unique situation as "mass monasticism" (Goldstein 1998; Tambiah 1976: 266–7). This arose from a unique combination of religious, social, political, geographic, and economic forces, and made the monkhood the most powerful estate within Tibetan society.

In Tibet, the pattern of the sangha's reliance on the laity would take a different form. Rather than go on itinerant begging rounds (which may have been impractical because of the distances between settlements, or the sheer imbalance of numbers, in which a monastery of thousands may be situated nearby a hamlet of only hundreds), at certain times of the year, monks would be sent out to travel to more distant locales to gather offerings and/or taxes: grain following the autumn harvest and dairy products during

FIGURE 4.6 *Burmese monks walking with their begging bowls.* Source: *Getty Images.*

the summer. It has also been very common for monks to be commissioned to visit a lay home to perform rituals, for which they are given food and other material support as payment. Due to the extremely cold weather on the Tibetan plateau, Tibetan monks and nuns modify the standard monastic dress by wearing boots, hats, and fur-lined jackets.

While Buddhism began to arrive in China from the first century CE, it was not until the beginning of the fifth century that a complete Chinese translation of a version of the Vinaya became available (this was the Dharmaguptaka Vinaya, with 250 rules). Even then, the importation of the Vinaya into China was difficult because of both cultural and linguistic factors. Monasteries thus had reason to compose their own regulations for life in the sangha, which were shorter than the Vinaya, and more tailored to the local environment. For example, in the eighth century, the Chinese monk Baizhang Huaihai established a monastic code that would become normative in Chan Buddhism in China, and then carry over into Zen in Japan (Foulk 1995: 455–72). Monks would be expected to sleep communally, in a grand hall, on the same straw mat on which they would meditate and eat their meals. Monks would also be expected to engage in farming or other kinds of labor on a daily basis. In China, Korea, and Japan there would form a particular school of Buddhism devoted to following the full Dharmaguptaka Vinaya, but this constituted an exception rather than the norm.

In Japan it became common for monks serving in the role of temple priests in the True Pure Land School (Jōdo Shinshū) to marry. While in this case celibacy ceased to serve its traditionally crucial role in maintaining the division between monk and layman, a division of spiritual labor was nevertheless still maintained between the laity and the sangha (Jaffe 2001).

Vegetarianism became an important facet of monastic life in China (and then Japan), in a manner unlike anywhere else in Buddhist Asia. This is despite the fact that the Vinaya texts nowhere mention a rule against eating meat. For the rest of the Buddhist world, the overriding logic is that as mendicants, sangha members should eat whatever has been offered, and not indulge in the luxury of being overly discriminatory (Lopez 2001: 135).

The Nunhood

The history and the future of the Buddhist nunhood are highly contested, bringing into relief important questions about what we reliably know about the formation of the early sangha and the future outcomes of Buddhism's encounter with modernity.

Tradition maintains that a few years after the initiation of the male sangha, the Buddha's maternal aunt and foster mother, Mahāprajāpatī, approached him to request that he allow a sangha for women, parallel to that of the men. There are competing versions of what happened next and how to interpret it. One version maintains that the Buddha denied her request two times, but somewhat begrudgingly assented on the third occasion, at the urging of the Buddha's attendant and paternal cousin,

Ānanda (Ven. Anālayo 2011). Some say that the Buddha prophesied that as a result of his allowing the formation of a community of nuns, the eventual disappearance of Buddhism from the world would be sped up by 500 years, cutting in half the time of Buddhism's existence in the world. It is maintained that at this time the Buddha instituted eight additional rules that fully ordained nuns would be required to follow. These include the rule that a monk should be at the head of every community of nuns; that any discipline for a nun be handed down by a monk; and most galling of all, that within this extremely hierarchical culture, every monk would necessarily be regarded as more senior than every nun. In other words, a woman who had followed the discipline for thirty years would assume a position subservient to a boy who had been a monk for only a single day.

There has been considerable debate about the true reasons behind this expression of seeming misogyny on the part of the Buddha. Was this an expression of his own feelings toward women? Did he see men and women as not having the same spiritual capabilities—and women's participation as in fact likely to prove harmful to Buddhism? Was he perhaps merely being pragmatic in accounting for the challenges that would inevitably arise from having communities of sexually abstinent men and women directly beside and in close proximity to one another? Was the Buddha speaking not from his own feelings but as an expression of the attitudes of South Asian society at the time? Or may it be that these clearly misogynistic aspects of the story represent interpolations at the hands of the male sangha, from centuries after the fact, and thus do not necessarily represent the Buddha's sentiments whatsoever? This question cannot be separated from the broader question of the extent to which the early record of Buddhism—in particular the contents of the sutras and other early literature such as the Vinaya—represents a reliable record of the Buddha's words and events as they took place, or the extent to which they reflect the work of later generations.

The position of nuns in Buddhist societies has always been more precarious than that of their male counterparts. In the context of the economy of merit, where the merit accrued is directly proportional to the religious standing of the recipient, nuns have always received less material support, and thus have often found themselves in a position of having to spend their time working to support themselves (and in some communities, act as servants to the male sangha). Nuns have also typically been given fewer educational opportunities and less, if any, instruction in meditation (Gutschow 2004). All of these factors have contributed to a vicious cycle placing nuns in an unfavorable position relative to monks and from which it has been difficult to escape.

The question of what the future holds for Buddhist nuns is also far from certain. While there have been robust traditions of women taking novice vows, the lineage of fully ordained nuns has died out in both Southeast Asia and in the Tibetan tradition. Because of the necessity of receiving one's vows from a fully ordained member of a lineage stretching all the way back to the first nun, Mahāprajāpatī, from a fully traditionalist perspective, these lineages cannot be revived. Only in East Asia has the tradition of full ordination for nuns been maintained. There are proponents of Theravadin and Tibetan Buddhist nuns taking full ordination from East Asian nuns (which has begun to occur on a limited scale in the last few years) or via some other means (see Figure 4.7). These possibilities have been taken up most thoroughly by the International Congress on Buddhist Women's Role (n.d.) in the Sangha. Meanwhile others are opposed to this, whether because of the illegitimacy of crossing boundaries between differing Vinaya traditions, or because taking full ordination also entails taking the eight vows of subservience to monks (Salgado 2008). For those in favor, there is the challenge of determining the correct protocol for

FIGURE 4.7 *Tibetan Buddhist nuns living in India participate in a protest on International Women's Uprising Day, March 12, 2018.* Source: *Getty Images.*

doing something that is unprecedented in a context where tradition is everything. Amidst the competing aims of tradition and modernism, of feminism and Buddhism, there are strongly held opinions about the proper way forward for the nunhood. With the continued expansion and strengthening of the international network of female Buddhist monastics, there is reason to believe that the gains made over the past few decades are only just the beginning (Sakyadhita n.d.).

Conclusion

Monasticism has provided unbroken continuity within the Buddhist tradition from the time of the Buddha to the present. As a topic of inquiry, monasticism provides us with an avenue to consider how the religion has evolved over time, how it has been transformed by diverse Asian societies, and the challenging attitudes toward the female gender that it has espoused. We have also seen how an individual's participation in this religious pursuit, defined by vowing to adhere to more than 200 specific behavioral guidelines, enfolds a person within an institution that is perpetuated through the maintenance of a delicate relationship with the rest of society. Monasticism thus brings us from the personal to the sociological and back again, giving us a comprehensive way of understanding Buddhist practices and beliefs as inextricably tied to material and political realities.

Further Reading and Online Resources

Carrithers, M. (1983), *The Forest Monks of Sri Lanka: An Anthropological and Historical Study*, Delhi: Oxford University Press.

Clarke, S. (2013), *Family Matters in Buddhist Monasticisms*, Honolulu: University of Hawai'i Press.

Dreyfus, G. (2003), *The Sound of Two Hands Clapping: The Education of a Tibetan Buddhist Monk*, Berkeley: University of California Press.

Karma, L.T., ed. (1999), *Buddhist Women across Cultures: Realizations*, New York: State University of New York Press.

Schopen, G. (2004), *Buddhist Monks and Business Matters: Still More Papers on Monastic Buddhism in India*, Honolulu: University of Hawai'i Press.

Soko, M. (2004), *Novice to Master: An Ongoing Lesson in the Extent of My Own Stupidity*, trans. B. Attaway Yamakawa, Somerville, MA: Wisdom Publications.

Spiro, M. (1982), *Buddhism and Society: A Great Tradition and Its Burmese Vicissitudes*, Berkeley: University of California Press.

References

Borchert, T.A. (2017), *Educating Monks: Minority Buddhism on China's Southwest Border*, Honolulu: University of Hawai'i Press.

Congress on Buddhist Women (n.d.), "Homepage." Available online: http://www.congress-on-buddhist-women.org/21.0.html (accessed September 26, 2020).
Fogelin, L. (2015), *An Archaeological History of Indian Buddhism*, New York: Oxford University Press.
Foulk, T.G. (1995), "Daily Life in the Assembly," in D. Lopez Jr. (ed.), *Buddhism in Practice*, 455–72, Princeton, NJ: Princeton University Press.
Freiberger, O. (2006), "Early Buddhism, Asceticism, and the Politics of the Middle Way," in O. Freiberger (ed.), *Asceticism and Its Critics: Historical Accounts and Comparative Perspectives*, 235–58, New York: Oxford University Press.
Gethin, R. (1998), *The Foundations of Buddhism*, New York: Oxford University Press.
Goldstein, M. (1998), "The Revival of Monastic Life in Drepung Monastery," in M. Goldstein and M. Kapstein (eds.), *Buddhism in Contemporary Tibet: Religious Revival and Cultural Identity*, 15–52, Berkeley: University of California Press.
Goldstein, M. and P. Tsarong (1985), "Tibetan Buddhist Monasticism: Social, Psychological and Cultural Implications," *Tibet Journal*, 10 (1): 14–31.
Gutschow, K. (2004), *Being a Buddhist Nun: The Struggle for Enlightenment in the Himalayas*, Cambridge, MA: Harvard University Press.
His Holiness the XIV Dalai Lama ([1982] 2006), *Advice from Śākyamuni: An Abridged Exposition of the Precepts for Bikkshus*, Dharamsala: Library of Tibetan Works and Archives.
Jaffe, R.M. (2001), *Neither Monk nor Layman: Clerical Marriage in Modern Japanese Buddhism*, Princeton, NJ: Princeton University Press.
Lopez, D., Jr. (2001), *The Story of Buddhism: A Concise Guide to Its History and Teachings*, New York: HarperCollins.
Lopez, D., Jr., ed. (2004), *Buddhist Scriptures*, New York: Penguin.
Prebish, C. (2003), "Varying the Vinaya: Creative Responses to Modernity," in S. Heine and C. Prebish (eds.), *Buddhism in the Modern World: Adaptations of an Ancient Tradition*, 45–73, Oxford: Oxford University Press.
Ray, R. (1994), *Buddhist Saints in India: A Study in Buddhist Values and Orientations*, New York: Oxford University Press.
Sakyadhita (n.d.), "International Association of Buddhist Women." Available online: http://www.sakyadhita.org (accessed September 26, 2020).
Salgado, N. (2008), "Eight Revered Conditions: Ideological Complicity, Contemporary Reflections and Practical Realities," *Journal of Buddhist Ethics*, 15: 177–213.
Tambiah, S.J. (1976), *World Conqueror and World Renouncer: A Study of Buddhism and Polity in Thailand against a Historical Background*, Cambridge: Cambridge University Press.
Ven. Anālayo. (2011), "Mahāpajāpatī's Going Forth in the *Madhyama-āgama*," *Journal of Buddhist Ethics*, 18: 268–317.

Glossary Terms

Bhikṣu Distinguished from the novice, a *bhikṣu* is a fully ordained monk, expected to abide by between 227 and 253 rules for personal conduct (depending on which version of the Vinaya prevails in his particular monastic community). As members of the *sangha*, *bhikṣu*s are professionals whose vocation is to engage in religious activity, and who have traditionally been expected to refrain from productive labor and other worldly pursuits.

Bhikṣuṇī Distinguished from the novice, a *bhikṣuṇī* is a fully ordained nun, expected to abide by between 279 and 380 rules for personal conduct (depending on which version of the Vinaya prevails in her particular monastic community). Purportedly dating back to the time of the Buddha himself, *bhikṣuṇīs* have been subject to eight special vows that make them at all times subservient to *bhikṣus* in terms of their personal status.

Economy of merit A term coined by anthropologists to refer to a dynamic that is observed in most Buddhist societies, in which the laity supports the *sangha* materially (with food, clothing, housing, and so forth), in return for which they receive merit or good karma. *Sangha* members are thus able to abstain from productive labor, in pursuit of higher religious ideals. *Sangha* members are joined to lay society through a social contract, compelling them to continue adhering to the dictates of the Vinaya, to ensure that their donors can receive the merit that is due to them.

Novice Used to translate the Sanskrit terms *śrāmaṇera* for a male and *śrāmaṇerī* for a female, a "novice" is an individual who has formally entered into the *sangha* or monastic order, but has not taken the full ordination of a *bhikṣu* or a *bhikṣuṇī*. Novices are typically bound by a set of only ten vows, although they nevertheless wear monastic robes and have shaved heads.

Sangha A Sanskrit term meaning "group" or "community," *sangha* is used to refer to the community of Buddhist monks and nuns—the robed and for the most part celibate males and females who live in accordance with more than 200 vows that delimit their behavior, laid out in the Vinaya. More so than any particular practice, scripture, or point of doctrine, it is the *sangha* that has provided continuity to the Buddhist tradition for the past 2,500 years. The *sangha* is one of the three "refuges" of Buddhism (along with the Buddha, and his teachings, the Dharma).

Vinaya A Sanskrit term meaning "discipline," Vinaya is used to refer to the body of literature that lays out the extensive vows (between 227 and 253 for *bhikṣus*, and between 279 and 380 for *bhikṣuṇīs*) that members of the Buddhist *sangha* are expected to abide by. There are five separate versions of the Vinaya, which are prevalent in different parts of Asia. Purportedly dating back to the time of the Buddha himself, these vows concern such matters as sexual activity, theft, the harming of other living beings, lying, and stealing, as well as the personal comportment prescribed for monks and nuns, concerning mundane matters such as eating, sitting, and walking.

PART II

Practices and Beliefs

5

Buddhist Meditation

Napakadol Kittisenee

Note on Terms and Sources

This chapter refers to terms in Pali, the language usually found in the texts of the Theravada school of Buddhism dominant in mainland Southeast Asia and Sri Lanka. Since this writing draws on sources of meditation from the Theravada school, particularly from Thai Buddhism, the author therefore uses Pali terms with Sanskrit equivalents where necessary.

Buddhist Practice and Meditation

The general Buddhist process of education is apparent in three domains: *pariyatti* (theory), *patipatti* (practice), and *pativedha* (insight) (Sugunasiri 2005: 2–3) (see Figure 5.1). Learning from the Buddha's teachings is the first step so that practitioners will be well-versed in implementing it and eventually understanding clearly how to use it to find peace in their lives. One could even think about the way the Buddha himself acquired insight, which was primarily through his "practice" rather than theory. He was experimenting and learning things by doing them, until he found the right balance. The core method for this experimentation is meditation. This chapter will therefore mainly focus on meditation as a practice related to this mode of education. How does Buddhism talk about practice? What do those practices look like? And, ultimately, what is the purpose of practice?

The most commonplace activities of a Buddhist layperson in the Theravada tradition, located primarily in South and Southeast Asia, are serving monks food and donating money to construct buildings and temples with the main purpose of earning merit (Tambiah 1968: 51–2). Merit, also known as good karma, secures practitioners a better

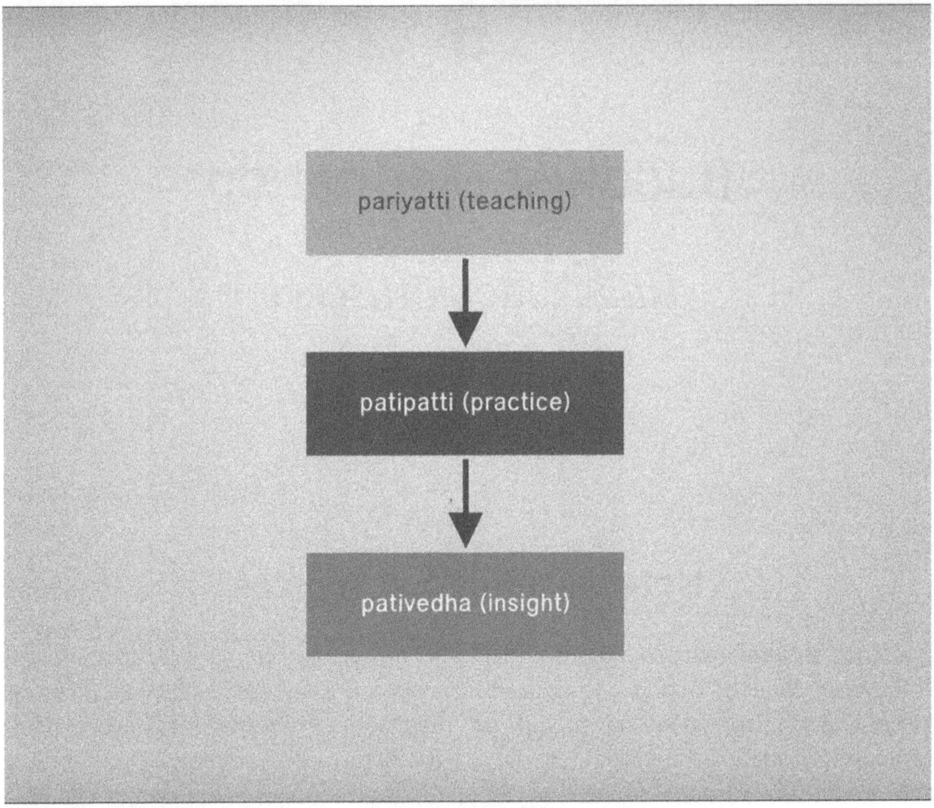

FIGURE 5.1 *Buddhist process of education.* Source: *Napakadol Kittisenee.*

future as good karma is the causative factor that results in both past and future life conditions (Keyes 1983: 265–71). This is, however, not the entire story of merit and dedicated action from a Buddhist perspective. There is another kind of practice that is a source of merit one can obtain supreme happiness from: self-purification.

Different Forms of Buddhist Practices

The Dhammapada records that on the full moon of the third lunar month at Veḷuvana (present-day Venu Van), the first temple was built in the bamboo forest of Rajgir, India, which marked the spontaneous assembly of the Buddha and his thousand enlightened disciples. The Great Teacher admonished his followers to pursue the three most essential teachings of Buddhism: abstention from evil, cultivation of the good, and purification of the mind. This doctrinal summary, known as the Ovādapātimokkha, is one prominent way of defining the essential Buddhist practices. It is also the abbreviation of the more elaborate codes of conduct (Vinaya) as it is regularly recited in the monastic assembly twice a month, particularly among Theravada monastics.

Abstinence from evil means observing the *sīla* (precepts). The term precept here is broader than its later narrow definition limited to monastic discipline. Precepts are designed as preventive mechanisms so that practitioners do not get involved with evil matters. More practically, it is the code of conduct to maintain one's life balance and social order. For instance, most lay Buddhists observe the five precepts: abstinence from killing, stealing, sexual misconduct, telling lies, and ingesting intoxicants. Buddhists believe that if one fails to observe one of these, they will cause harm for themselves and others.

Cultivation of the good stems from doing the opposite of what the precepts warn not to do, for example, promoting loving kindness instead of killing, earning a living rather than stealing, loyalty not betrayal, truthfulness not lying, and cultivating mindfulness instead of taking drugs and getting drunk. This mode of practice is, however, not a shortcut to the cessation of suffering in Buddhism but rather guides the practitioner onto the path of liberation.

After cultivating a dedication to avoiding wrong actions and pursuing right ones, the Visuddhimagga ("Path of Purification," a Pali commentary providing guidance for meditation) encourages practitioners to learn tactics of self-investigation, the "inner work" one has to process to recognize the hidden evils in one's mind (*Kilesa*; Skt: *Kleśa*). Like a barren field full of landmines beneath, practitioners must carefully and deliberately investigate the area and "de-mine" it one at a time. The mines are variously translated as: anger, hatred, lust, greed, etc. Purifying the mind is therefore delicate work, focusing on self-discovery and inward scrutiny. Once one detects anger in one's own heart, it is less dangerous and will not easily explode. Practitioners will learn how to avoid stepping on it because they clearly understand the damage this might cause. This purification of the mind is synonymous with meditation.

Noble Eightfold Path and Buddhist Practices

These three Buddhist ideals—abstaining from evil, cultivating the good, and purifying the mind—encourage Buddhists to think about their implementation. If this is the goal, what is the path? Buddhists focus on the three steps of training: *sīla* (precept), **samādhi** (concentration), and *pañña* (wisdom) (see Figure 5.2). Each one affects the others. When one observes precepts well, it is easy to develop concentration as the code of conduct maintains body equilibrium. With concentration, one can see things clearly, which enables wisdom to arise from the equanimous, unshaken state of mind (Maha Boowa 2018: 105–9). The three steps further serve and support each other as three different parts of the same wheel.

What kind of elements make this "wheel" roll? In what is considered to be the historical Buddha's first sermon, as recorded in the *Dhammacakkappavattana*

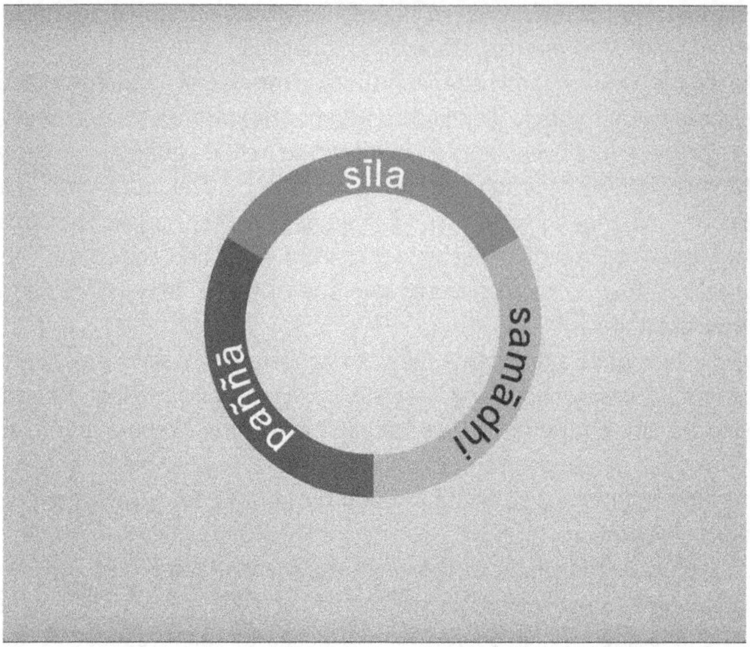

FIGURE 5.2 *Three steps of Buddhist training.* Source: *Napakadol Kittisenee.*

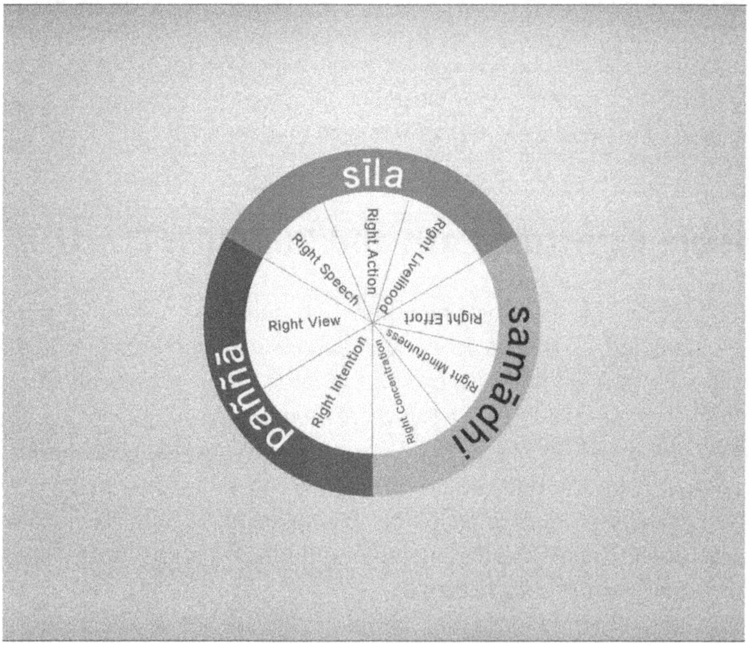

FIGURE 5.3 *Noble Eightfold Path in the context of Buddhist training.* Source: *Napakadol Kittisene.*

sutta (Setting the Wheel of Dhamma in Motion) taking place at the deer park in Sarnath, India, the Buddha ended his discussion of the Four Noble Truths with the teachings of the Noble Eightfold Path as the way leading to the end of suffering (see Figure 5.3). It includes, in order: right view, right intention, right speech, right action, right livelihood, right effort, right mindfulness, and right concentration. Even though they are explained as different paths, they are inseparable from each other. And all echo the threefold training; speech, action, and livelihood are prescribed by *sīla*, while effort, mindfulness, and concentration are developed through *samādhi*. The *pañña* training gives rise to right view and intention. If all works well, this wheel will move toward liberation.

Meditation and the Middle Path

Prior to becoming the Buddha, Siddhartha Gautama was a prince growing up in a proto-Hindu family and was likely familiar with meditative practices by Brahmins (Hindu priests) involved with court rituals. This is potentially why when the prince decided to leave behind his life of luxury, he decided to roam in search of spiritual mentors. Eventually he found himself among the students of two notable meditation schools at that time, named after two great teachers, "Āḷāra Kālāma" and "Uddaka Rāmaputta." From them, he learned how to achieve **jhānas** (Skt: *dhyāna*), or profound states of concentration. He excelled especially in the formless jhānas, which were considered to be the highest state of concentration. After being unable to find liberation through these states, he joined a group of five men who used extreme fasting and harsh asceticism to become enlightened (see Figure 5.4). He later realized this was not the right way, ate some food, and sat under the Bodhi tree to contemplate liberation, eventually attaining enlightenment. This part of Siddhartha's spiritual trajectory can be equated to his exposure to **samatha** (concentration meditation), which according to this life story, already existed before Siddhartha became enlightened as the Buddha.

In the renowned *Dhammacakkappavattana Sutta*, the first sermon after his enlightenment given to the five ascetics who doubted his spiritual discovery, the Buddha began with a warning to avoid the two extremes: *kāmasukhallikānuyogo* (self-gratification) and *attakilamathānuyogo* (self-mortification). The first one is the self-indulgence of looking only for pleasant things, impeding one's ability to encounter and understand the nature of suffering (*dukkha*). In contrast, the Buddha's years of self-mortification proved that this was also not the right way to enlightenment.

In place of these extremes, the Buddha suggests the Middle Way to retain balance in practice, which he explains through the Noble Eightfold Path. Within this eightfold complex, right mindfulness and right concentration are the two major threads related to meditation. What does right mindfulness look like when it comes to practice? What is right concentration?

FIGURE 5.4 *Buddha's extreme fasting*. Source: *Napakadol Kittisenee*.

Meditation of Right Mindfulness

The *Satipaṭṭhāna Sutta* (Majjhima Nikaya 10: The Discourse of Establishing Mindfulness) and *Mahāsatipaṭṭhāna Sutta* (Dīgha Nikāya 22: The Great Discourse of Establishing Mindfulness) are the basis for two of the most popular canons among meditation schools where the text delineates the Buddha's systematic and clear steps of meditation from the basic to advanced level, illuminating four approaches to meditative practice: body, pain, mind, and sensation. *Satipaṭṭhāna* means the location of mindfulness, so this approach encourages practitioners to observe and be aware of what occurs in the realm of the body, pain, mind, and sensation, which needs to be monitored during the four manners of daily life: standing, walking, sitting, and reclining.

In **vipassana** (insight meditation), the first step is awareness of the body (*kāyānupassanā satipaṭṭhāna*), which aims to observe the conditions of the body, for example, cool, warm, soft, hard, relaxed, tensed, ill, etc. The more continuously one observes, the more one will see the suffering and impermanence of the body. This method continues with further analysis of the thirty-two organs in the body, intended to focus the practitioner beyond outside appearance into the gross body comprised of blood, intestines, the lungs, and so on, which will make us less affectionate for a world of impermanence and suffering.

Realizing this truth of the body enables a broader view: that all humans are made up of these processes. Even those that are physically beautiful, young, and fit are potentially suffering from sickness and aging. Thus, when they truly accept this physical reality, they will learn little by little how to let go of the sense of belonging to the body. Practitioners will be less depressed when they get sick and be able to accept this is the physical reality. When getting old, they will not suffer from their lost beauty and when death comes, they will peacefully embrace it, because impermanence is the law of nature.

The second location of awareness is pain (*vedanānupassanā satipaṭṭhāna*). This method is the continuous observation on physical pain. In life, no one can avoid hurt. At the same time, physical pain is temporal: it comes and goes, on and off. Buddhists argue that taking a deep look into pain enables us to find that it is also impermanent. For example, pain will appear when sitting in meditation for a long time. But using this method, practitioners will change their response to it. Instead of blaming others or feeling self-pity, meditators can contemplate the duration of pain. Will they hurt every second of twenty-four hours? Perhaps, but more likely, it will come and go, which they can use as a way to cultivate tolerance for pain and equanimity in the face of uncertainty. The more they practice, they can come to deal with it peacefully.

Cittānupassanā satipaṭṭhāna (mind observation) is the next location of right mindfulness practice. This method is monitoring the mind as the location of the development of feelings: joy, boredom, sadness, anger, etc. All are indicators of mental health. Along with physical pain, feelings and emotions are always changing. When practitioners continuously observe this, they can gradually comprehend emotions as impermanent. Oddom Van Syvorn (1962–2018), a lay practitioner and the prime mover of the peace walk in Cambodia, is an exemplary figure for this practice. She experienced famine, displacement, and imprisonment under the Democratic Kampuchea (known as the Cambodian Genocide, 1975–1979). She engaged in mindfulness practice, to deal with her trauma as suggested by her master, Maha Ghosananda (1924–2007). Her feelings of loss, anger from torture, and desire for revenge later became the "objects of observation," which she was able to confront, especially when she did walking meditation. In an interview with Syvorn, she stated that she realized her trauma is perpetuated when she lacks focus in her mind; emotions tend to prevent us from seeing things clearly.

The last location of awareness is sensation (*dhammānupassanā satipaṭṭhāna*). The term "dhamma" in Pali or "dharma" in Sanskrit conveys several meanings but here it aims to focus on sensation (*dhamma-ramana*: sensational condition). Similar to the other focuses, the purpose of the observation of sensation is to learn of its impertinent nature. In daily life, one experiences countless sensations. Each of them triggers and resonates with the Three Poisons: craving, aversion, and ignorance. The sensations cause the mind to be busy and unhealthy, overloading it, which incapacitates it. The practice of awareness of sensation is the way to be immune to these emotional arousals. A healthy mind is not easily shaken by worldly and sensational matters, falling instead into a state of equanimity where wisdom can easily prosper.

The four locations of mindfulness practice according to Satipaṭṭhāna Sutta are interconnected. In observing the body, practitioners can also notice pain, feeling, and sensation. This often happens in actual meditation where the practitioner is thus the observer; anything that arises first is the object of consideration. And the object of consideration will lead to an exploration of impermanence. The meditation school that primarily uses this method, vipassana, argues there is no need to be equipped with the fundamental practice of meditation; one can work on this from the start. This view is challenged by the school focusing on concentration, which I will now discuss.

Meditation of Right Concentration

Sammā Samādhi (right concentration), the last of the eightfold path, refers to calming of the mind. Right concentration is often interpreted to mean the *jhāna*, a profound state of concentration. As mentioned above, the renunciate prince who became the Buddha learned the jhānas from the two notable meditation mentors in ancient India. The metaphor of mind from Chinese and Japanese sources is often compared to a monkey ("heart-/mind-monkey"): always playing around, moving, unsettled, and untidy (Cleary 1987: 198). Concentration training is the method to tame this monkey to help it work well because the work of meditation is self-scrutiny, which works best with a settled mind. There are several techniques to concentrate on something, including reading, chanting, and walking, with the output varying according to its intensity.

Four Rupa jhānas (jhāna with form) rely on the practitioner noticing this type of profound concentration via visualized sensations. They are:

1 *Pathama jhāna* (focused mind)
2 2. *Dutiya jhāna* (deep joy)
3 3. *Tatiya jhāna* (deep relaxation)
4 4. *Catutha jhāna* (equanimity)

Four Arupa jhānas (formless jhāna) meaning profound concentration without a concrete reference point:

1 *Ākāsāyañcāyatana* (boundless feeling like air)
2 *Viññāṇañcāyatana* (deep senselessness)
3 *Ākiñcaññāyatana* (realm of void)
4 *Nevasaññānasaññāyatana* (deep disconnection with memory and recognition)

In the Buddha's life story, he attained the formless jhāna before he discovered the Middle Path and attained enlightenment. It is, however, only the fourth jhāna (equanimity) that is necessary to fulfill right concentration (Parisuddho 2009: 61). With an equanimous mind, one is able to observe clearly what to improve about oneself in the process of self-scrutiny. This method of training is synonymous with what is later perceived as samatha.

Samatha versus Vipassana

There has long been a debate amongst the meditation schools whether one should begin and delve into vipassana or samatha. Vipassana schools contend that vipassana only is enough to develop concentration and self-scrutiny (Bond 1992: 167). Conversely, Samatha schools argue that without the samatha foundation, how can one do vipassana effectively? With the "monkey mind," how would it be possible to concentrate on such a profound self-reflection? The practitioner needs to tame the monkey first.

Gombrich (1997: 96–144) and Brooks (2006) argue that this conflict is primarily caused by samatha's interpretation of the texts. It is noteworthy here that the popularized form of vipassana in the twentieth century among Theravada schools was sparked by the "vipassana movement" of Buddhist modernism in 1950s Burma (McMahan 2008), spearheaded by Ledi Sayadaw (1846–1923), U Vimala (1899–1962), Mahasi Sayadaw (1904–1982), and S.N. Goenka (1924–2013) (King 1992: 132–7), who focused on the dissemination of the Satipaṭṭhāna Sutta. This movement created popular waves of vipassana meditation across Theravada Asian countries and became appealing to Westerners, including the American vipassana teacher, Jack Kornfield

(McMahan 2008). A celebrated Thai meditation master, Venerable Suang Parisuddho (2009: 61) contends that if practitioners do value the Noble Eightfold Path, of which right mindfulness and right concentration are inseparable elements, they cannot let go of either. Rather, Buddhists should cultivate both in their practice.

Kammaṭṭhāna: Hidden Insights in Foundation

Kammaṭṭhāna (Skt: *Karmasthana*) in the Buddhist canon means the basic deed (for meditation). The most acclaimed meditation text is Visuddhimagga (Path to Purification) by the fifth-century Theravada Buddhist commentator Buddhaghosa. According to Visuddhimagga, there are forty basic approaches to meditation, divided into seven overarching categories: object study, decayed body, reminders, virtues of Brahma (a Buddhist god), the four formless jhānas discussed earlier, impermanent facts about food, and consideration of the four elements (Nyanamoli 2011).

The first of these is the *Kasiṇa* (staring at an object) method, which requires the meditator to consider the following objects to formulate concentration: earth, water, fire, wind, blue, yellow, red, white or sky, enclosed space, and bright light. This method turns the dynamic into static mind induced by materiality. It is considered to be the most basic and accessible form of practice because it focuses on observable phenomena that are not inherently repellent to the practitioner, unlike the second style, *Asubha*.

Literally translated as "the ugliness," Asubha practitioners examine and consider a corpse from its immediate postmortem swelling to its end as a fleshless skeleton. This method encourages meditators to develop an appreciation for the impermanence of the body and how the decayed corpse will one day be them. In ascetic forest traditions, popular historically in Thailand and Southeast Asia, monks often roamed around the forest in search of silent places for meditation, sometimes finding their place in graveyards (Tiyavanich 1997). In certain Buddhist countries, corpses are not fully buried or cremated, which provides the meditator with a chance to overcome fear and discontent when staring at and meditating on this object. Some Buddhist temples include the scenes of these meditative techniques in their temple mural paintings to educate practitioners.

This type of meditation is still used today. In twenty-first-century Thailand, some pictorial books of corpses are printed for dissemination of meditation practice, such as *Asubha Pictures: For Practitioners Only* by meditation master Venerable Maha Bua Ñanasampanno (1913–2011). It can also be linked to sky burial ("bird-scattered") among Vajrayana Buddhists particularly in Tibet, Mongolia, Bhutan, and parts of China where the corpse is seen as a reminder of impermanence and source of generosity for other beings by becoming food for scavenging animals (Goss and Klass 1997: 385). Maha Ghosananda (1992) details how a deep sense of impermanence and compassion resulted from his journey on the way to refugee camps along the Thai–Cambodian border where two sides of the road were laid with corpses from the genocide in the

1970s. The decomposed material for meditation on impermanence can be something beyond the human body. It can be some common objects in our daily life as suggested by Thich Nhat Hanh (1926–) (2008: 90):

In the garbage, I see a rose.
In the rose, I see the garbage.
Everything is in transformation.
Even permanence is impermanent.

The third method of meditation is *Anussati* (reminder), which uses aspects of Buddhist values and concepts as the subject of meditation. It helps practitioners recognize the meaning of these values while at the same time evoking a sense of commitment to and veneration of: Buddha, Dharma, sangha, *sīla* (precepts), cāga, the kindness of *devata* (heavenly beings), awareness of the body, awareness of death, awareness of breath, and the supremacy of nirvana (end of suffering). Among these subcategories, awareness of breath is one of the most popular meditation methods. It also appears in many suttas when referring to meditation (Anālayo 2003: 125).

Fourth are the Virtues of Brahma (Brahma Vihara), where "Brahma" in this particular Buddhist context refers to specific virtues instead of one of the gods with the same spelling. These virtues include *Mettā* (loving-kindness), *Karuna* (compassion), *Mudita* (sympathy), and *Upekkhā* (equanimity). Loving-kindness meditation (*mettā*) in particular has become increasingly popular globally and shown to treat mental illness (Galante et al. 2014).

The fifth main area is the Formless jhānas already discussed in relation to samatha meditative practices: Ākāsāyañcāyatana (boundless feeling like air), Viññāṇañcāyatana (deep senselessness), Ākiñcaññāyatana (realm of void), Nevasaññānasaññāyatana (deep disconnection with memory and recognition).

The sixth is impermanent facts about food (*Āhāre-paṭikūlasaññā*). It accounts for contemplating how our delicious intake ultimately becomes disgusting garbage.

Last is the consideration of four elements (*Catudhātuvaṭṭhāna*), what Buddhists consider to be the elemental factors of life: fire, water, earth, and wind. The human body in particular is composed of the four elements. Fire means warmth and life energy, while water refers to all kinds of liquids within the body. Earth signifies the flesh and organs, while wind is directly related to breath. By always acknowledging this interpretive reality, practitioners are directed toward a different way of thinking about matter. When a Buddhist is sad, meditation on the four-element reflection will enable her to detach from that emotion. She can see that she is the aggregation of the four elements rather than a complete "self." How can fire feel sad? How can water, earth, or wind? It is solely the mental craft of suffering that causes depression. So the same applies to the case of anger or hatred. Because this method requires recognition that all people are combinations of the four elements, suffering disappears not because of forgiveness but the insight one acquires from meditation. It lets go of strong mental attachment by envisioning and objectifying suffering.

Concerning the debates between the schools of meditation, samatha versus vipassana, it is noteworthy here that when taking a close look at the forty techniques of kammaṭṭhāna, some techniques are difficult to define as purely vipassana or samatha. The case of meditation on the decayed body focuses on developing concentration when staring at corpses but in the process one has to confront several mental processes: calming the mind when seeing unpleasant images and making sense of what one can learn from emotions such as fear and disgust. This indicates the interlacing spectrum of vipassana and samatha at play on the meditator's consciousness, which lessens the differences between the two techniques. For many practitioners, right mindfulness and right concentration are equally articulated (Parisuddho 2009: 61). The Kammaṭṭhāna (the basic deed/foundation) helps resolve the tensions between the meditation schools. In this light, samatha and vipassana work together like two human legs: moving back and forth, pushing the practitioner forward.

Transcending Techniques: Mahayana and Vajrayana Perspectives on Meditation

I have focused the bulk of this chapter on the Theravada Buddhist sources and understanding because many meditative practices and schools across the globe in the late twentieth and twenty-first century are deeply rooted in the Theravada tradition, including the vipassana schools of S.N. Goenka and Ajahn Chah Subhaddo. The latter school in particular drew a number of lay practitioners and Westerners to be ordained as monks. Some of them became known as notable dharma teachers such as Sumedho Bhikkhu (former abbot of Amaravati temple, London), Pasanno Bhikkhu (whose book recounts the conversation with a Thai prisoner facing a death sentence renders a deep sense of mindfulness), and Jayasaro Bhikkhu who wrote *9–11: A Buddhist Reflection on the Tragedy of September 11*. These prominent Western monks eventually returned to their place of spiritual origin and gained huge popularity among Thai lay Buddhists.

Nevertheless, Mahayana Buddhism has long developed traditions of meditation in the West as well, particularly in late nineteenth-century America. The primary example is rooted in Zen (Ch.: Chan) Buddhism, one of the sects of Mahayana Buddhism popular throughout East Asia. Zen meditation is not limited to particular forms and techniques. For many practitioners, one should embody the practice deeply in daily life experience, such as washing the dishes, sweeping the floor, or working in an office. It is not about sitting in silence to make one aware of their sensation. Instead, meditation infuses every single moment. Sudden wisdom, the state of awakening or enlightenment (*satori*), may arise from the unexpected click of experiential learning (Suzuki 1994: 259).

This school of meditation believes that inside everyone, there is Buddha-nature. Enlightenment is not waiting as a transcendental state but instead is ready to bloom when the conditions are right. Once practitioners fully comprehend mindfulness and self-scrutiny, like a fruit, enlightenment will naturally ripen when it has been well fertilized. This idea of practice can be traced to the teaching of a Japanese Zen master Dōgen Zenji (1200–1253) who also pointed out that there is no gap between practice and enlightenment. There is only oneness, no separation (Yukoi and Victoria 1990: 47). This idea therefore contradicts the step-by-step meditation widely embraced by Theravada meditative traditions.

One of the most prominent recent Chan meditation masters is Thich Nhat Hanh, a Vietnamese monk who advocated for this method of practice in the community called Plum village, primarily in France and later widespread to several corners of the world (Taylor 2007: 299). He decided to return to Vietnam and grow his community of mindfulness at Tu Hieu (Root Temple) in Hue (see Figure 5.5). Although he is situated within Mahayana Buddhism, he still embraces the ideas discussed above, such as meditation on decomposition.

With regard to the influence of Vajrayana (Thunderbolt/Diamond vehicle) meditation, the idea of practice is rooted in the mixture of Yogacāra tradition, whose core belief is based upon the supremacy of mind over matter, and at the same time adhering to Mādhyamika philosophy, which values non-duality and understanding that everything is void. Vajrayana meditation is often seen as a Tantric/Esoteric practice—a highly symbolic ritual enactment that tends to evoke the inner experience of the practitioner to process the perceived reality. The visual image as a sacred mandala, for instance, represents the culmination of the universe directly channeled to meditation (see Figure 5.6).

The rising popularity of Vajrayana practice in the West began in the 1950s when Tibetan Buddhists escaped suppression by the Chinese communist government. The Dalai

FIGURE 5.5 *Half-moon pond for meditation at Tu Hieu Temple, Vietnam.* Source: *Napakadol Kittisenee.*

Lama (1935–) was among these Buddhist asylum seekers. Based in Daramshala, India, the Dalai Lama disseminated Tibetan Vajrayana Buddhist teachings across the globe and is recognized as an ambassador of world peace and interfaith dialogue. Meanwhile in North America, Chögyam Trungpa (1939–1987) was a notable influencer of Vajrayana meditation practice. His idea of the Shambhala training method and "crazy wisdom," utilizing unexpected, outrageous, or unpredictable ways of religious and ritualistic pursuit, sparked controversy among the public (Divalerio 2015: 239). In this regard, Trungpa's teaching, however, carries many essential facets of Vajrayana meditation.

Buddhadasa (1906–1993), another great meditation mentor and thought-provoking monk from Thailand, grew up in the Theravada tradition but is often conceived of as Zen (Gabaude 2000). When lay persons claimed they had no time to take meditation courses or retreats, he reminded them every moment could be their meditation as they do not need to find time for breathing. Buddhadasa extended his teaching style from conventional preaching to a dharma talk. Rather than writing commentaries on the Buddhist canon, he turned dharma into poems, cartoon, and exhibits, which are intended to inspire thought and meditation. This reoriented dharma practice coincides with his view on the ontological nature of dharma (Sirikanchana 1985).

From these examples, it is clear that the idea of meditation not only transcends the conventional form of practice but also goes beyond the boundaries of Buddhist traditions. What matters is whether it fulfills the common purpose of meditation itself: mindfulness, concentration, and wisdom.

FIGURE 5.6 *Buddhist sand mandala.* Source: *Pascal Deloche/GODONG/Getty Images.*

Contemporary Forms of Meditation

In the late twentieth and early twenty-first centuries, new vocabularies have become a regular part of society; things such as yoga, retreats, and life coaching all offer a sense of meditation in disguise.

Modernity assumes that society, especially in the Western context, has gone through secularization (the removal of religion from all spheres of life) and Buddhist meditation is no exception. Ouyporn Khuankaew a prominent Buddhist feminist activist explained that people tend to think about meditation as an old-fashioned activity. She argues that young people of the twenty-first century find the term "stress reduction workshop" more familiar, despite being a mindfulness meditation course in its nature (Ouyporn Khuankaew, personal interview). Her life coaching methods also combine her former S.N. Goenka school vipassana training and her inspiration from Thich Nhat Hanh's way of listening (Feungfusakul 2020: 37; Khuankaew 2014: 61) as well as yoga. In Thailand, the Willpower Institute is a famous meditation center that originated as a temple in the downtown area of Bangkok and organizes meditation courses at other facilities outside the temple complex across the country (Willpower Institute 2020).

The center of Buddhist meditation is therefore moving out of the temple to various locations within and around the urban landscape, ranging from government buildings to the private homes of individuals who welcome guests to sit and meditate. It is common to see after retreat courses many practitioners from the S.N. Goenka school of vipassana meditation regularly organize themselves for group sitting sessions by inviting friends to join in meditation at home or a condominium near a busy part of town. "He was really representative of a lay person's lineage [...]. He was very much a spokesman for the possibility of having a profound practice even while you stayed in the world with responsibilities," one of his students expressed (Gelles 2019). In Burma in 1969, when S.N. Goenka started teaching meditation, most schools were led by monks and nuns.

During the 2020 Covid-19 pandemic, many practitioners found it difficult to participate in meditation courses at temples or retreat centers (see Figure 5.7). There is an initiative by the followers of Wat Tri Visuddhidham, a prominent Buddhist healing temple in central Thailand closed during the government lockdown, to create alternative meditation spaces. Starting an online campaign via a Facebook fanpage, members were inspired by the abbot Phra Khru Pitak Sasanawong saying, "Tham Baan Hai Pen Wat" (Turning Home into Monastery). Like "work from home," the practitioners managed to meditate from home and share their "cultivation of good" to their virtual meditation community. Instead of feeling depressed from the socio-economic downturn, they are encouraged to move on with their lives, boosted by the force of meditation and digital membership in a community of support and sharing (Making a House into a Temple n.d.).

After reviewing perspectives on change and dynamics in Buddhist meditation, it is interesting to see the adaptation of spirituality in new contexts. Despite the changing grammar and vocabularies for new audiences, it serves the same, universal needs: the way to deal with suffering.

FIGURE 5.7 *Buddhist practice in the "New Normal."* Source: *sutiporn somnam/Getty Images.*

Further Reading and Online Resources

Access to Insight (n.d.), "Readings in Theravada Buddhism." Available online: https://www.accesstoinsight.org (accessed June 29, 2020).
Amaravati Temple (2002–2020), "Home." Available online: https://www.amaravati.org/ (accessed June 30, 2020).
Audio Dharma (n.d.), "Beth Goldring." Available online: https://www.audiodharma.org/teacher/63/ (accessed June 30, 2020).
Chah, A. (n.d.), "Venerable Ajahn Chah." Available online: https://www.ajahnchah.org/ (accessed June 29, 2020).
Eifring, H. (2016), *Asian Traditions of Meditation*, Honolulu: University of Hawai'i Press.
McConnell, J.A. (1995), *Mindful Mediation: A Handbook for Buddhist Peacemakers*, Bangkok: Buddhist Research Institute.
Panyaprateep Foundation (n.d.), "Venerable Ajahn Jayasaro." Available online: https://www.jayasaro.panyaprateep.org/ (accessed June 30, 2020).
Pugh, E. (2015), *Even the Crazy Man Wept: Reflections Following the War in Cambodia*, UK: Sharp Edge Publishing Movements.
Shaw, S. (2014), *The Spirit of Buddhist Meditation*, New Haven, CT: Yale University Press.

References

Access to Insight (1993), *Dhammacakkappavattana Sutta: Setting the Wheel of Dhamma in Motion*, trans. T. Bhikkhu. Available online: https://www.accesstoinsight.org/tipitaka/sn/sn56/sn56.011.than.html (accessed October 24, 2020).
Anālayo (2003), *Satipaṭṭhāna: The Direct Path to Realization*, Birmingham: Windhorse.
Assavavirulhakarn, P. (2010), *The Ascendancy of Theravada Buddhism in Southeast Asia*, Chiang Mai: Silkworm Books.
Bond, G.D. (1992), *The Buddhist Revival in Sri Lanka: Religious Tradition, Reinterpretation and Response*, Delhi: Motilal Banarsidass Publishers.
Brooks, J.S. (2006), "A Critique of the Abhidhamma and Visuddhimagga," *Great Western Vehicle*. Available online: http://www.greatwesternvehicle.org/criticism/abhidhamma.htm (accessed June 29, 2020).
Cleary, T. (1987), *Understanding Reality: A Taoist Alchemical Classic*, Honolulu: University of Hawai'i Press.
Divalerio, D. (2015), *The Holy Madmen of Tibet*, Oxford: Oxford University Press.
Feungfusakul, A. (2020), "Religion and Feminist," *Stance*, 7 (1): 29–38 [in Thai].
Gabaude, L. (2000), "Bouddhismes en contact: Un zeste de Zen dans le bouddhisme thaï," *Bulletin de l'Ecole française d'Extrême-Orient*, 87 (2): 389–444.
Galante, J., I. Galante, M.J. Bekkers, and J. Gallacher (2014), "Effect of Kindness-Based Meditation on Health and Well-Being: A Systematic Review and Meta-Analysis," *Journal of Consulting and Clinical Psychology*, 82 (6): 1101–14.
Gelles, D. (2019), "Overlooked No More: S.N. Goenka, Who Brought Mindfulness to the West," *The New York Times*, April 3. Available online: https://www.nytimes.com/2019/04/03/obituaries/sn-goenka-overlooked.html (accessed October 24, 2020).
Gombrich, R.F. (1997), *How Buddhism Began: The Conditioned Genesis of the Early Teachings*, New Delhi: Munshiram Manoharlal Publishers.
Goss, R.E. and D. Klass (1997), "Tibetan Buddhism and the Resolution of Grief: The Bardo-Thodol for the Dying and the Grieving," *Death Studies*, 21 (4): 377–95.

Keyes, C. (1983), "Merit-Transference in the Karmic Theory of Popular Theravada Buddhism," in C. Keyes and E.V. Daniel (eds.), *Karma: An Anthropological Enquiry*, 261–86, Berkeley: University of California Press.
Khuankaew, O. (2014), "Listening to the World: Engagement with Those Who Suffer," *Buddhist-Christian Studies*, 34: 59–62.
King, W.L. (1992), *Theravada Meditation: The Buddhist Transformation of Yoga*, Delhi: Motilal Banarsidass.
Lowe, S. (2011), "Transcendental Meditation, Vedic Science and Science," *Nova Religio*, 14 (4): 54–76.
Maha Boowa, V.Ā. (2018), *Kammaṭṭhāna: The Basis of Practice*, 4th edn., Bangkok: Silpa Siam Packaging & Printing.
Maha Ghosananda (1992), *Step by Step: Meditations on Wisdom and Compassion*, Berkeley, CA: Parallax Press.
Making a House into a Temple (n.d.), @Dhammagohome, Facebook community. Available online: https://www.facebook.com/Dhammagohome?_rdc=1&_rdr (accessed September 26, 2020).
McMahan, D.L. (2008), *The Making of Buddhist Modernism*, Oxford: Oxford University Press.
Nyanamoli, B. (2011), *The Path of Purification, Visuddhimagga*, Kandy: Buddhist Publication Society.
Ostler, N. (2005), *Empires of the Word: A Language History of the World*, New York: HarperCollins.
Parisuddho, Venerable S. (2009), *Life and Works of Phrakhru Bhavanabhirom (Venerable Suang Parisuddho): Cremation Book*, Bangkok: Wat Tham Khwan Muang [in Thai].
Sirikanchana, P. (1985), "The Concept of 'Dhamma' in Thai Buddhism: A Study in the Thought of Vajiranana and Buddhadasa," PhD diss., University of Pennsylvania.
Sugunasiri, S.H.J. (2005), "Pariyatti, patipatti and pativedha (Theory, Praxis and Insight)," *Canadian Journal of Buddhist Studies*, 1: 2–3.
Suzuki, D.T. (1994), *An Introduction to Zen Buddhism*, New York: Grove Press.
Tambiah, S.J. (1968), "The Ideology of Merit and the Social Correlates of Buddhism in a Thai Village," in E.R. Leach (ed.), *Dialectic in Practical Religion*, 41–121, Cambridge: Cambridge University Press.
Taylor, P., ed. (2007), *Modernity and Re-enchantment: Religion in Post-revolutionary Vietnam*, Singapore: Institute of Southeast Asian Studies.
Thich Nhat Hanh (2008), *The World We Have: A Buddhist Approach to Peace and Ecology*, Easyread Super Large 20pt edn., Surrey Hills, NSW: Read How You Want.
Tiyavanich, K. (1997), *Forest Recollections: Wandering Monks in Twentieth-Century Thailand*, Honolulu: University of Hawai'i Press.
Willpower Institute (2020), "Home Page." Available online: http://www.samathi.com/2016/ (accessed September 26, 2020).
Yokoi, Y. and B. Victoria, trans. and eds. (1990), *Zen Master Dōgen: An Introduction with Selected Writings*, New York: Weatherhill.

Glossary Terms

Āamatha (Sanskrit) or Samatha (Pali) The practice of concentration meditation focusing on having one's own mind focused on the moment or object of interest. The main goal for this type of meditation is to calm the mind from the busy mind. The term itself also suggests another connotation meaning of frugality as portrayed in the practice of forest ascetic monks who wander around all places, not clinging to one particular place and having only basic needs for their modest living condition during the meditation practice. Moreover, this frugal sense of being is directed to the observation of precepts since some precepts prescribe not to use cosmetics or sleeping on the fluffy bed. This enables one to be away from the sensual pleasures. One can easily gain the concentrated mind without worrying about other things. The practice of Śamatha bears fruit as *Samādhi* (concentration) or in some cases as *Dhyāna* (insight concentration). The well-known examples of Śamatha are breathing observation and unwinking staring at an object. Śamatha is often considered as the foundation for *Vipaśyanā* (insight meditation).

Dhyāna (Sanskrit) or Jhāna (Pali) Insight concentration. The concentration in general term (*Khaṇika Samādhi*; momentary concentration) can be obtained by ordinary practice in daily life activities namely reading, cooking, playing sports; but Dhyāna or insight concentration will specifically be achieved through the practice of *Śamatha* (concentration meditation) and in some cases from extreme fasting or other ascetic acts as exemplified by the Buddha's life story when he was in search of enlightenment. As seen before and during Buddha's lifetime this term is usually associated with the supernatural or magical power endorsed by Dhyāna, later known as "Esoteric Buddhism." The insight concentration can be further classified as *Rūpa Dhyāna* (form concentration) and *Arūpa Dhyāna* (formless concentration) depending on the object of focus when practicing it. Each type combines another four stages.

Karmasthana (Sanskrit) or Kammaṭṭhāna (Pali) Literally, foundation of practice. It is the basics of meditation to prepare one's state of mind ready for the more sophisticated spiritual cultivation. There are forty techniques or methods of Karmasthana advised by the Buddha. It varies from breathing observation, mantra/syllable recitals, staring at certain objects to visualization of dead bodies and skeletons. All are categorized into two major fields: *Śamatha Karmasthana* (concentration meditation) and *Vipaśyanā Karmasthana* (insight meditation)

Samādhi The concentration of the mind. The busy mind is the symptom of having no Samādhi. Śamatha is not the only method of achieving Samādhi but also some daily activities such as reading. There are three stages of Samādhi: *Khaṇika* (momentary), *Upacāra* (periodic), and *Appanā* (firm). The latter two can regularly be acquired through meditation practice. Both can be developed into *Dhyāna* (insight concentration) but in the Noble Eightfold path toward the end of suffering, it only requires *Sammā Samādhi* (right concentration), which can be loosely interpreted as useful concentration for *Vipaśyanā* (insight meditation).

Vipaśyanā (Sanskrit) or Vipassanā (Pali) Seeing things clearly. It is the insight meditation in which mindfulness is the key in observing how the mind functions. After being trained in *Śamatha*, one's state of mind is now ready for inspection. The ordinary/untrained mind is unclear because it is covered by hatred, greed, delusion, and illusion. Vipaśyanā is meant to be coping with this. In general, Vipaśyanā involves three actors: the observer, the observed, and the observation. All are interrelated but the meditation practitioner will work ceaselessly to have them broken up via observation. Concentration is important yet not the essential part of Vipaśyanā. Rather, the practitioner will be trained to realize the impermanence, the suffering, and the non-self until the mind has learnt to let go on its own—free itself from clinging to emotions and thoughts that are the projection of hatred, greed, delusion, and illusion.

6

Buddhist Ritual

Matthew Hayes

Introduction

Buddhist ritual practices vary as widely as the regional traditions that comprise the religion. While we can identify a few shared doctrinal features across ritual practices within Buddhism, such as the centrality of merit-making and devotional expression, ritual motive, form, and purpose range so widely that it becomes impossible to examine Buddhist ritual in monolithic terms. As Buddhism spread from India across the Silk Road to East Asia and beyond, practices and doctrines changed according to new cultural, geographical, and social demands. As part and parcel of Buddhist practice and doctrine, therefore, ritual was no exception to this transformation.

This section recognizes the importance of these demands by taking an anthropological approach to Buddhist ritual practices. The anthropological approach places the human practitioner at the center of ritual activities and perceives of them both as the central actors in rituals and as the recipients of ritual result; Buddhist practitioners are performers, observers, vectors, and targets of ritual expression. This approach thus takes seriously the role and influence of ritual participants, observers, and recipients as meaningful shapers of ritual processes. Buddhists across the world depict ritual activity in their writings and art; they maintain architectural spaces dedicated to ritual; they set aside special days or times for ritual; they construct ritual languages; and, in some regions, ritual has become a means of economic stability. Buddhist ritual thus begins and ends as a human endeavor.

This human-driven feature is not particular to Buddhist ritual. In fact, anthropologists (Gluckman 1954; Goffman 1974; Turner 1985) have long depicted ritual as *social action* across a variety of religious and nonreligious social groups. Several implications have emerged through this depiction. At a basic level, ritual is *social* insofar as it involves, whether physically or conceptually, more than one individual. This can directly involve individuals who are a part of the ritual performance itself or it may involve individuals indirectly related to the performance, such as a distant sponsor, a recipient of transferred **merit**, or a long-deceased ancestor. Ritual is also *active* insofar as it involves a mode of prescribed or choreographed *action* to bring about a result; rituals are performed on a spectrum of protocol, formality, and innovation but are ultimately aimed at producing a state of change. This collective recognition of ritual as a social means to an end operates on many legitimating frameworks to which human beings attach meaning. These include, but are not limited to, the broad categories of social organization, symbolism, and power exchanges.

Dominant theoretical approaches to ritual have emerged from the fields of sociology, anthropology, and religious studies. Sociologist Émile Durkheim (1858–1917) established an early framework for thinking about religion as a social effort and his arguments generally engage the role of ritual practice in shaping that effort. Durkheim concluded that collective religious action creates and expresses a unified religious worldview among a society, which he calls the "collective consciousness." This action can take many forms, one of which is ritual practice, and it allows for social solidarity in and an expression of collective moral vitality, among other social behaviors. Anthropologist Clifford Geertz (1926–2006) built upon Durkheim's approach by investigating the ritual mechanisms through which human beings establish religious worldviews. For Geertz (2017: 14), symbols are "interworked systems of construable signs" that can signify a range of potential meanings for the observer. One major implication of Geertz's work is that ritual is a symbolic act particular to human communities, and its symbolic meaning is always under human control. Religious Studies scholar Catherine Bell (1953–2008) synthesized and advanced many of the views put forth by Durkheim and Geertz. While she recognized the social and symbolic imperatives to ritual behavior, she pointed out an implicit problem in the process of ritual theorization, which is that too many theoretical approaches to anthropology and sociology tend to obscure, rather than illuminate, the motives and beliefs of ritual actors. Bell reminds us that theory may not account for the social, political, ideological, and economic factors that shape the form and tenor of ritual practice across religious traditions.

While the work of these scholars is but a small sample of the varied approaches to the study of ritual across fields, they remain standards for their nuanced considerations of the integrative roles that rituals play in our lives. Above all, each of these scholars reveals the multifunctionality of ritual in both theorization and practice. In the case of Buddhism, it is precisely through this multifunctionality that ritualized social action supports a larger framework of Buddhist belief and doctrine. What follows is an overview of the form, function, and meaning of rituals within monastic and lay communities across a variety of Buddhist traditions, and each of the examples below reflect a close relationship between Buddhist ritual and the actors and observers that they involve.

Rituals in Monastic Life

Just as Durkheim argues that ritual helps to organize human societies, ritual practices also help to organize Buddhist monastic communities. Rituals work in several ways to organize this social group: they mark the entrance of a monastic into the Buddhist community (functionally similar to a baptism or confirmation in the Christian traditions), distinguish the monastic community from the lay community, and in some Buddhist traditions they may mark certain stages of advancement within monastic ranks. In other religious traditions where the identification of religious individuals is important for establishing a sense of communal belonging, Buddhist rituals also establish a new identity for the individual whereby the individual formally commits to a life governed by monastic practices, studies, and ethical systems.

The Sanskrit term for this marked entrance into monastic life is *pravrajyā*, or "going forth" into a collective religious community. In Buddhist East Asia, this term was translated as "to leave one's family" (Ch. *chūjiā*; Jpn. *shukke*). In English, these terms are usually rendered as "ordination," or the conferral of a religious status onto an individual. From a ritual perspective, ordination is a performed conferral (from an officiant) and acceptance (by the initiand) of an official religious status contingent, especially, on their observance of established Buddhist rules of discipline (Bodiford 2005: 3–4). Ordination rituals mark the adoption of an entirely new worldview from the perspective of the Buddhist order. These rituals thus have an initiatory and transformative quality; they formally "begin" a monastic life for an individual and signal a change from one ethical mode of life to another.

While ordination rituals differ across Buddhist sub-traditions, two major stages tend to comprise the process. The first stage is novice ordination, during which an aspirant as young as seven or eight years old may become a novice monk (Sk. *śrāmaṇeraka*) or novice nun (Sk. *śramaṇerī*). During this procedure, there occurs a ritual shaving of the head, or tonsure (Sk. *tuṇḍa-muṇḍana*; Ch. *tìxū*; Jpn. *teishu*), which is a physical symbol of an abandonment of vanity (see Figure 6.1). There also occurs, through vocal recitation, the adoption of ten behavioral precepts meant to guide the ethical actions of the new members. In addition to head-shaving, novices also don colored robes that visually distinguish them as members of the Buddhist community. In the Theravadin traditions of Sri Lanka and Thailand, these robes are usually orange, yellow, or ochre, whereas in Tibetan traditions they are usually a deep red. In China, Korea, and Japan, robes are usually gray or black. Novice monks and nuns also receive an alms bowl, which is a deep, rounded container used for the collection of alms and for taking meals. Finally, in most traditions, newly ordained Buddhists adopt a religious name, which is conferred by the prospective teacher or the supervising ritualist, with a meaning usually tied to a cherished Buddhist quality, adopted from a well-known Buddhist figure, or partially adopted from one's primary teacher (Harvey 2013: 293–5). These ritualized physical transformations and bestowals of identifying items usually occur within the precincts of the temple to which the new member will belong and before a group of witnesses comprised of monastics. In some traditions, such as in the Sri Lankan

Therāvada tradition, the ritualized handing over of monastic implements and clothing is performed by the family of the novice inductee. The participation of the parents, in this case, further underscores the dramatic departure of the novice from their home (Samuels 2013: 239–40). In most traditions, parental support for young initiands is considered a highly meritorious act.

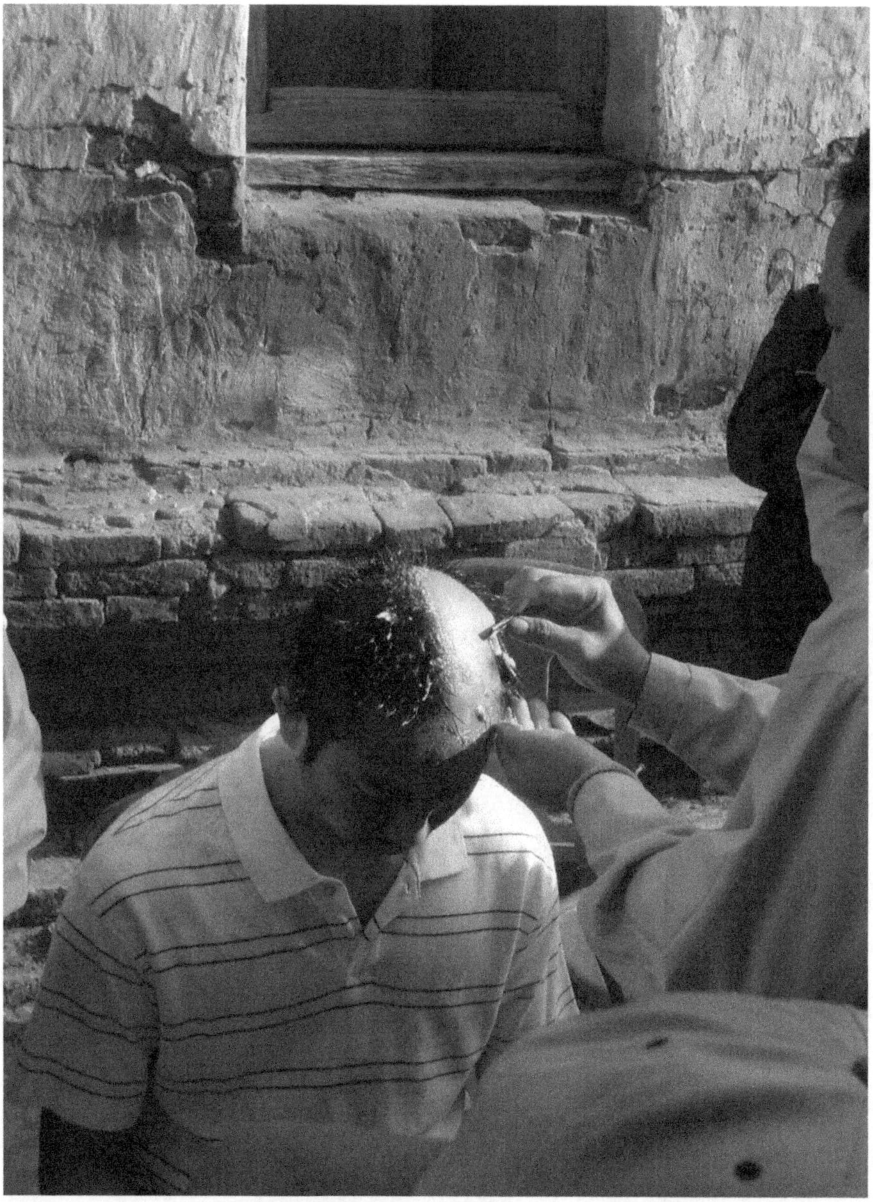

FIGURE 6.1 *Performance of the tonsure ceremony in the Thai Therāvada tradition.* Source: *Americanthai via Wikimedia Commons.*

Once the new member advances to the age of twenty, he or she may then take a higher ritual ordination as a fully ordained monk (Sk. *bhikṣu*) or nun (Sk. *bhikṣuṇī*). This advancement means the adoption of additional behavioral precepts and a ritualized recognition of a member's maturity in discipline and practice. While rituals for full ordination may mark a new and important stage in monastic life, there are yet other rituals that some Buddhists participate in to demarcate substages of spiritual advancement thereafter. In some East Asian traditions, such as the Japanese True Word (Shingon) and Heavenly Terrace (Tendai) schools, monks will engage in question-and-answer format oral examinations to advance to various ranks within the monastery (Ambros 2011: 1081–2; Groner 2002: 139–41). Rituals such as these, which demand an intellectual mastery over central doctrine within the tradition, reveal the importance of self-governance in religious study as well as the importance of community-wide support and recognition for discipline in Buddhist scholasticism.

In Tibetan traditions especially, monastic intellectual hierarchies are one means of signifying and organizing the Buddhist community according to doctrinal understanding. In these contexts, one practical purpose of hierarchizing the monastic community around scholarly mastery is for maintaining a cohesive body of teachings that reflect scholastic precedent within the tradition. The attainment of the *géshe* degree in the Gélug school of Tibetan Buddhism is one example of this monastic emphasis on scholasticism as a means to organize the community. At the age of twenty, following full ordination, clerics may enter a fifteen- to twenty-year additional course of study and mastery of texts surrounding monastic discipline as well as teachings in philosophy, cosmology, and metaphysics. Monastics who complete this course of study are thereafter eligible to compete for the *géshe* degree, the success of which consists of victory in performative intellectual debates between the candidate and high-ranking teachers recognized as spiritual incarnates (**lamas**). During these oral debates, a candidate must quickly field an array of philosophical attacks from these challengers who seek to destabilize, refute, and eventually overturn the positions held by the candidate (see Figure 6.2). Debates adopt a performative style insofar as they involve jumping, clapping, shouting, and expressions of intimidation aimed at either opponent. The winning candidates are then eligible to advance even further to several tutorship appointments among inner intellectual circles close to the Dalai Lama, the current and foremost spiritual leader in the Gélug tradition. The final selection process of this advanced stage is highly ritualized and marks the pinnacle of the scholarly hierarchy within the Gélug school: the names of finalists are written on paper, placed within barley flour balls, and offered to a Buddha image. The ball containing a name that falls from the ornamental bowl during a ceremonial handling identify the new junior tutor to the Dalai Lama (Powers 2007: 478–80). The Gélug school's emphasis on competitive scholasticism drives much of the ceremonial aspects of advancement and orders the monastic community based on doctrinal mastery. Core doctrine is studied and internalized, and its expression is then performed and ritualized.

Ritual is expressive and demonstrative in many contexts in the Buddhist tradition and, just as in other religions, is a mechanism for organizing a community. For Buddhists,

FIGURE 6.2 Géshe *debate underway at Sera Mey Monastery in Lhasa, Tibet.* Source: *Evan Osherow via Wikimedia Commons.*

ritual can establish a hierarchy that reflects a spectrum of study and practice and it can help to identify and mark the tradition by highlighting certain facets of doctrine. On the path of practice, these ritual occasions ultimately mark a stage of advancement for the practitioner and demonstrates that progress before fellow monastics.

Ritual in Lay Life

For lay Buddhists, or those who join the Buddhist community but continue to lead livelihoods, rituals also play an integrative role in establishing and expressing religious imperatives. Whereas monastics are typically able to devote time to practice while residing at a monastery, time devoted to secular livelihoods means that lay Buddhists must engage in practice in consolidated ways that take advantage of, for example, close proximity to a temple that offers regular services to the Buddhist community. One among these ways is through ritual practice, which offers the **layperson** an opportunity to narrowly express devotion, interact with and among the clergy, and provide support for the Buddhist community through merit-making activities.

Typically, a layperson will attend to secular obligations (e.g., jobs, family life) that require time and energy and thus will be unable to engage in regular, rigorous practice in the same way as monastics. One of the primary ways that laity are able to remain engaged and steadily connected to the tradition is through devotional acts such as giving (Sk. *dāna*). Buddhists recognize giving as one of the highest acts of virtue within the program of practice and as an inroad to benefits during this life and the next. This is made possible through giving because the act is understood to produce wholesome merit (Sk. *puṇ.ya*). In the Mahāyāna tradition, giving is described first among the ten perfections on the bodhisattva path. During moments when the Buddha encountered potential followers who had not yet come to know his teachings, he delineated eight types of offerings best suited for proper merit-making and for the support of the Buddhist community. These include food, water, and clothing (Buswell and Lopez 2014: 211–12). Ritualized giving can therefore work toward many ends in the Buddhist tradition. It can sustain the Buddhist monastic community, which orients itself toward sustained and standardized practice, and it can produce wholesome merit for laity, for whom practice may be difficult to regulate with discipline outside of monastery walls.

For laity, the ritual act of making offerings (Sk. *pūjā*) is one formalized example of virtuous giving. During this act, proper offerings are presented before an image of a Buddha, Buddha **relic**, bodhisattva, Arhat, or teacher in an expression of devotion or veneration. Ritualized offerings made after a purificatory prerequisite or alongside a ritual gesture, prayer, incantation, or recitation, are the lay practitioner's mark of confidence in the target of devotion (e.g., the Buddha) as a spiritual refuge. This act is also an expression of the practitioner's fidelity toward that object of devotion, and an embodiment of nonattachment to the offering itself. Offerings made in this ritual context, as Kevin Trainor (1997: 152–5) notes of offerings made to relics housed within stupas in the Sri Lankan Theravada tradition, constitute an "orientation to the Buddha's presence" insofar as it establishes a dependent relationship shared between the practitioner and the Buddha. This expressive component is important for understanding ritual agency wielded by laity and how the act of making offerings is an embodiment of their devotion; laity are in complete control of what is offered, where and when it is offered, and to whom an offering is made. In this way, ritual offerings are a devotional expression of the lay practitioner's own effort to "take refuge" (Sk. *śaraṇa*) in the Buddha as a source of religious comfort and aid and as a prime teacher. Laity identify as Buddhist followers, in part, through a performative giving that connects them to the Buddha (see Figure 6.3).

In some cases, laity may wish to set aside time from their secular lives to travel to an important Buddhist site. As Ian Reader (2005: 90–2) describes of Buddhist pilgrims who travel Japan's 88-temple circuit around Shikoku island, devotion to Japanese esoteric founder Kōbō Daishi, also known as Kūkai (774–835) is one of the primary motivations for embarking on the journey, and in some cases completing it multiple times. To express their gratitude to him for having established the esoteric teachings in Japan, many pilgrims wish to commit to the Shikoku pilgrimage, whether a portion of the circuit or the full circuit. If completed in a single period, the Shikoku pilgrimage

FIGURE 6.3 *Chinese lay Buddhists presenting offerings of incense at a temple.* Source: *Mind Meal via Wikimedia Commons.*

usually takes many months to complete. Pilgrims wear and carry distinguishing equipment fit for travel, namely a white shirt, conical bamboo hat, a bag for storing votary slips and incense, and they usually carry a walking staff and prayer beads (Jpn. *juzu*) (Reader 2005: 12–13) (see Figure 6.4). Some also carry religious texts, such as the *Heart Sutra*, for recitation before Buddhist images at each temple stop.

FIGURE 6.4 *Shikoku pilgrim nearby Iwamotoji, nearly halfway through the 88-temple circuit.* Source: *Jpatokal via Wikimedia Commons.*

In return for the devotional act of religious travel, Shikoku pilgrims earn merit that may, similar to the ritual examples outlined in the section above, yield favorable rebirths in future lives. They may also yield "this-worldly benefits" (Jpn. *genze riyaku*), such as protection from illness and disaster, prosperity, and auspicious blessings. This latter benefit tends to play an important role in the lives of lay Buddhists, for whom there are ever-present challenges and risks in maintaining a stable livelihood outside of a monastery.

Anthropologist Victor Turner (1920–1983), whose work on pilgrimage in Christian culture has been foundational to studies on religious travel in general, understands pilgrimage as a transformative experience with a liminal quality. The pilgrim breaks away from the common structures of society and sets out between the powerful centers and the indiscernible peripheries of society. Religious travel thus occurs in a liminal state, or "between" these spaces, insofar as the pilgrim temporarily belongs neither to their place of origin nor to their intended destination. For this reason, pilgrimage can be transformative and renewing as the pilgrim imputes religious and symbolic meaning onto the experience of travel and, as they approach their destination, onto the religious site itself (Turner and Turner 1978: 1–39). Lay Buddhists, for whom pilgrimage requires a deliberate severance from the secular world to embark on pilgrimages, especially large-scale ones, seek out similar opportunities for meaning-making during their journey.

An arrival to a final pilgrimage destination, or one among many sites that dot a pilgrimage circuit, usually presents additional opportunities to ritually purify one's body or hands before making ritual offerings to images of important Buddhist figures. Destinations may include Buddhist temples, or other architectural or natural formations associated with major figures or events within the pilgrim's own tradition. Pilgrims may offer food, water, flowers, or incense at these sites, and may commit to many circumambulations, or clockwise walking rotations, around the site itself. This is considered yet another merit-making activity that can accompany offerings made to various images.

For laity, rituals function as a socially organizing mechanism insofar as they allow for inclusion in the same doctrinal and practical frameworks enjoyed by Buddhist monastics. Indeed, laity remain outside of the monastery, but rituals focused on giving and religious travel are just two of many alternate routes toward spiritual progress for them (Copp 2014; Gouin 2010; Hardacre 1984). In this way, laity establish their identity as practicing Buddhists included in the potential benefits of practice.

Rituals for the "Next Life"

While ritual practice organizes and orients both monastics and laity in their respective roles as Buddhists during the present lifetime, rituals can also hold purpose at the end of a practitioner's life. Some Buddhist rituals are soteriological in the sense that they can modulate karmic merit and demerit in active and purposeful ways. In many traditions, these types of rituals are referred to as "deathbed rites," and they often involve karmic expiation, purification, and confession to produce a favorable rebirth in the following lifetime. In the same way as merit-making and repentance rituals undertaken during one's lifetime, deathbed rites play an influential role in steering the accrued results behind a lifetime of ethical (or unethical) action.

While this late-stage control over karmic accrual may seem surprising, it operates well within the broader framework of Buddhist moral causation. That is, Buddhists across sub-traditions perceive of karmic merit and demerit as ritually malleable and fluid. Buddhists perform rituals to amplify and dedicate karmic merit, while they also expunge and expiate karmic demerit. In this way, the end of a practitioner's life provides perhaps the final opportunity to modulate the fruits of one's ethical decisions prior to the next rebirth.

In the Tibetan tradition, rituals surrounding death help to guide the deceased as though they were aimlessly wandering into the next life. *Great Liberation Upon Hearing in the Between* (*Bardo Thodol*), popularly known in the West as the *Tibetan Book of the Dead*, is a ritual manual for stewarding the deceased to a favorable rebirth into one of the upper realms (gods, asuras, and human beings) by delivering navigational guidance and instructions aloud to the deceased, or its effigy, during a multistage ritual. Correct guidance toward a favorable rebirth hinges on proper purification of unwholesome karmic accrual, especially during the preparatory period. *Bardo Thodol* belongs to a category of texts recognized as treasures (Tib. *terma*) in the sense that they are prized teachings usually discovered by an individual (Tib. *tertön*) who then reveals them to the world. Authorship of *Bardo Thodol* is attributed to Padmasambhava, referred to as

FIGURE 6.5 *A 45-meter statue of Padmasambhava in Namchi, India.* Source: *Subhrajyoti07 via Wikimedia Commons.*

Lotus Guru, who is believed to have hidden away various treasures in remote regions of Tibet during a visit in the eighth century (see Figure 6.5). These treasures, among which were included esoteric Yogic manuals, maṇḍalas, and early writings that would later comprise *Bardo Thodol*, are said to have been discovered by a mystic named Karma Lingpa nearly six centuries after Padmasambhava hid the treasures. This status of *terma* and its connection to Padmasambhava drew Tibetan scholastics to later expand on the early work in the fourteenth century, and today's basic ritual sequence is the by-product of centuries of influence and eventual scholastic systematization of several funerary texts across Tibet and Northern India (Cuevas 2003: 14–17).

According to *Bardo Thodol*, two or three days after death, the family is notified, and the body left in the position in which it last rested. The body is not to be touched, for improper contact could release the consciousness too early. A high-ranking lama then completes an initiatory ritual for properly drawing out the consciousness, monastics recite protective chants and incantations, and the body is bound and ritually disposed of. Later, and after horoscopy rituals to determine auspicious timing, *Bardo Thodol* is read to the consciousness of the deceased, which is housed in a clay-pot effigy during the ritual. It is believed that the consciousness of the deceased cannot navigate the labyrinthine journey through the *bardo*, or the liminal state between sequential lives, and can only avoid the lower realms with the aid of a skilled lama and the spiritual support of surviving relatives. This assisted navigation unfolds as the lama reads aloud from *Bardo Thodol* and instructs the consciousness of the deceased in how to perceive and discern the various visions of deities appearing at each crossroads (Cuevas 2003: 69–77).

Similar to how the lama guides and allays the internal fears of the deceased in the Tibetan traditions, early medieval Japanese Buddhist communities also established ritual systems to oversee affective states in the dying. Jacqueline Stone (2008) has explored how *Essentials of Pure Land Birth* (*Ōjōyōshū*), sets of ritual instructions for deathbed practices written by the medieval Tendai Buddhist monk Genshin (942–1017), brought Buddhist confraternities together to steer and comfort the dying in their final moments. These confraternities were one major reason Pure Land Buddhism spread during the eleventh century, though it was not until the end of the century that *Essentials of Pure Land Birth* eventually became a standard model for deathbed practices in the school (Horton 2004). The ritual sequence includes the necessary presence of a "good friend" (Jpn. *zenchishiki*) to assist the dying person as they attempt to maintain right-mindfulness while chanting Amida Buddha's name in recollection (Jpn. *nenbutsu*) during the final moments before death. Genshin, along with others such as medieval Shingon cleric Kakuban (1095–1143), understood the effectiveness of chanting while setting one's thoughts on Amida Buddha. From their perspective, such an act establishes a connection to Amida and forges a clear avenue to a favorable rebirth into his Pure Land (Sk. **Sukhāvati**). Birth in Amida's Pure Land is not a terminal destination, but rather an opportunity to expedite and foster further practice on the Mahāyana path without the distractions and challenges of our defiled world (see Figure 6.6).

FIGURE 6.6 *Amida Buddha in descent, welcoming the dying to the Pure Land.* Source: *Cleveland Museum of Art, John L. Severance Fund.*

A "good friend," usually a dharma teacher close to the dying, will oversee the transfer of the dying individual to a discreet room or hall set apart from other activities, and will attend to the burning of incense and the scattering of flowers to create a ceremonial atmosphere. To allay any feelings of attachment within the dying individual, austere clothing should be worn by all in attendance and any personal objects belonging to the dying should be removed from sight. The dying is then seated facing west, or laid down with the head facing north, just as the historical Buddha Śākyamuni took his final breath. Images of Amida Buddha are then positioned opposite west and east of the room to symbolize Amida's descent into the world and his eventual escort of the dying into the Pure Land. In some esoteric versions of this ritual, meticulously prepared threads are strung from the Buddha images and held in the hand of the dying as a further symbol of a connection struck and maintained between the dying and Amida Buddha. The "good friend" oversees this entire process and assists the dying in sustaining their thoughts and vocalizations on Amida, his Pure Land, and eventual delivery there through to the final breaths of life (Stone 2008: 71–5).

As these and many other examples attest, Buddhist ritual practice performed at the end of a practitioner's life is a communal affair. The dying receives the support of close friends and relatives, but also the expertise of trained ritualists who assist in the navigation of the final moments and transitional periods into the next life. If we are to take the above anthropological models into consideration as guides for ritual purpose and motivation, we can see that deathbed rites are yet another mode of ritual organization for the dying; they help to situate the dying in relation to their lifetime of karmic accrual, ceremonially separate the dying from the living, and prepare the dying for entrance into a future lifetime on the Buddhist path.

Conclusion

The above overview highlights the role of human experience and concern in shaping the delivery, meaning, and function of Buddhist ritual. The examples provided here reflect many of the classification schemes advanced in the field of ritual studies by Durkheim, Geertz, Bell, and others. Accordingly, Buddhist rituals have a profound influence on the religious worldviews of followers, as well as on their roles and perspectives within a religious community. We can therefore observe at least three major features of Buddhist rituals across various sub-traditions.

First, we can see how ritual organizes the Buddhist community and formally punctuates certain moments of induction or advancement. In these contexts, ritual serves both a religious and practical purpose for the monastic community; it grows the following while maintaining a systematic and organized structure. Second, we can see that in many cases of ritual expression, the symbolic power of founder figures or central texts is a driving force behind ritual meaning. Ritual expression captures the power of these symbols insofar as participants focus their collective effort and energy on formally acknowledging this power and its role within the religious community.

Finally, we can see how ritual is deployed for specific liberatory purposes. In these contexts, ritual functions as an active force in the exchange of religious merit that can influence future rebirths. Thus, while some Buddhist ritual performances only last a few hours, their effects are perceived to transcend space and time. Taken together, we can see that Buddhist rituals help the practitioner to identify with their tradition and their community by participating in social acts of great religious power.

Further Reading and Online Resources

de la Perrière, B.B. (2015), "Religious Donations, Ritual Offerings, and Humanitarian Aid: Fields of Practice According to Forms of Giving in Burma," *Religion Compass*, 9 (11): 386–403.

Heine, S. and D. Wright (2008), *Zen Ritual: Studies of Zen Buddhist Theory in Practice*, Oxford: Oxford University Press.

Lowe, B. (2017), *Ritualized Writing: Buddhist Practice and Scriptural Cultures in Ancient Japan*, Honolulu: University of Hawai'i Press.

Sharf, R. (2005), "Ritual," in D. Lopez Jr. (ed.), *Critical Terms for the Study of Buddhism*, 245–70, Chicago: University of Chicago Press.

Shinohara, K. (2014), *Spells, Images, and Mandalas: Tracing the Evolution of Esoteric Buddhist Rituals*, New York: Columbia University Press.

Stone, J.I. (2018), *Right Thoughts at the Last Moment: Buddhism and Deathbed Practices in Early Medieval Japan*, Honolulu: University of Hawai'i Press.

References

Ambros, B. (2011), "Shingon Buddhism in the Early Modern Period," in C.D. Orzech, H.H. Sørensen, and R.K. Payne (eds.), *Esoteric Buddhism and the Tantras in East Asia*, 1009–17, Leiden: Brill.

Bell, C. (1992), *Ritual Theory, Ritual Practice*, Oxford: Oxford University Press.

Bodiford, W., ed. (2005), *Going Forth: Visions of the Buddhist Vinaya*, Honolulu: University of Hawai'i Press.

Buswell Jr., R.E. and D.S. Lopez Jr. (2014), *The Princeton Dictionary of Buddhism*, Princeton, NJ: Princeton University Press.

Copp, P. (2014), *The Body Incantatory: Spells and the Ritual Imagination in Medieval Chinese Buddhism*, New York: Columbia University Press.

Cuevas, B. (2003), *The Hidden History of the Tibetan Book of the Dead*, Oxford: Oxford University Press.

Durkheim, É. (1965), *The Elementary Forms of the Religious Life*, New York: Free Press.

Geertz, C. and R. Darnton (2017), *The Interpretation of Cultures: Selected Essays*, 3rd edn., New York: Basic Books.

Gluckman, M. (1954), *Rituals of Rebellion in South-east Africa*, Manchester: Manchester University Press.

Goffman, E. (1974), *Frame Analysis*, New York: Harper Books.

Gouin, M. (2010), *Tibetan Rituals of Death: Buddhist Funerary Practices*, London: Routledge.

Groner, P. (2002), *Ryōgen and Mount Hiei: Japanese Tendai in the Tenth Century*, Honolulu: University of Hawai'i Press.
Hardacre, H. (1984), *Lay Buddhism in Contemporary Japan: Reiyūkai Kyōdan*, Princeton, NJ: Princeton University Press.
Harvey, P. (2013), *An Introduction to Buddhism: Teachings, History and Practices*, 2nd edn., Cambridge: Cambridge University Press.
Horton, S. (2004), "The Influence of the *Ōjōyōshū* in Late Tenth- and Early Eleventh-Century Japan," *Japanese Journal of Religious Studies*, 31 (1): 29–54.
Powers, J. (2007), *Introduction to Tibetan Buddhism*, Ithaca, NY: Snow Lion Publications.
Reader, I. (2005), *Making Pilgrimages: Meaning and Practice in Shikoku*, Honolulu: University of Hawai'i Press.
Samuels, J. (2013), "Ordination (*Pabbājja*) as Going Forth? Social Bonds and the Making of a Buddhist Monastic," in V.R. Sasson (ed.), *Little Buddhas: Children and Childhoods in Buddhist Texts and Traditions*, ch. 9, Oxford: Oxford University Press.
Stone, J.I. (2008), "With the Help of 'Good Friends': Deathbed Ritual Practices in Early Medieval Japan," in J.I. Stone and M.N. Walter (eds.), *Death and the Afterlife in Japanese Buddhism*, 61–101, Honolulu: University of Hawai'i Press.
Trainor, K. (1997), *Relics, Ritual, and Representation in Buddhism: Rematerializing the Sri Lankan Theravāda Tradition*, Cambridge: Cambridge University Press.
Turner, V. (1985), *On the Edge of the Bush: Anthropology as Experience*, edited by E. Turner, Tucson: University of Arizona Press.
Turner, V. and E. Turner (1978), *Image and Pilgrimage in Christian Culture: Anthropological Perspectives*, New York: Columbia University Press.

Glossary Terms

Lama (bla ma) Tibetan term, often used in translation to refer to the Sanskrit term *guru*, that refers to a high priest who teaches within the Tibetan tradition. The term "Lamaism" is now considered outdated and a misuse of the term to denote Tibetan Buddhism in general. Widely, the term lama refers to any high-ranking adept with the tradition and, narrowly, to a specific individual within a lineage of other lamas. The Geluk (dGe-Lugs-Pa) school, for example, recognizes a lineage of incarnate lamas that includes the fourteenth Dalai Lama, Tenzin Gyatso, himself believed to be the incarnation of Avalokiteśvara, the bodhisattva of compassion.

Layperson A member of the Buddhist community unaffiliated as a monk or a nun. This status of belonging includes those who have vowed to take refuge in the Three Jewels, and who have taken five lay precepts against killing, theft, sexual misdeeds, false speech, and intoxication. As unordained members of the Buddhist community, laity often maintain livelihoods outside of the monastery. As a result of this connection to secular life, laity often engage in alternative merit-making practices because they are unable to devote the time and energy to discipline and learning in a monastery. Such practices include making donations, observing the lay precepts, chanting, and embarking on pilgrimage, among others.

Merit The pool of karmic fruits that have resulted from wholesome physical, verbal, or mental actions. Merit is the by-product of virtuous deeds, according to the doctrine of karma, and may accumulate over several lifetimes. Merit is fluid in the sense that, once it is accrued, it can be dedicated to sentient beings for fortunate rebirths or for their eventual awakening. Since merit offsets the accrual of negative karma that results in unwholesome actions, merit is one of the central features of practice in the Buddhist tradition. Making donations to the Buddhist community remains one of the major merit-making practices for laity.

Relic (śarīra) The bodily remains of the Buddha Śakyamuni or other eminent Buddhist individuals. Relics can take the form of finger bones, teeth, or other crystalline substances thought to be the condensed remains of the Buddha or another eminent individual after cremation. Less often, relics can take the form of the mummified remains of eminent individuals, called a "whole-body relic." Relics are said to represent the continuing presence of the Buddha in the living world and are often enshrined in stupas. Nearing a relic and presenting offerings to them is considered a highly meritorious activity for laity and monastics.

Sukhāvatī (Pure Land) A Sanskrit term that means "bliss" or, as translated in Chinese sources, "ultimate bliss." It refers to a celestial realm, or "buddha field," presided over by the Buddha Amitābha and described in sutra literature as filled with light and replete with jewels, lotuses, and other precious substances. In East Asia, this realm is said to exist in the West. The Pure Land does not provide a terminal destination for Buddhist practitioners after death, as is sometimes thought, but rather a site of rebirth meant to expedite future practice, free of the distractions and defilements of the mundane world.

7

Death and the Afterlife in Buddhism

Alyson Prude

The problem of death is central to Buddhism, and Buddhism's philosophical and ritual attention to death played an important role in its spread from India throughout Asia. From the time of its introduction into Asian societies and continuing in the present day, Buddhist monks are "specialists in death" (Ladwig and Williams 2012: 1).

Samsara, Karma, and Nirvana

All lives, including our current human life, are afterlives. That is to say, in our universe of impermanence and constant change, nothing is stable—not even death. Just as no life lasts forever, according to Buddhist philosophy, neither does any death. Instead, death leads to rebirth, and we have all been born before in an ever-churning washing machine of rebirths called samsara. For evidence substantiating these beliefs, especially for people to whom this seems a little far-fetched, Buddhists point to cases of children speaking of past lives, the experience of déjà-vu, and the phenomenon of people who seemingly die and return to life.

The kind of body and circumstances that someone will find in the next life are determined by karma. Karma is defined most simply as "action." In Buddhism, however, karma is created not only by actions but also by words and thoughts. In other words, it is not simply what one *does* that determines the type of karma—positive or negative—that one creates. One's *intentions*, regardless of whether or not one is successful in carrying them out, as well as one's *thoughts about the results* of what one does or says, are important determinants of karma.

In the circle of samsara, beings carry their karma from one life to the next. That is, the effects of karma do not manifest immediately. Neither does karma from one's current life necessarily ripen in one's next. Like popcorn kernels that do not all pop at the same time, karma ripens at varying rates, and both positive and negative karma can be carried over, unripened, throughout many lifetimes. So it is as if we all carry a karmic backpack that we cannot see. Only an enlightened being can know when a particular karma will bear fruit: maybe tomorrow or maybe not for hundreds of future lifetimes. We can only know that our past, present, and future are affected by the thoughts, words, and deeds in which we continually engage.

Because we have been taking rebirth in samsara since beginningless time, we have lived innumerable lives in innumerable different bodies and experienced innumerable pleasures and pains. Even the Buddha lived many, many lifetimes, some of which are described in the popular Jātaka tales. During his previous lives as, for example, a prince, a merchant, a god, a rabbit, and an elephant, he developed great compassion and generated good karma. Only after numerous lifetimes of developing wisdom and engaging in good deeds was he born as Siddhārtha Gautama.

Buddhist doctrines concerning rebirth have much in common with the teachings of other Indian traditions, including Hinduism and Jainism. Instead of continuing to circle in samsara, the goal of these religions is to attain a permanent state of peace that ends the cycle of death and rebirth. The Buddhist term for this is nirvana.

Death of the Buddha

Awareness of the fact of death and its attendant sufferings was one of the realizations that motivated Prince Siddhārtha to renounce royal life and begin his quest for enlightenment. As he told his disciples after his awakening, it was understanding the suffering that is inherent in aging, illness, and death that led him to seek "the aging-less, illness-less, deathless" state, which he described as "unborn, unexcelled rest" (Bhikku 2004). The word "unborn" is important here. We know from experience that everything that is born must die. Instead of teaching a path said to lead to eternal life, therefore, the Buddha taught a method for avoiding (re)birth.

"'This is the last birth. There is now no further becoming,'" he proclaimed after he attained enlightenment (Bhikku 2004). Buddhist teachings posit that only nirvana is permanent and offers freedom from repeated births and deaths. This is the state that the Buddha attained upon his enlightenment. In common usage, nirvana refers to both a state of awakening that can be achieved during life and a transcendent state of no-more-suffering that is attained at death. A more precise term for the latter is parinirvāṇa, often referred to as "complete nirvana" or "nirvana without remainder." This is what the Buddha attained when he died, when all of his mental and physical constituents (**skandha**) ceased.

The death of the Buddha at the end of his teaching career is described in the *Mahāparinibbāṇa Sutta*. According to this important Buddhist scripture, when the Buddha was eighty years old, he lay down in what is called the lion's posture: on his right side with his legs outstretched and his right hand supporting his head (see Figure 7.1). As his death grew immanent, the Buddha's disciple Ānanda became distraught. The Buddha told Ānanda not to grieve his passing, because everything that comes into being must perish. Following his last words of advice, the Buddha entered the first level of meditative absorption (*dhyāna*). From there, he passed through deeper and deeper meditative states and then returned to the first level. He then again went deeper and deeper into meditation and passed away (Davids 1881: 86–116).

For six days, local people paid their respects to the Buddha's body, after which it was cremated in accordance with his instructions. The bone fragments that remained after cremation were divided into portions, and reliquary mounds called stupas were erected across northeastern India to house the relics.

The Buddha is distinctive because when he died, he was not reborn. So where is the Buddha now? The existence or nonexistence of the Buddha after passing into **parinirvāṇa** is a difficult question to which the Buddha did not offer a clear answer. What can be said with certainty is that his relics, the small jewel-like bits that were left after his cremation, are regarded as sacred and powerful. They are not treated as mere reminders of the Buddha but as holy objects imbued with the Buddha's living presence (Schopen 1987). The Temple of the Sacred Tooth Relic in Kandy, Sri Lanka, provides a notable example of relic veneration. Three times a day, offerings of food, water, music, flowers, and even toothpicks are ceremoniously presented to a small golden stupa said to contain the Buddha's left canine tooth (Sri Dalada Maligawa 2019).

FIGURE 7.1 *Buddhists in Dhaka, Bangladesh, gather in front of a statue of the Buddha resting in lion's posture.* Source: *NurPhoto/Getty Images.*

FIGURE 7.2 *This stupa in Kathmandu, Nepal, is a Buddhist center of religious practice, commerce, and tourism. Photograph by the author.* Source: *Alyson Prude.*

Today, in much the same way that the Buddha's relics were preserved for veneration, when a respected Buddhist adept or teacher dies, the body or its relics may be enshrined in a stupa or distributed among devotees (see Figure 7.2).

The Realms of Rebirth

For those who do not attain enlightenment, Buddhist cosmology imagines a hierarchy of three realms for rebirth. At the pinnacle is the formless realm populated by highly realized beings that have no physical form. Correspondingly, the formless realm has no physical location. Next is the form realm where divine beings, including several gods adopted from the Vedic pantheon, live free from sensual desire. These gods have very subtle bodies that are invisible both to humans and to lesser gods. At the bottom of the hierarchy is the desire realm, which itself is divided into five or six realms (see Figure 7.3). These five or six realms are ranked according to the amount of pleasure and/or pain that beings born into them experience (Harvey [1990] 1998: 33–6).

FIGURE 7.3 *This Wheel of Life image depicts six realms of rebirth inside a circle (wheel) that a demon, usually identified as Māra, holds in its jaws. Māra's tight grasp represents the clinging of beings to existence, a primary cause for rebirth in samsara.* Source: *Mistvan/ Wikimedia Commons.*

The desire realm of greatest pleasure is that of the gods (*deva*). Gods live exceedingly long lives free from worry or unhappiness in one of many heavens. Two noteworthy heavens are Trāyastriṃśa, the Heaven of the Thirty-Three, where the Buddha's mother was reborn, and Tuṣita, the heaven inhabited by the bodhisattva destined to become the next buddha. A being is reborn into the god realm as a result of practicing kindness and generosity. As is the case with all rebirths in the desire realm, life as a god is finite. Eventually the gods die and are reborn into samsara.

Sometimes included among the gods and sometimes located in a realm of their own are the demi-gods (*asura*). When posited as a distinct class of beings, demi-gods are said to enjoy lives almost as long and pleasant as those of the gods. The demi-gods' jealousy of the gods, however, leads them to constant fighting as they try to force their way into the god realm. Envy and competitiveness, the characteristics that demi-gods manifest, lead to rebirth as a demi-god.

The last of the favorable rebirths is rebirth as a human, a rebirth that entails both pleasure and pain. Pleasure offers a taste of nirvana; pain acts as a motivator to strive for liberation. As is also the case in the other realms, not all human births are equal. Due to the privileges that men enjoy, birth as a male, for example, is more desirable and requires more positive karma than birth as a female. The same is true for birth into a wealthy or well-respected family as opposed to birth into a poor family or despised class of society. Rebirth as a human is gained by ethical conduct and religious practice.

Among the three unfavorable rebirths is the realm of animals. Although life as a domestic dog may seem fortunate and enjoyable, from a Buddhist perspective, rebirth as a dog is unfortunate. Dogs have little control over their lives; they may be chained outside in the rain or neglected by their human owners. Other animals, such as oxen, may be worked beyond their strength. Antelopes may be hunted and killed by tigers, while tigers may be hunted and shot by humans. Most importantly, animals are not believed to have the cognitive abilities necessary to understand the principle of karma or other Buddhist doctrines. As a result, they are unable to reach enlightenment. Laziness and willful ignorance cause rebirth as an animal.

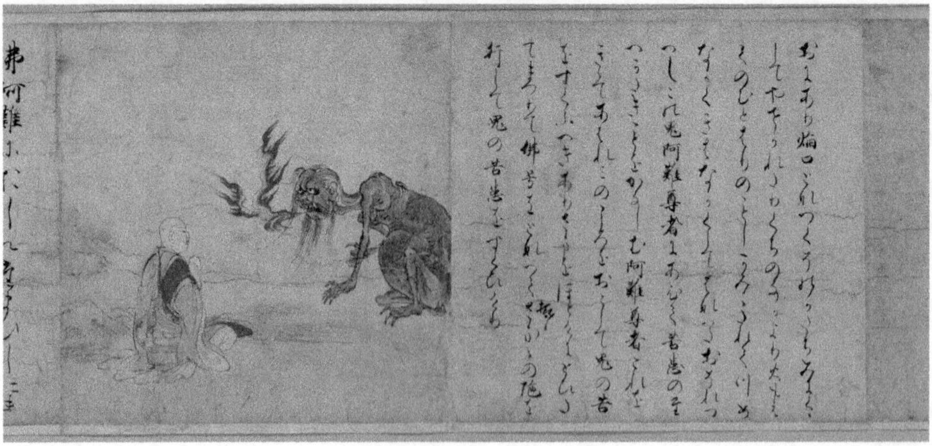

FIGURE 7.4 *In this twelfth-century Japanese scroll painting, a hungry ghost is shown with fire blazing from its mouth.* Source: *Kyoto National Museum/Wikimedia Commons.*

Worse than rebirth as an animal is rebirth as a ghost (*preta*), particularly as a hungry ghost. Hungry ghosts are imaged as human in form but with enormous bellies and extremely thin necks (see Figure 7.4). Their distended bellies represent the extent of their desires. Their tiny necks signify their inability to find satisfaction for their desires. Ghosts live at the margins of the human world where they wait for humans to assuage their suffering. This is the rebirth of beings who were stingy or greedy in a past life. It can also be the fate of those with strong attachments or those who die an untimely death, such as death in childbirth.

The lowest realm of rebirth is hell. Buddhist texts describe numerous hells, both hot and cold. In one hell, beings have molten metal poured down their throats. In another, their bodies are crushed to a bloody pulp by boulders. In another, they are exposed to an icy wind that freezes the skin, causing it to blister and crack open (P. Rinpoche [1994] 1998: 63–71). Violence and hatred lead to rebirth in hell.

The one positive feature of a life in hell is the fact that, eventually, it will end. That is, a being remains in hell until the bad karma that caused the hellish rebirth is exhausted. This is also the case for the other realms within the desire realm. Among the animals, for example, a cockroach remains a cockroach until its cockroach karma runs out. For this reason, it is not an act of compassion to kill a cockroach, because squashing it does nothing to remove its unfinished cockroach karma.

Precious Human Birth

Because gods live the most enjoyable lives, one might think that the god realm is the "best" place to be reborn, but this is not the case. Because they do not experience suffering, the gods are seen as lacking motivation to study and practice Buddhist teachings. As a result, they have little chance of attaining liberation. It is the human realm, instead, that is the best rebirth, since it is the realm that offers the greatest opportunity to achieve nirvana.

Rebirth as a human is difficult to attain, however. In the *Chiggala Sutta*, the Buddha describes an earth completely covered by water and a blind sea turtle that rises to the water's surface once every hundred years. Suppose, says the Buddha, that a person tosses something like an inner tube onto the ocean. As winds from the four directions blow the inner tube here and there, what are the chances that the sea turtle, coming up for air only once a century, pokes its head through the middle of the inner tube? The chances of being reborn as a human in a time and place where one has the opportunity to practice the Buddhist teachings is as unlikely as the sea turtle surfacing in the center of that inner tube (Bhikku 1998).

The point of the sea turtle analogy is to emphasize the rarity of a human rebirth. The significance of a human birth has ethical implications, particularly in regards to suicide and euthanasia. Because death does not erase the negative karma that causes suffering, seeking an end to pain by ending one's life is considered ignorant and pointless, because the karma that gives rise to extreme grief or agony will only continue to manifest in future lives until it has been exhausted. Instead of trying to escape the consequences of one's negative karma, therefore, one should endeavor to accept one's suffering as evidence of the First Noble Truth, the truth of suffering.

Other Buddhist teachings advocate maintaining a constant awareness of death. Mindfulness of death (*maraṇānusmṛti*) practices are said to be especially powerful antidotes for people afflicted with attachment and desire. Monks are instructed to meditate on death in a variety of ways. One technique involves imaginatively visualizing the process of dying and the decay of the physical body. Another method is to go to a charnel ground and, surrounded by skeletons and decaying corpses, contemplate the fact that one's own body will one day also cease functioning and decompose (Klima 2002: 172–88).

This may sound depressing, but from a Buddhist perspective, it is craving for permanent life—in other words, the desire to deny death—that robs people of happiness. The purpose of always thinking about death is to remain undistracted by and unattached to worldly things, so that one can work wholeheartedly toward liberation. Numerous Buddhist scriptures emphasize the certainty that *we will die* so that we do not waste the opportunity to attain enlightenment that a precious human birth offers. In the words of Geshe Potowa, "Once you are certain that you are going to die, you will no longer find it hard to put aside harmful actions, nor difficult to do what is right" (P. Rinpoche [1994] 1998: 58). Reflecting on the inevitability of death is intended to inspire a higher quality of life, a factor Buddhist teachings posit as more valuable than a long lifespan.

Pure Lands

The six possibilities for rebirth in the desire realm are complicated in Mahayana cosmology by the existence of **Pure Lands**. Pure Lands are paradisiacal realms filled with flowers, jewels, and wish-fulfilling trees presided over by a buddha or celestial bodhisattva. Pure Lands exist apart from the various realms of the desire realm and are ideal places for hearing the Dharma and progressing toward enlightenment.

Buddha Amitābha's western Pure Land, called the Land of Bliss (Sukhāvatī), is the most popular among Pure Land practitioners (see Figure 7.5). As described in the *Longer Sukhāvatīvyūha Sūtra*, in the distant past before he attained enlightenment, Amitābha was a monk called Dharmākara. In front of the buddha of that time period, Dharmākara made a series of vows regarding his future Pure Land. The eighteenth of these vows is known in East Asia as the Fundamental Vow (Jpn. *hongan*). It stipulated that any being who had faith in him and desired to be reborn in his Pure Land had only to call on him ten times. By the power of the vast amount of merit that he accrued on his path to Buddhahood, he would bring any being who wished and who had faith in him to his Pure Land.

FIGURE 7.5 *Amitābha's Pure Land, the Land of Bliss.* Source: *Metropolitan Museum of Art.*

By repeatedly chanting the name of Amitābha, a practice known as *nenbutsu* in Japanese and *nianfo* in Chinese, Pure Land Buddhists secure their rebirth in the Land of Bliss. Even people who do not engage in Buddhist practice during their lives or who have created much negative karma can call on Amitābha at their moment of death, and he will rescue them, causing them to be reborn into his Pure Land.

Pure Land practice was popularized in Japan by the teachings of the master Hōnen (1133–1212) and his disciple Shinran (1173–1263). According to their view, the world had entered a time when the Dharma was in decline (Jpn. *mappō*) and it was no longer possible for people to achieve awakening through their own efforts. For Shinran, even faith in the buddha Amitābha was not something that people could generate themselves; it was a gift bestowed by Amitābha (Ingram 1968). The view of Hōnen and Shinran, that it is currently impossible to attain liberation through practicing the path set out by Buddha Śakyamuni, runs counter to the Buddha's injunction to "be lamps unto yourselves." Japanese Pure Land Buddhists, however, argue that times have changed since Śakyamuni set out the Noble Eightfold Path. Today, people must rely on the power and grace of the buddhas for salvation.

The Intermediate State

When does rebirth occur? Is it instantaneous at the moment of death or is there an interlude, an intermission between lives? This is a debate that remained unresolved among Indian Buddhists, with the Theravadins and Nagārjuna rejecting the existence of an intermediate state (*antarābhava*) and Vasubhandu and the Mahayana schools arguing in its favor (Wayman 1974).

The idea of an intermediate state between death and rebirth is highly developed in Vajrayana, or tantric, Buddhism. Called bardo (*bar do*) in Tibetan, it begins the moment someone dies and lasts for seven to forty-nine days. During this time, the deceased encounters final opportunities to attain enlightenment, thus avoiding rebirth into samsara. Extended descriptions of the **bardo** are found in the text popularly known as the *Tibetan Book of the Dead*, more accurately translated as *Liberation upon Hearing while in the Bardo* (*Bar do thos grol*).

The *Liberation upon Hearing* explains that, when a person dies, consciousness coalesces at the center of the chest. When this happens, the dying person experiences a bright luminosity known as the clear light of death. This is the first opportunity, at death, to attain liberation: if a person is able to recognize that the light does not originate from an external source but is a manifestation of their own innate wisdom, they immediately achieve enlightenment. For those who are unsuccessful at recognizing the clear light of death, consciousness encounters colorful visions and incredibly loud sounds as forty-two peaceful and fifty-eight wrathful deities appear in sequence. If consciousness does not turn away from these fearsome appearances but is able to identify them as its own projections, enlightenment ensues. Most of the time, however, the lights and sounds of the *bardo* are overwhelming, and consciousness faints in terror. When it reawakens, it is blown about here and there, arriving wherever its thoughts take it. Thinking of home, it sees its family and calls to them, but they do not hear. Then, consciousness longs to be reborn and finds itself in front of Yama, the Lord of Death. Its deeds reflected in the mirror of karma, it is sent to its next birth in one of the realms of samsara (Dorje 2005).

When a person is near death, Tibetan Buddhists read the *Liberation upon Hearing* aloud and continue reading even after the person has died. This practice is based on the belief that while in the *bardo*, consciousness is clairvoyant and thus able to understand the meaning of the text (S. Rinpoche 1993: 305). This makes the intermediate state an important last chance to receive religious instruction.

Preparing for Death

Buddhists attempt to maintain a calm and peaceful demeanor in the presence of someone who is dying. Although this might give the impression that they do not care about the person, this is not the case. After two of the Buddha's closest disciples, Śāriputra and Maudgalyāyana, passed away, the Buddha is said to have extolled their excellence and told the other monks that the community now felt empty to him. But he did not grieve. Anything that is born, the Buddha said, is subject to dissolution. Therefore, even the best disciples must die. The fact that he accepted the inevitable without lament, he continued, was both wonderful and marvelous (Thera 1995).

A further reason for restraining one's emotions when a loved one is dying is that a person's state of mind at death greatly affects their rebirth. A peaceful mind is likely to activate positive karma, leading to rebirth as a human or god. A mind gripped by anguish, fear, or attachment, in contrast, risks triggering the ripening of negative karma and thus leading to rebirth as an animal, ghost, or hell being (Langer 2007: 14–15). Consequently, in an effort to direct the thoughts of the dying, Buddhist monks and lamas will read scriptures or chant prayers to someone believed to be on their deathbed.

The importance of one's state of mind at death has implications for end-of-life medical decisions. Aggressive or painful treatments, especially those that impair one's ability to think clearly, are seen as spiritually dangerous as they have the potential to trigger negative emotions such as anger and frustration in the person who is dying (S. Rinpoche 1993: 372–3; Tsomo 2006: 218–19).

After Death

Customs and superstitions surrounding the treatment of dead bodies stem from widespread fears of ghosts and zombies. In Cambodia, for instance, a corpse is considered both polluting and dangerous. The danger lies in the belief that it takes a week for the deceased to realize that they are dead. For the first seven days after death, the deceased is confused and may wish to harm the living. If someone disturbs the corpse during this time, the spirit may escape the body and cause problems for the living (Davis 2016: 148). Tibetan Buddhists avoid touching a corpse for similar reasons: touch is believed to draw the consciousness to the part of the body that is touched, decreasing the likelihood that consciousness will exit the body through the top of the head and thus achieve liberation or, at least, a favorable rebirth.

Vajrayana adepts may also practice consciousness transference (Tib. *'pho ba*). Through this ritual, an accomplished meditator is able to mentally direct the consciousness of a dead or dying person out of the body through the fontanel and toward a favorable realm or Pure Land.

Buddhist funerals are not short or insignificant events. In many Buddhist countries, funerals are the most expensive and elaborate of all life cycle rituals. Himalayan Buddhists, for example, try to put aside substantial sums of money during their lives to ensure that they will receive a proper funeral, and in Japan, many Buddhist temples are financially dependent upon funeral-related income (Bodiford 1992: 150; Covell 2005: 140–8).

The reason for spending large sums of money on funeral rituals is tied to the idea of **merit transfer**. Acts such as feeding monks and other funeral attendees or offering gifts to the Sangha generate merit that can be transferred to the deceased, further aiding them in securing a fortunate rebirth. The idea of merit as "a kind of spiritual bank account from which one can make payments to others" runs counter to Buddhism's individualistic theory of karma and was likely adapted from Hindu customs (Gombrich 1971: 204). Transfer of merit is made doctrinally acceptable in Buddhism by denying that merit is actually given away or received by one person from another. Instead, it is posited that when the deceased (or anyone, for that matter) witnesses a good deed and delights in it, their joy creates additional merit. It follows that just as lighting a candle from the flame of another candle does not diminish the first candle's light, merit created on behalf of the dead in no way decreases the giver's stock of merit. Instead, the dead create their own merit by rejoicing in the generosity of the living.

For Mahayana Buddhists who posit an intermediate state between lives, merit transfer can occur for up to seven weeks after a person's death, hence extended funerary rituals. In cases in which the deceased has already been reborn, merit can shorten the length of an unfortunate rebirth, as seen in the legend of Maudgalyāyana rescuing his mother. In this story, one of the Buddha's foremost disciples, Maudgalyāyana, or Mulian, as he is called in Chinese, uses his psychic powers to search for his parents in their next lives. He finds his mother suffering in the lowest hell, his offerings on her behalf having failed to benefit her. Mulian begs the Buddha to intercede, but when the Buddha dissolves the hell realms, Mulian's mother is reborn as a hungry ghost. Mulian attempts to assuage her hunger by feeding her rice, but the rice turns to fire in her mouth. Distraught, Mulian again seeks the help of the Buddha. This time, the Buddha informs Mulian that instead of attempting to aid his mother directly, he should make offerings to the monastic Sangha. In this way, Mulian enables his mother to be reborn as a dog. Finally, through Mulian's recitation of Buddhist scriptures, his mother is reborn in heaven (Waley [1960] 2005: 216–35).

The Chinese story of Mulian has parallels in Southeast Asia and precedents in the Pali canon's *Petavatthu*, a collection of tales extoling the benefits that those reborn as ghosts accrue when, on their behalf, the living offer food and robes to monks. Although the dead are unable to benefit from gifts made directly to them, by making offerings to the monastic community, the living are able to provide for the deceased.

Festivals and Material Culture

The legend of Mulian provides the narrative foundation for the popular Ghost Festival (Ullambana) that is celebrated across East and Southeast Asia (see Figure 7.6). This festival marks the day each year when the gates of hell are believed to be thrown open, allowing the dead to visit the living. People attempt to assist the wandering spirits by setting out offerings of food and, in China, burning incense and paper money, and releasing floating lanterns. Often, families will prepare elaborate meals and create table settings for their family's dead, treating them as if they are physically present. In this way, the living strive to hasten their ancestors' rebirths into better forms.

In Mahayana Buddhist temples, altars for the dead are guarded by statues of Kṣitigarbha (see Figure 7.7). Kṣitigarbha is considered the special bodhisattva of hell beings due to his vow to postpone Buddhahood until all realms of hell have been emptied. Kṣitigarbha

FIGURE 7.6 *A woman prepares offerings during Hong Kong's 2015 Ghost Festival.* Source: *Lam Yik Fei/Stringer/Getty Images.*

FIGURE 7.7 *Kṣitigarbha guards an altar for the dead in Buu Dai Son Temple, Danang, Vietnam.* Source: *Alyson Prude.*

works to ease the suffering and shorten the sentences of those serving time in hell. In Buddhist iconography, Kṣitigarbha is depicted as a monk with a halo surrounding his head. He carries a large six-ringed staff to break open the gates of hell and a wish-fulfilling jewel to light the darkness of the underworld.

Kṣitigarbha is especially popular in Japan where he is known as Jizō and serves as the guardian of expectant mothers, children, and aborted, miscarried, and stillborn fetuses. Stone images of him are common in cemeteries where parents dress him in bibs or other children's clothing as they ask him to protect their dead child in the afterlife or thank him for curing their child of a life-threatening illness (Glassman 2012).

Coming Full Circle

Death preparations and funerary rituals vary widely among Buddhist cultures and societies. What holds true across the Buddhist world is that death marks the end of one life and the start of another. Since death is inevitable, Buddhist teachings stress the importance of accepting the fact of death. Doing so fosters renunciation of material things, including the body, and lends a sense of urgency to one's spiritual goals. Nonetheless, for people who do not take full advantage of the opportunities that a precious human birth presents, death provides additional opportunities to escape the endless cycle of rebirths, whether through one's own efforts or those of others.

Further Reading and Online Resources

Dorje, G., trans. (2005), *The Tibetan Book of the Dead*, New York: Penguin.

Ingram, P. (1968), "Hōnen's and Shinran's Justification for their Doctrine of Salvation by Faith through 'Other Power,'" *Contemporary Religions in Japan*, 9 (3): 233–51.

Qin, W. (2001), *To the Land of Bliss*, Watertown, MA: Documentary Educational Resources.

Rinpoche, P. (1994), "The Defects of Saṁsāra," in P. Rinpoche (ed.), *Words of My Perfect Teacher*, 61–99, Boston: Shambhala Publications.

Williams, P. and P. Ladwig, eds. (2012), *Buddhist Funeral Cultures of Southeast Asia and China*, Cambridge: Cambridge University Press.

References

Bhikkhu, T., trans. (1998), "Chiggala Sutta: The Hole," *Samyutta Nikaya*, 56. Available online: https://www.accesstoinsight.org/tipitaka/sn/sn56/sn56.048.than.html (accessed August 25, 2019).

Bhikkhu, T., trans. (2004), "Ariyapariyesana Sutta: The Noble Search," *Majjima Nikaya*, 26. Available online: https://www.accesstoinsight.org/tipitaka/mn/mn.026.than.html (accessed September 5, 2019).

Bodiford, W. (1992), "Zen in the Art of Funerals: Ritual Salvation in Japanese Buddhism," *History of Religions*, 32 (2): 146–64.

Covell, S. (2005), *Japanese Temple Buddhism: Worldliness in a Religion of Renunciation*, Honolulu: University of Hawai'i Press.

Davids, T.W.R., trans. (1881), "The Book of the Great Decease" (Mahâ-parinibbâna Suttanta), in T.W.R. Davids (ed.), *Buddhist Suttas*, 1–136, Oxford: Clarendon Press.

Davis, E. (2016), *Deathpower: Buddhism's Ritual Imagination in Cambodia*, New York: Columbia University Press.

Dorje, G., trans. (2005), *The Tibetan Book of the Dead*, New York: Penguin.

Glassman, H. (2012), *The Face of Jizō: Image and Cult in Medieval Japanese Buddhism*, Honolulu: University of Hawai'I Press.

Gombrich, R. (1971), "'Merit Transference' in Sinhalese Buddhism: A Case Study of the Interaction between Doctrine and Practice," *History of Religions*, 11 (2): 203–19.

Harvey, P. ([1990] 1998), *An Introduction to Buddhism: Teachings, History and Practices*, Cambridge: Cambridge University Press.

Ingram, P. (1968), "Hōnen's and Shinran's Justification for Their Doctrine of Salvation by Faith through 'Other Power,'" *Contemporary Religions in Japan*, 9 (3): 233–51.

Klima, A. (2002), *The Funeral Casino: Meditation, Massacre, and Exchange with the Dead in Thailand*, Princeton, NJ: Princeton University Press.

Ladwig, P. and P. Williams (2012), "Introduction: Buddhist Funeral Cultures," in P. Ladwig and P. Williams (eds.), *Buddhist Funeral Cultures of Southeast Asia and China*, 1–20, New York: Cambridge University Press.

Langer, R. (2007), *Buddhist Rituals of Death and Rebirth: Contemporary Sri Lankan Practice and Its Origins*, London: Routledge.
Rinpoche, P. ([1994] 1998), *Words of My Perfect Teacher*, New Delhi: Vistaar Publications.
Rinpoche, S. (1993), *The Tibetan Book of Living and Dying*, San Francisco: HarperCollins.
Schopen, G. (1987), "Burial 'Ad Sanctos' and the Physical Presence of the Buddha in Early Indian Buddhism: A Study in the Archaeology of Religions," *Religion*, 17: 193–225.
Sri Dalada Maligawa: Temple of the Sacred Tooth Relic (2019), "Daily Service (Tevana)." Available online: http://www.sridaladamaligawa.lk/Rituals (accessed September 4, 2019).
Thera, N., trans. (1995), *Cunda Sutta: At Ukkacela. Access to Insight.* Available online: https://www.accesstoinsight.org/tipitaka/sn/sn47/sn47.014.nypo.html (accessed 25 August, 2019).
Tsomo, K.L. (2006), *Into the Jaws of Yama, Lord of Death: Buddhism, Bioethics, and Death*, Albany: State University of New York Press.
Waley, A. ([1960] 2005), "Mu-lien Rescues His Mother," in A. Waley (ed.), *Ballads and Stories from Tun-Huang*, 216–35, New York: Routledge.
Wayman, A. (1974), "The Intermediate-State Dispute in Buddhism," in L. Cousins, A. Kunst, and K. Norman (eds.), *Buddhist Studies in Honour of I. B. Horner*, 227–39, Dordrecht: D. Reidel Publishing Company.

Glossary Terms

Bardo A Tibetan term referring most commonly to the intermediate state (*antarābhava*) between lives. Mahayana Buddhism posits a period of up to forty-nine days between death and rebirth. During this time, consciousness "wanders in the *bardo*" as it encounters bright lights, terrifyingly loud noises, and images of both peaceful and wrathful deities. *Bardo*'s literal meaning is "in between," and according to Tibetan Buddhism (also called Vajrayana and Tantric Buddhism), there are four *bardo*s: (1) the natural *bardo* of one's current life, (2) the painful *bardo* of dying, (3) the luminous *bardo* of reality, and (4) the karmic *bardo* of becoming. This schema encompasses all moments of a person's life and death such that the entirety of a person's existence occurs within a *bardo* or transitory state.

Merit transfer The dedication, or transfer, of wholesome karma, or merit. Many Mahayana rituals conclude with a formal dedication of the merit generated by the ritual to all sentient beings. Dedicating merit for the benefit of others has a compounding effect on the quantity of merit produced. In other words, the dedication of merit is not a zero-sum game. Instead, dedicating merit results in an overall increase of merit. Merit transfer is also an important component of Buddhist funerals. This ritual transfer of good karma offsets negative karma that the deceased may have and helps the deceased attain a favorable rebirth.

Parinirvāṇa "Complete nirvana." The release from suffering that is attained upon death when an enlightened being leaves behind both physical and mental constituents. *Parinirvāṇa* is different from *nirvāṇa* in that *nirvāṇa* can be attained during life. A person who has attained *nirvāṇa* (i.e., an *arhat*), remains embodied and thus possessed of the five *skanda*s. This state is referred to as "*nirvāṇa* with remainder." When a person who has attained *nirvāṇa* dies and the aggregates cease functioning, the person attains "*nirvāṇa* without remainder," or *parinirvāṇa*. "Reclining Buddha" images in which the Buddha Śakyamuni is shown lying on his right side with his hand supporting his head depict his entrance into *parinirvāṇa*.

Pure Lands (general) Celestial realms, posited in Mahayana Buddhism. Each Pure Land or "buddha field" (*buddhakṣetra*) is presided over by a celestial buddha or bodhisattva who guides the beings of the Pure Land toward Buddhahood. Pure Lands are advantageous environments for Dharma practice, and beings born into a Pure Land are guaranteed enlightenment at the end of their time in the Pure Land. For this reason, Pure Lands are ideal places for rebirth, and many East Asian Buddhists center their practices on prayers to be reborn in a particular buddha's Pure Land. The most popular Pure Land is Sukhāvatī, or "Land of Bliss," the western Pure Land of the Buddha Amitābha.

Skandha A Sanskrit word meaning "heap" or "collection." In the absence of a self (*ātman*), the *skandha*s are the five mental-physical constituents that, from a Buddhist perspective, make up a person. They are: form (*rūpa*, the physical body), sensations (*vedanā*, the feelings one has as a result of contact with other forms), perception (*saṃjñā*, the part of a person that identifies and labels), volition (*saṃskāra*, the part of a person that decides to take action), and consciousness (*vijñāna*, the mental processes that organize sensory and emotional information). The aggregates are impermanent. Nevertheless, they form the basis of humans' sense of identity and are therefore objects of attachment and thus a fundamental cause of suffering.

PART III

Critical Issues

8

Buddhism and Women

Gurmeet Kaur

Buddhism is among the oldest and most traveled religions of the world. As a tradition, it started with the teachings of Buddha Sākyamuni (Siddhartha Gautama) who is popularly referred to as "The Buddha" (see Figure 8.1). Buddhism has engaged people from all over the world due to its vibrant, evolving, and human-centric approach to existence.

FIGURE 8.1 *Statue of the Buddha in Norbulingka Institute, Himachal Pradesh, India.* Source: *Gurmeet Kaur.*

Buddhism originated in the northern Indian states such as Uttar Pradesh and Bihar. It reached the remotest regions of Asia through three ways or vehicles (yāna). These are

- The Theravada or Hinayana (the Elders way)
- The Mahayana (the Great way)
- The Vajrayana (the Thunderbolt's or Esoteric way)

The followers of Theravada Buddhism trace their imprints from the original descents of the *sangha* (community) who were ordained and followed the Buddha. Mahayana Buddhism originated between the first century BCE to the first century CE and is credited as being a more progressive form of Buddhism that is accessible to monks, nuns, and non-monastics alike. Vajrayana Buddhism grew out of Mahayana and spread like wildfire in the Upper Himalayas, including Tibet.

Siddhārtha Gautama, the Buddha: A Biographical Sketch in Scriptures

There are numerous stories associated with the birth of Siddhārtha Gautama. Most accepted among all stories in India's philosophical tradition is about his birth into a royal family in the small Kingdom of Kapilvastu in Lumbinī (in present-day Nepal) between 573–432 BCE. Geographically and culturally, it was part of the Indian subcontinent. The father of Siddhārtha was King Śuddhodana and his birth mother was Queen Mahamāyā of the Śākyaclan.

According to the Lalitavistara Sūtra, while Queen Mahamāyā was pregnant, she had a vision of a white elephant with six white tusks entering her womb from the right side. To decipher this dream, King Śuddhodana consulted the astrologer of his royal court. The astrologer predicted and interpreted the dream as evidence of the birth of a great being. After roughly ten lunar months, when Queen Mahamāyā was traveling to her parents' home, Siddhārtha was born in a garden between sāla trees (see Figure 8.2). Stories claim that she underwent no bodily discomfort; indeed, she felt physical pleasure during pregnancy (Powers 2009). All the Buddhist sources stress the idea that his conception and birth were unnatural. According to the *Majjhim Nikāya* sutra, Queen Mahamāya never had sensual thoughts regarding any man and that no man with a lustful mind could approach her. She also chose strict celibacy from the moment of conception.

According to Vasubandhu (Buddhist scholar of the fourth and fifth century), the Buddha chose to be born from the womb for three main reasons:

- because he knew that the powerful Śākya clan would welcome the dharma (teachings) because of its association with him;
- because he was born from the womb-like them, humans could relate to him; and

FIGURE 8.2 *Birth of the Buddha, eleventh century.* Source: *Met Musuem, New York. Public domain.*

- because he was a physical being, his remains could be cremated after death, and thus his relics could be worshipped by succeeding generations, allowing them to make merit.

The birth of the Buddha is commemorated widely in Buddhist societies and celebrated as the full moon day of Vesak (thrice-auspicious day).

Siddhārtha grew up in a very guarded environment because the royal astrologer proclaimed to his parents that he would be either the most influential sovereign king or a sage. Thus, King Śuddhodana made every imaginable endeavor to raise Siddhārtha in an extremely luxurious and protective environment and it is said that Siddhārtha was not familiar with unhappiness, grief, or sorrow. During his teens and twenties, he lived in the women's portions of the palace, surrounded by thousands by courtesans who were proficient in erotic techniques. To keep his son busy in worldly affairs, King Śuddhodana married him to a royal girl of similar social status—Yaśodharā, the Koliya Princess. Soon after, she gave birth to a son named Rāhula.

However, the Four Sights changed his view toward life. For the first time in his life, he encountered the old, sick, and dead. One evening, he noticed a young hermit who was on his way to collect alms-food. The face of the hermit was gleaming and he seemed very happy. Prince Siddhārtha asked his charioteer Chandaka to explain this situation. The reply came that the young hermit had left household affairs and desires and now leads a righteous life to help humanity. Encounters with all these people created a turning point in Gautama's life. He realized that no material object or property would stay with him for eternity. Eventually, he would end up in suffering. So, to pursue truth, at the age of twenty-nine, he renounced his luxurious life and left his wife and son while they slept.

Women and Buddhism

As the life of the Buddha makes clear, women were central to his early life. Yet gender has often been ignored as a line of inquiry within Buddhism. This has changed with the advent of feminism within the study and practice of Buddhism.

Feminism as a movement started during the nineteenth century in developed countries such as the United States and the UK (see Figure 8.3). It demands equal access to resources for women belonging to various segments of society. Proponents argue that the reevaluation of men and women's socialization and/or social conditioning is necessary to ensure this equality. In Buddhism, the socialization of its followers is under the scrutiny of many feminist scholars. Buddhism has a complicated history related to women, however, there are plenty of instances of women within Buddhist history and scriptures for people to look to when reading Buddhism through a gendered lens. In other words, feminism can be seen as a pathway for Buddhists to eliminate gendered barriers in the pursuit of religious self-realization. Feminism demands rethinking socialization practices promoted by social and religious orders.

In many religions of the world, women are stereotyped as manifestations of lust, considered to be major hurdles in the path of salvation. Likewise, in Buddhist traditions, the Buddha is regarded as the patriarch of all whose teachings, rules, and regulations should not be subject to inquiry despite their absence of promoting gender equality. In

FIGURE 8.3 *Suffrage parade, United States, March 3, 1913.* Source: *Library of Congress.*

other words, Buddhism is not a gender-neutral religion. To examine this, we will look at Buddhism in two phases:

- pre-Buddha or Vedic period
- post-Buddha or post-Vedic period

Pre-Buddha Period/Ancient Indian Period

India is a land of numerous religions but the two of importance for this discussion are Hinduism and Buddhism. Hinduism, earlier known as the Vedic religion, is sometimes referred to as Sanātana Dharma by scholars. It is among the oldest religions of the world. Nearly 80 percent of India's population is Hindu (Central Intelligence Agency [CIA] 2019) and nearly 94 percent of Hindus worldwide live in India (Majumdar 2019). Traditional Hindu thinking rests largely with two schools of religious philosophy—Vedānta (the Upaniṣadic tradition) and Sāmkhya (the enumeration school). These two theological schools attempt to solve the riddles of the universe and human life. Sometimes, they are considered to be contrasting to each other. Yet the beginnings of both their philosophies are found in the Upaniṣads, a set of treatises that are part of the ancient writings known as the **Vedas**.

The position of women in the earliest Veda, the Rig Veda, was seemingly good. During Rig-Vedic times, women and men equally were allowed to perform sacrifices during marriage ceremonies. Unfortunately, in the later Vedas, the position of women deteriorated slowly and gradually. In the Atharva-Veda, the final Veda, nuptial hymns indicate that the husband was the absolute master of his wife.

Later writings (400–1250 BCE) further lowered women's position. According to one of the most famous, the **Laws of Manu** (Manu Smriti), "In childhood, she must be subject to her father, in youth to her husband, and in old age to her sons" (Radhakrishnan and Moore 1957). In other words, women must never be independent even in their own households. Further, it states, "Women have no sacrifices of their own to perform nor religious rites or observances to follow. Obedience to the husband alone would exalt the woman in heaven" (Barua 2011).

The Laws of Manu was also important because it articulated the caste hierarchy in Indian society. Manu himself supposedly divided the social orders into four castes (*varṇas*):

- Brahmans (priests and teachers)
- Kṣatriyaḥ (warriors and emperors)
- Vaishya (traders and farmers)
- Shudras (laborers and menial-job workers)

In the Ram Charita Manas of the Hindus, it is written that "Drum, dumb, lower caste, animal and women all are entitled to thrashing."

The principles of Vedic-Upaniṣadic traditions that prevailed in the Buddha's time were extremely androcentric. Such dominance explains the omission of women from social and spiritual activities on their own. In contrast to this widespread attitude, which reserved spiritual achievement to males, the Buddha declared a message considered to be universal for all people. In my opinion, Buddhism had the least biased attitude toward women compared to other religious traditions. The *Therīgāthā* documents how the Buddha pointed out women's strengths and weaknesses to lead them to full religious lives. There is no doubt that the Buddha initiated and ensured the admission and participation of women in its religious order, which was later known as the Bhikkhunī Sangha (order of nuns). Even though Buddhism was started by a man, many Buddhists argue its essence lies in the universal law of compassion.

Post-Buddha Period

The post-Buddha or post-Vedic period follows the physical death (*parinirvāṇa*) of Śakyamuni Buddha in the fifth century BCE. In this era, speculation raised questions about the existence and possibility of female buddhas. While those who follow Mahayana and Vajrayana agree to the existence of female buddhas (like the cults of Guanyin in China and Tara in Tibet), others keep this line blurred.

To answer the question about the possibilities of a female buddha, the right approach is to ask whether females in Buddhism can break out of worldly phenomenon. The **anātman** (no-self) doctrine, which argues that there is no persistent personal identity over continuous rebirths, is central for this investigation. Despite this idea and much literary evidence for Buddhism's inclusive attitude toward women, the contrary view, that men are superior to women, has gained popularity in many Buddhist countries and is enshrined in prominent texts such as Jataka Tales.

The Buddha's View of Women's Nature

Most concretely, the Buddha was able to elevate the status and position of women in Indian society through the introduction of the nun's order, known as the Bhikkhunī Sangha. This Sangha allows for the full ordination of female monastics in Buddhism. To lay women, the Buddha often gave advice for how both genders should live, taking into account what he saw as the social and physiological differences between men and women. According to the *Aṅguttara* and *Saṃyutta Nikāya*, the duties of men were to pursue knowledge, development, and refinement, while women were to look after their homes and husbands. These passages in Buddhist canonical literature have perpetuated gender stereotypes and the public and private sphere dichotomy (Kerber 1988).

The Buddha's Advice to Unmarried and Married Women

In *Anguttara Nikaya*, the Buddha advised unmarried girls to respect their future in-laws and serve them lovingly, as they would their biological parents (Dhammananda 1987: 4). They were requested to honor and respect their husband's relatives and friends, thus creating a harmonious atmosphere in their new homes. In addition, they were advised to study their husband's nature and temperament so as to be useful and cooperative at all times in their new homes. They should be polite, kind, and watchful in their relationships with servants and safeguard their husband's earnings, using them properly.

Mātugāma Saṃyutta also deals with women. The Buddha says that a woman has to undergo five special sufferings:

- a woman at tender age goes to her husband's family
- leaves her relatives behind
- is subject to pregnancy
- has to bring forth (children), and
- has to wait upon a man.

In revealing the nature of women, the Buddha pointed out not only their weakness but also their abilities and potential. He advised married women to maintain peace and harmony in their homes, a wife

- should not hold destructive ideas and thoughts toward her partner
- should not be ruthless, rude, and tyrannical
- should not spend extravagantly and live within her means
- should vigorously safeguard and save her husband's property and hard-earned income
- should always be righteous, ethical, and moral in mind and actions
- should be gentle in doing and speech
- should be gentle, venturesome, and hardworking
- should be considerate and sympathetic toward her partner, like a loving mother protecting his son
- should be reasonable and courteous
- should be relaxed, patient, and mindful, helping not only as a wife but also as a friend and confidant to her partner whenever required.

The above points might make it seem that the Buddha only counseled married women. But in the *Sīgālaka Sutra*, he enumerates that a husband

- should be honest
- should be gracious
- should be courteous and not disdain
- should give authority to his wife
- should present adornments to his partner from time to time.

In part 1 of *Saṃyutta Nikāya*, the Buddha said that a "Wife is [her] husband's Best Friend." Other practical advice was given to women on different occasions under different circumstances. The *Mātugāma Saṃyutta* clearly mentions that a woman is reborn in purgatory if she is faithless, shameless, unscrupulous, wrathful, and of weak wisdom. Conversely, a woman is reborn in heaven if she is faithful, modest, scrupulous, moral, knowledgeable, and avoids wrath, envy, and adultery.

Buddhist Approaches Toward Marriage

In ancient India, there were various forms of marriages and unions, in particular the Āvāha and Vivāha (marriage). Commenting on caste concerning marriages, the Buddha himself said: "There is no reference to the question of birth, caste, or prestige, which says, you are held as worthy as I and you are not held worth as I." In Hindu societies, one's status was expressed in the terms birth and caste.

In Buddhism, marriage is an individual concern not based on birth or caste, although incidental references to inter-caste marriage, especially between those in the top two rungs of the caste hierarchy, are found in the Sutra Piṭaka. Buddhist texts do not prohibit inter-caste marriages, monogamy, or polygamy; however, Buddhist laypeople are generally advised to have only one spouse and the texts warn against the negative consequences of polygamy.

Buddhist Motherhood

This study of familial relations brings us back to the question as to why the Buddha left his wife and child in slumber. He could have done the same in broad daylight. At the least, Siddhartha could have informed them before his departure. However, this decision seems to be an imitation of the path chosen by hermits belonging to the ascetic/Vedic tradition at that time. Sadly, no sutra in the Pali canon describes the plight of Yaśodharā and Rāhula after he left them without a word, although other traditions developed explanations for Yaśodharā and Rahula where both take monastic vows and Rāhula becomes an arhat (Mahathera 2010: 70). The famous Indian Hindi poet Maithili Sharan Gupt (1886–1964) tried to gather the emotions of Yaśodharā in his poem:

> Oh dear, if he would have told me,
> Would he still have found me a roadblock?
> He gave me lot of respect,
> But did he recognize my existence in true sense?
> I recognized him,
> If he had this thought in his heart
> Oh dear, if he would have told me.

Yaśodharā does appear in the Buddha's view of marriage. The main distinction between Buddhism and Hinduism is that Buddhism doesn't consider marriage as religiously binding, making it an individual concern. Looking carefully, the onus of maintaining the marriage is largely on women. So, the basic rules given by the Buddha are highly androcentric and don't intend to emancipate household women. There is no written rule on how many children Buddhists can have, which means they can have as many as they want, but in turn, it puts women in a condition where they might face significant barriers to their reproductive health. It is interesting to note that Buddhist canonical scripture glorifies the generosity of women who endure the discomfort of delivery, give birth, and bear the responsibility of parenting a child, but it never asserts a mother's agency over her unborn children. In fact, the opposite is found in Buddhism: that the mother is not the owner of the being she carries in her womb because the fetus is playing out its individual karma.

Buddhist canonical texts do not directly reflect on the issue of abortion. However, the Buddha is believed to talk about abortion in the Mahayana "Dharani Sutra," when he argues that the five kinds of evil karma are difficult to end, even if one were to repent of them. The first is killing the father, the second is killing the mother, the third is abortion, the fourth is to cause injury to the Buddha, and fifth is to create disharmony among the community assemblies. "These five types of evil and sinful karma are difficult to extinguish" (BuddhaSutra n.d.).

Order of Nuns

Although the life of a wife and mother is commonly discussed within Buddhism, the vast majority of Buddhist texts concerning gender focus on the Bhikkunī Sangha, the female monastic order (see Figure 8.4). The Bhikkuṇī Saṃyutta of Saṃyutta Nikāya provides references to ten nuns, including Mahāprajāpatī Gotamī, Uppalavaṇṇā, and Vajirā, considered the first women to enter the Buddhist order of nuns.

This order started with ordination of the Buddha's aunt and step-mother Mahāprajāpatī. Her entrance in the Buddhist monastic order and her acceptance of the basic rules for a female monastic community constitute the point of reference for the development of the first Buddhist nunneries. However, the establishment of a nun's community was not a foregone conclusion; three times, the Buddha denied Mahāprajāpatī full ordination. Finally, he answered affirmatively to the monk Ānanda's question on whether or not women can become arhats and thus obtain enlightenment. The Buddha then allowed women to create the Bhikkhunī sangha on the condition that they accept and follow eight basic principles (garudhamma):

1. A nun who has been ordained even for a hundred years must greet respectfully, rise from her seat, salute with joined palms, do proper homage to monk ordained but that day.

FIGURE 8.4 *Buddhist nuns of Jampa Choeling Nunnery, Dharamshala, Himachal Pradesh, India.* Source: *Wikimedia Commons.*

2 A nun must not spend the rains in a residence where there are no monks.

3 Every half month a nun should desire two things from the order of monks:

   a The asking as to be the date of the observance day

   b The coming for the exhortation (appeal)

4 After the rains a nun must invite before both orders in respect of three matters:

   a What was seen

   b What was heard

   c What was suspected

5 A nun, offending against any important rule, must undergo manatta discipline (probation) for half a month before both orders.

6 When, as a probationer, she has trained in six rules for two years, she should seek higher ordination from both orders.

7 A monk must not be abused or reviled in anyway by nun.

8 From today, admonition of monks by nuns is forbidden, admonition of nuns by monks is forbidden. (Sharma and Dubey 2011: 88)

The initial bhikkunī accepted these rules and many eventually attained enlightenment. Buddhist nuns such as Kisāgotamī and Paṭācārā are prominent in stories of early Buddhism. Kisāgotamī spent her life dealing with inferior robes (robes made of inferior cloth, sewn in inferior thread, and dyed in an inferior pale color) while Paṭācārā acquired the knowledge of monastic rules (Vinaya) from the Buddha and delivered thoughtful decisions on matters related to them.

Accounts of such stories can be found in the Pali canon's *Therīgāthā*, which compiles seventy-three poems of elder nuns that depict various nuns' journeys toward nirvana. In these poems, we also find a glimpse of the families of elder nuns and society at large:

- **Somā**

  Spoken by Mara to Somā: It is hard to get to the place that sages want to reach,
  It's not possible for a woman, especially not one with two finger's worth of wisdom
  Somā replies: What does being a woman have to with it?
  What counts is that the heart is settled
  And that one sees what really is
  What you take as pleasures are not for me,
  The mass of mental darkness is split open.
  Know this, evil one, you are defeated, you are finished.

  (Hallisey 2015: 44–5)

This poem depicts gender equality in early Buddhist traditions. Somā was one early convert to the Buddha's teachings. In this conversation, Marā, the personification of evil forces (or death or rebirth or desire), is striving to provoke and discourage Somā but only reveals delusion. The "two fingers of wisdom" refers to the domestic task in Asian countries of checking if rice is cooked by examining it between the fingers. However, in this matter, it is used to negatively portray that women are less capable of liberation. Somā not only refrains from getting offended but calmly points out how absurd the statement is when viewed in light of the Buddha's higher teachings about the nature of personhood. The poem shows the mental strength of Therī Somā who skillfully defeats Mara's attempts to demean her on the basis of her gender.

- **Kisāgotamī**

  The Sage commended having good friends
  For anyone anywhere in the universe,
  By keeping company with good friends
  Even a fool becomes wise.

> Keep company with good people
> Wisdom increases for those who do.
> By keeping company with good people
> One is freed from every suffering.
> One should know suffering,
> The origin of suffering and its cessation,
> The eightfold path.
> A female deity speaks about the state of being a woman:
> Being a woman is suffering,
> That has been shown by the Buddha,
> The tamer of those to be tamed
> Sharing a husband with another wife is suffering for some,
> While for others, having a baby just once is more than enough suffering.
> (Hallisey 2015: 110–11)

Kisāgotami was one of the famous Bhikkunī of her time. In this poem, she shares her innermost feelings about spiritual development, arguing that the company of an individual should be good and thus, provides criteria for good friends. In addition, she clearly shows her adoption of the traditional view that women are imbued with suffering that permeates much of Buddhism. Nevertheless, Kisāgotami shows empathy and illustrates women's different kinds of suffering due to the presence of patriarchal norms.

From the above poems, it is clear that elder Therīs shared their point of view on life as both nuns and laywomen. Lamentably, the monastic rules in the Theravada tradition lack reciprocity between males and females, which many Buddhists who follow the Mahayana tradition in the twentieth and twenty-first century argue do not suit the present age. It should be mentioned here that on his deathbed, the Buddha gave permission to revise the less important rules of the Vinaya, but the offer was never taken. Thus, the subordination of Bhikkuṇī should be seen as one relating to protocol rather than to spiritual progress.

Analyzing the Place of Buddhist Nuns

The Buddha's own biases seem to have trickled down into the sangha, where women were seen as obstacles and secondary to Buddhist men, especially monks. We find ample evidence in the eight garudhamma (rules) where nuns are subordinated to monks regardless of age, class, and so on. On closer examination of these rules, it becomes apparent that Bhikkuṇī are expected to recognize the spiritual leadership of Bhikkhu. In the matter of Bhikkhunovada too, it was a Bhikkhu who was appointed to regularly remind the Bhikkuṇī of the proper observance of the eight garudhamma. Thus, due to Bhikkuṇī's complete dependence on the leadership of a Bhikkhu, the second of this eight garudhamma forbade Bhikkuṇī from going into residence during the annual rains

FIGURE 8.5 *Statue of the Buddha in DhakpoShedrupling Monastery, Kullu, Himachal Pradesh, India*. Source: *Gurmeet Kaur.*

retreat in a place with no Bhikkhu. The third garudhamma too implies the reliance of the Bhikkuṇī on the order of Bhikkhus in the performance of the two ritual functions of *uposathapucchaka* (observance) and *ovadupasankamana* (exhortation).

Bhikkhu were given the right to advise and assist the Bhikkuṇī in their affairs, and thus regulate the destinies of the female monastic order. Public opinion about women' status in the religious orders must have played a considerable part in bringing Bhikkuṇī under the wing of the Bhikkhu Sangha. At any rate, it appears to have been considered wise to have all the important monastic activities of the Bhikkuṇī aligned with a more established and senior group of the Bhikkhu Sangha. This doesn't have to be interpreted negatively, however, because the Buddha took every necessary precaution to avoid possible abuse of privilege on the side of Bhikkhus (see Figure 8.5).

The first, seventh, and eighth garudhamma ensure that Bhikkuṇī do not under any condition assert their superiority over the Bhikkhs. To justify this attitude of Buddha, the Theravada tradition attempts to argue that the organization of the monastic order vis-à-vis the social order of the time combined with moral and ethical values, loomed large in the mind of the Buddha. Dhirasekera argues:

> In the *Cullavagga*, Buddha states: "Not even the Titthiyas who propound imperfect doctrines sanction such homage of men towards women. How could the Tathagata [Buddha] do so? Besides, the Chinese version of the Dharmagupta Vinaya has a chapter entitled Bhikkuṇī Khandhaka wherein the question is asked whether Bhikkuṇ īs cannot accuse the Bhikkhus under any circumstances. The Buddha replies clarify that nuns could not do so even if the Bhikkhus violated the rules of discipline or were guilty of offences. These two protests on the part of Bhikkuṇīs seem to show that the Bhikkuṇī Sangha, or at least a section of it, resisted what is considered by both historical and modern standards to be harsh and unfavourable legislation.
>
> (1964: 477)

The Pali records of the Theriya tradition, which belongs to an earlier phase of the history of the Sāsanaseem, recall Anānda's chastisement of the Buddha, which ultimately led to the admission of women into the order. The Mahīśāsaka Vinaya contains a story where Anānda apologizes to the Buddha for having requested him to permit women to enter the order. But the Buddha absolves him saying that he did so unwittingly under the influence of Māra, the king of demons. This demonstrates that at the time of the crystallization of the Theriya tradition, two ideas regarding the establishment of the Bhikkṇī Sangha stood out clearly: those women who deserved to be in the sangha and those that did not. However, once the order of Bhikkuṇī was founded, a large number of distinguished women from various social backgrounds came to participate in this order, attracted by the power of the Buddha's teaching and the freedom the new order offered them.

Unfortunately, in neither society nor the monastic order are women recognized as spiritual leaders above the authority of men. Bhikkuṇī are systematically taught and told to follow the footsteps of Bhikku through an institutional mechanism that is so strong that whosoever tries to challenge it faces backlashes from the Buddhist community. One such incidence is shared by Eun-su Cho:

> Tonghwa-sa Temple was discussed as the prospective site for such a bhikṣuṇī monastic headquarters in 1954. In preparation, a group of nuns who participated in the movement took charge of Tonghwa-sa for one year, after it was recovered from a married monk. Immediately, opposition arose from the bhikṣus. It is said that a particular senior monk protested, arguing that Tonghwa-sa Temple could not be entrusted to nuns because it was inconceivable that a woman could become the matriarch of a monastic headquarters. In the end, the backlash was too strong, and plans for a bhikṣuṇī headquarters never came to fruition.
>
> (2014: 135)

It is clear that the Bhikku sangha and even sometimes Bhikkuṇī promote patriarchal norms within the Buddhist community and as a result, the monastic orders spread these biased teachings among the laity. This not only supports patriarchy but also strengthens its roots in Buddhism, which may lead to further oppression of both nuns and laypeople in Buddhist communities.

Conclusion

It is commendable that Buddhism was the first among the ancient Indian traditions to formally introduce women to the monastic order. It broke some of the serious myths in relation to women's potential as spiritual beings. Indeed, the Buddha not only abandoned the prevailing ideology of superiority based on birth but he also uplifted the status of women in his tradition to some extent. There is no doubt that Buddhism's place as a relatively practical religion presents a less religious secular viewpoint on the matters related to marriage, divorce, remarriage, and so on. It has contributed widely to both uplifting and subordinating women in Buddhist societies. Women have always been an integral part of Buddhist society but it is only through examining the gendered ways that women have been treated and interpreted within a supposedly egalitarian tradition that the patriarchal and androcentric nature of Buddhism across various Asian contexts has been brought to light.

Further Reading and Online Resources

Barua, D. (2003), *An Analytical Study of Four Nikāyas*, New Delhi: Munshiram Manoharlal Publishers.

Collett, A. (2006), "Buddhism and Gender: Reframing and Refocusing the Debate," *Journal of Feminist Studies in Religion*, 22 (2): 55–84.

Faure, B. (2008), *The Power of Denial: Buddhism, Purity, and Gender*, Princeton, NJ: Princeton University Press.

Singh, V.K. (2019), *Buddhism, Tibetan Traditions, and Indian Path: An Anthology of Selected Essays on Buddhist Studies*, Bilaspur: Sankalp Publication.

Tsomo, K.L. (2000), *Buddhist Women across Cultures*, Delhi: Sri Satguru Publications.

References

Barua, B. (2011), "Position of Women in Buddhism: Spiritual and Cultural Activities," *Arts Faculty Journal*, 4: 75–83.

Bihar Government (1960), *Suttanipāta*, Patna: Pali Publication Board.

BuddhaSutra (n.d.), "The Dharani Sutra of the Buddha on Longevity the Extinction of Offences and the Protection of Young Children." Available online: http://www.buddhasutra.com/files/dharani_sutra_of_the_buddha_1.htm (accessed June 30, 2020).

Central Intelligence Agency (CIA) (2019), "South Asia: India — The World Factbook - Central Intelligence Agency." Available online: https://www.cia.gov/library/publications/the-world-factbook/geos/in.html (accessed June 30, 2020).

Cho, E. (2014), "A Resolute Vision of the Future: Hyechun Sunim's Founding of the National Bhikṣuṇī Association of Korea," in K.L. Tsomo (ed.), *Eminent Buddhist Women*, 125–42, New York: State University of New York Press.

Dhammananda, K. (1987), *A Happy Married Life: A Buddhist Perspective*, Malaysia: The Buddhist Missionary Society.

Dhirasekera, J. (1964), "Buddhist Monastic Discipline: A Study of Its Origin and Development in Relation to the Sutta and Vinaya Pitakas," PhD diss., University of Ceylon.

Feer, M. (1991), *Saṃyutta-Nikâya of the Sutta-Piṭaka*, Oxford: Pali Text Society.

Gupt, M. (n.d.), सखि, वेमुझसेकहकरजाते (यशोधरा) - मैथलीशरणगुप्त| Sakhi, Ve Mujhse Kahkar Jaate – Maithilisharan Gupt. काव्यालय| Kaavyaalaya: House of Hindi Poetry. Available online: https://kaavyaalaya.org/sakhi_ve_mujshe_kahkar_jaate (accessed June 30, 2020).

Hallisey, C., trans. and ed. (2015), *Therigatha*, Cambridge, MA: Harvard University Press.

Kerber, L. (1988), "Separate Spheres, Female Worlds, Woman's Place: The Rhetoric of Women's History," *Journal of American History*, 75 (1): 9–39.

Maha Thera, V. (2010), *The Buddha and His Teachings*, 3rd edn., Kandy: Buddhist Publication Society.

Majumdar, S. (2019), "5 Facts about Religion in India," *Pew Research Center*, June 29. https://www.pewresearch.org/fact-tank/2018/06/29/5-facts-about-religion-in-india/ (accessed June 30, 2020).

Powers, J. (2009), *A Bull of a Man: Images of Masculinity, Sex, and the Body in Indian Buddhism*, Cambridge, MA: Harvard University Press.

Radhakrishnan, S. and C. Moore, eds. (1957), *A Source Book in Indian Philosophy*, Princeton, NJ: Princeton University Press.

Sharma, A. and J. Dubey (2011), *Woman and Religion: An Encyclopedia on Women in Different Religions of the World*, 1st edn., New Delhi: Regal Publications.

Singh, V.K. (2006), *Sects in Tibetan Buddhism*, New Delhi: D.K. Printworld.

Tong, R. (2013), *Feminist Thought*, New York: Routledge.

Glossary Terms

Anātman Buddhist philosophy renders anàtman as the absence of an independent self. The fitting translation of it in English is "a doctrine of non-self." It appears in Anattālakkhana Sutta of Samyukta Nikaya. According to this doctrine, things or beings don't originate by themselves. They depend on others to originate, they do not have their origin. Self is merely a designation as there is no self. This doctrine is in contrast to the Vedic philosophy of permanent self. Buddha said, if anything ceases to exist, it arises after being affected by previous karma and vice versa.

Laws of Manu The Sanskrit term for Laws of Manu is Manu Smriti. Smriti implies memory. So, Manu Smriti or Laws of Manu is thought laid down by Sage Manu. Every sage in the Vedic period has written their memory (*Smriti*), for example, Yagwal Smriti and Bhardwaj Smriti. Vedas are also Smritis. In ancient India, passing knowledge to one's disciples and society was on trend. It was done through oral tradition. So, one had to memorize the sayings of their guru and sages. Laws of Manu are often misinterpreted as Hindu law.

Vedas The word Veda comes to from Sanskrit word "vid," which means to know. It is thought to be the oldest book, and verses are in the form of hymns. The hymns are in praise of nature. There are four: Rig Veda, Sama Veda, Yajur Veda, and Atharva Veda. The Hymns of the Rig Veda are considered the oldest and most important of the Vedas, having been composed in the period of 1500 to 900 BCE. There are more than one thousand hymns organized into ten mandalas or circles. Sama Veda contains melodies or music for chants used from the Rig Veda for sacrifices. Almost all of its recorded verses are traceable to the Rig Veda. Yajur Veda a distinct Veda diverge more from previous Vedas in its collection of the ritual methods that were used by the priests in the various ceremonies and sacrifices. The latest and fourth Veda, Atharva Veda, provides magic spells and incantations.

9

Buddhism and Economics

Courtney Bruntz

In 1973 British economist E.F. Schumacher's book *Small is Beautiful: Economics as if People Mattered* was published and introduced the term Buddhist economics. While the expression appeared in the essay "Buddhist Economics" published in 1966, it was the 1973 text that became greatly influential. In it, Schumacher criticized Western economics (especially capitalism) and provided alternatives, including Buddhist economics based on the teachings of the Buddha. Inspired by travels to Burma in the 1950s, he used Buddhist economics to create a proposed shift in perspective regarding consumptive behavior and markers of economic growth. He encouraged individuals and societies to measure standards of living not by the amount of materials consumed per year but instead by one's overall well-being (Schumacher 1973).

Studies of Buddhism and economics include a variety of examinations. Ones like Schumacher's focus on intersections between Buddhist teachings, ethics, and economic activity, and are concerned with constructing a "right" (i.e., ethical) way to enact economic activity based on the teachings of the Buddha. In these constructions of Buddhist economics the central question for research is: how *should* individuals act in accordance to/with the teachings of the Buddha? This is an ethical question, and as such, scholars often draw on the discipline of Buddhist ethics to construct responses based on values. Western economists also draw on their backgrounds to theorize that a Buddhist economic stance is rational. And finally, Buddhist intellectuals make use of textual analysis to justify their position, and do so by examining key Buddhist sutras (scriptures).

Other approaches within the field include uncovering Buddhism's entrenchment in its surrounding economic systems. In this approach, scholars emphasize the importance of revealing how Buddhist community formation, practices, and beliefs alter in response to shifting market economies, and they additionally focus on the ways in which Buddhists too have shaped their economies. Investigations of this kind locate histories of Buddhism within socio-economic and political realities and emphasize the development of religious communities as related to shifting economic patterns and political power. In terms of methodology, studies of Buddhist communities as they are rooted in economic realities often come from historians, and scholars make use of archival materials to determine how Buddhists affected their economic contexts while also being shaped by them. Furthermore, to uncover Buddhism's contemporary relationship with surrounding market economies, scholarship frequently incorporates sociological and anthropological methods. Drawing on interviews and participant observation, this work emphasizes the ways in which global market economies in Asia affect Buddhist practice. Both directions of examination—Buddhism in its socio-economic contexts and Buddhist economics as ethical consumption—are important for understanding the topic of Buddhism and economics, and each will be introduced in the following chapter.

Buddhism and Socio-Economic Contexts

Within Buddhist traditions, there exists a unique economic feature known as dāna (gift, gift-giving, generosity). ***Dāna*** is an act in which an individual provides: alms (donations of food and clothing) to monastic communities (monks and nuns), financial support to temples, charity to those who are poor or sick, and hospitality to strangers. *Dāna* is part of a Buddhist ethical ideal of nonattachment, and there are stories of the Buddha in previous lives giving up even his own life for the sake of saving others. Giving to others embodies the ideal of nonattachment to self, and is a practice that helps one along their path toward enlightenment.

Acts of *dāna* have an economic implication. As a result of their generosity, the individual who gives to others consequentially receives merit (beneficial karma). Across Buddhist Asia, practices of *dāna* become merit-making activities. For example, one of the key Buddhist guidelines is to not harm (and thus not kill) other living beings. Instead, one should strive to save life. One Buddhist ritual in many Asian nations (including China and Japan) based on this belief is the act of releasing captive animals (see Figure 9.1). Such a ritual gives life back to the animal (an act of *dāna*), and it is believed that the person who releases the animal earns merit.

In both **Theravada** and **Mahayana** contexts, Buddhism therefore has its own internal economy. In addition to practices such as the one described above that generate merit, giving to monastic communities creates merit for the actor. Lay Buddhists (individuals who are not ordained as monks or nuns) support the monastic community through the giving of food and clothing (*dāna*), and the monks and nuns serve as a "field of merit." Monks and nuns themselves do not give the lay Buddhists merit, but instead through their ascetic lifestyle, monks and nuns are a field in which the lay person's giving results in the acquisition of merit (Freiberger 2000). This is Buddhism's internal merit economy, and it is one centered on gifts. Based on Buddhist beliefs, practitioners give gifts to monastic communities, and merit earned positively benefits the person's current situation while also negating the effects of past evil deeds.

FIGURE 9.1 *Hojo-e ritual.* Source: *Masahiro Makino/Getty Images.*

Such merit-making leads to "beneficial future conditions, especially a good rebirth" (Adamek 2005: 135). Additionally, given that Buddhist monks and nuns are required to give up worldly possessions, they depend on the lay community to sustain them (see Figure 9.2). Lay Buddhists therefore need to supply monastic communities with food, clothing, shelter, and medicine, but to do so, lay Buddhists need to have an economic surplus to accommodate donations. Buddhism's historical development across Asia therefore has had a reciprocal relationship with economic advancement. Economic surplus is necessary for gift giving and sustaining the monastic community, and such donations in turn result in the actor acquiring merit.

To detail the importance of *dāna* (giving) further, it is helpful to examine the historical development of Chinese Buddhism. Chinese Buddhism includes a variety of traditions from the Mahayana branch of Buddhism and, as such, emphasizes the activities of lay Buddhists and the significance of bodhisattvas. In the religion's development, donations to temples from lay Chinese had such a profound effect that scholar Michael Walsh (2007) argues that without merit as a transaction exchange mechanism, Chinese Buddhist monastic culture would not have survived. Within the Chinese religious view of merit, the notion existed that to receive that which the individual felt they needed (wealth, social recognition, salvation after death), the person had to donate that which they had (land, harvest, money, labor, and time). This belief not only inspired non-elite Chinese to donate to monks but also motivated emperors to support monks as well. Walsh explains that some emperors were attracted to the salvational or philosophical aspects Buddhist monks offered (i.e., being able to discuss Buddhist teachings with them), but emperors also desired protection and the stability of their rule. The practice of donating to a monastery was believed to bring about this protection (Walsh 2007: 358). And in addition to providing monasteries with money and land, it was common for individuals to write poems and essays about well-known monasteries. Such actions were important to monks because they provided the monastery with greater prestige. Reciprocally, the gift was significant to the patron, scholar, or emperor who offered the poem or essay because they received a karmic reward (i.e., merit). Imperial economic support of Buddhism also helped to establish pilgrimage sites, which were additionally supported by lay Buddhists through their acts of pilgrimage and donation.

What this history shows is the importance merit-making had on the development of Buddhist traditions, specifically in China. But in addition to financially supporting the monastic community, according to Chinese Buddhist thought, individuals could also acquire merit by sacrificing time. This included the giving of time to go on pilgrimage. During medieval Chinese history, for example, four sacred Buddhist mountains were identified as the physical residences of bodhisattvas, and over time, miracle tales circulated regarding pilgrims having visions of a bodhisattva at their resident mountain. These tales were one inspiration for individuals to go on pilgrimage, as it was believed that their sacrifice of time would result in receiving some sort of spiritual benefit—perhaps a miraculous healing. Mount Putuo in China's Zhejiang Province, for example, became known as the home of the Bodhisattva Guanyin (Bodhisattva of Compassion), and the Cave of Tidal Sound in particular, was identified as a site where Guanyin

FIGURE 9.2 *Women giving monk alms, Laos.* Source: *Manan Vatsyayana/AFP/Getty Images.*

appeared to pilgrims. From the Song period (960–1279) onward, officials, scholars, poets, and writers visited the site and wrote about the island and their encounters (Yü 1992: 205). These compilations of writings (known as gazetteers) included collections of miracle tales about Guanyin and miraculous actions the bodhisattva performed, including stories of the bodhisattva reciting the dharma (teachings of the Buddha) surrounded by heavenly dragons (208) (see Figure 9.3). Such myths helped establish sites of Buddhist pilgrimage, as it was believed that by sacrificing time and money to go, the individual spiritually benefited. Over time, financial funding provided by ordinary pilgrims, elites, and emperors helped support the creation of four sacred Buddhist mountains.

What this very brief overview of Chinese Buddhism indicates is the importance of Buddhist monasteries, temples, and sacred sites as locations of exchange. Buddhist locations have always been entrenched in fields of commerce, and various forms of support (land, harvest, money, and time) specifically aided Chinese Buddhism's development. This short history furthermore reveals the importance of financial donations to monastic communities plus the significance of Buddhist sites gaining prestige in the realm of arts. Acts of *dāna* (giving) that generated merit thus came not only through financial support but also from artistic patronage.

In addition to shaping contexts of Mahayana Buddhism, merit economies were also pertinent to the development of Theravada Buddhist locations. To make sense of this, it is helpful to turn to the situation of Burma (Myanmar). Scholar Melford Spiro has

FIGURE 9.3 *Bodhisattva Guanyin, Mount Putuo, Zhejiang Province, China, 2016.* Source: *Courtney Bruntz.*

detailed the ways that merit-making activities shaped Buddhism's rise in Burma, with particular concern on how merit-making has guided social norms. In Burma, he reveals, an ideology of merit influences finances. As stated above, merit can be acquired through acts of charity, but acts of morality and meditation are also mechanisms for merit-making. To be charitable means to be reborn as a wealthy human in a future life, being moral creates rebirth in heaven, and practicing meditation generates in the attainment of nirvana (Spiro 1966: 1167).

In Theravada beliefs, nirvana is understood as almost impossible for the ordinary person, and since being moral is often quite difficult, charity is the foundational ideology and practice for lay Buddhists. In particular, religious charity through financially supporting monks, helping to maintain monasteries, and building **stupas** (known as pagodas in East Asia) is of particular significance (Spiro 1966: 1167) (see Figure 9.4). In Burmese culture, instead of increasing one's capital by saving their earnings, "the Burman who wishes to satisfy his desire for material pleasure can choose instead to increase his merit by spending his earnings—on religion [...] religious spending is the Burman's soundest financial investment" (1167). Acts of religious charity are believed to be a profitable investment for the future and the present, thus "for the average Burman, then, the choice between economic saving and religious spending is a simple

FIGURE 9.4 *Shwesigon Pagoda in Burma (Myanmar).* Source: *By DIMMIS via Wikimedia Commons.*

one" (1168). Overall, just as we saw in the case of China, acts of religious charity were also considered to be a useful investment in Burmese culture, and this belief was foundational for Buddhism's development. In both contexts, correlations between *dāna* and merit-making inspired support for monastic communities, including financial donations for constructing Buddhist temples. In both Mahayana and Theravada regions, Buddhist views regarding an economy of merit shaped surrounding socio-economic realities, especially regarding investment of one's time and money.

In recent scholarship concerning contemporary settings, researchers of Buddhism have noted how global markets of exchange, in particular market capitalism, have shaped Buddhist practice. Capitalist economies are not, however, unique to contemporary Asia. Sociologist Randall Collins, for example, contends that the foundations for capitalism in Asia, particularly Japan, came from Buddhist monastic economies. "The temples were the first entrepreneurial organizations in Japan [...] to combine control of the factors of labor, capital, and land so as to allocate them for enhancing production" (Collins 1997: 855). While capitalism may not be unique to contemporary settings, what are distinct are the global economic markets influencing Buddhist practice. This pointedly includes international tourism, which provides a useful insight into the ways in which Buddhist communities are affected by global economies, while also participating in contemporary global networks of exchange.

In the first decades of the twenty-first century, Buddhist monasteries, temples, and sacred sites across Asia have been incorporated into tourism circuits that draw visitors from around the world, and in many cases, governments have developed Buddhist tourism as a means of financial gain. In India, local governments and tourism management companies now market Buddhist locations as "cultural" destinations, and in this process of rebranding Buddhist sites, nonreligious organizations emphasize a location's connections to Buddhism in terms of cultural heritage. Locations in India are marketed for their connections to the historical Buddha, and to attract Buddhists from other regions of Asia, India is advertised as Buddhism's "homeland" (Bruntz and Schedneck 2020). Constructions of World Heritage Sites via UNESCO

FIGURE 9.5 *Mahabodhi temple, Bodh Gaya.* Source: *By Bpilgrim via Wikimedia Commons*

have furthermore transformed locations across Asia into sites of global tourism. For economic development, governments participate in the revitalization of Buddhist-related locations to emphasize connections between a physical site and its cultural and historical importance. In modern settings of global mobility, the aim of such revitalization has been to increase tourism for financial gain, and thus, partnering with UNESCO is strategic (UNESCO n.d.). At Bodh Gaya, the site holds legendary importance as the location of the Buddha's enlightenment, but recent developments have furthermore connected it to an imaginary of peace—a proliferated image of Buddhist meditation and practice (Geary 2020) (see Figure 9.5).

In addition to UNESCO developments, national tourism organizations promote Buddhist sites in the hope of gaining visitors. The tourism Organization of Thailand began after the Second World War to promote Buddhist sites and boost the nation's economic sector and in South Korea, a temple-stay program welcomes visitors (regardless of religious adherence) to log onto their templestay website, reserve an overnight stay at a temple in Korea, and choose their location based on the historical information provided, videos, photographs, and the choice of program (Cultural Corps of Korean Buddhism 2016). Korea's temple-stay program offers the chance to live among monks or nuns, which is still a unique opportunity in modern settings.

These alterations to Buddhist temples, sacred sites, and monasteries are just a glimpse into the ways in which socio-economic contexts alter Buddhist practice. Opening up to global tourism has been one of the ways in which Buddhist sites have responded to global market economies, and such alterations shape how Buddhist sites are experienced and by whom. In addition to global economies, advancements in technology and convenience of travel and accessibility also shape Buddhist communities. In Japan, for example, changes in pilgrimage practice include accommodating travelers who do not have the time to undertake a traditional walking pilgrimage. With advancements in mobility and transportation, pilgrims may choose to visit difficult-to-reach sites by car, bus, or even helicopter. In the late 1960s, Shikoku—the famous eighty-eight temple circulatory pilgrimage on the island of Shikoku—received 1,500 pilgrims each year, but by the 1980s there were 100,000. By the late 1990s this number continued to rise, and such growth is linked to the modifications regarding accessibility (Reader 2005).

These short overviews make clear that Buddhists have affected surrounding economic markets in Asia while also being shaped by them, and this first section of inquiry provides an introduction to ways in which this has occurred. Buddhist beliefs regarding merit-making have importantly influenced investment activities, but Buddhist practices too have responded to changing demands based on shifts in surrounding economic contexts. Below is an introduction to Buddhist economics—an economic theory based on key Buddhist principles. While this first section comes from historians and scholars utilizing sociological and anthropological methodologies, this next section arises out of conversations between economics and Buddhist ethics.

Buddhist Economics

As stated in the above introduction, the term Buddhist economics refers to individuals and societies approaching economic activity by aligning to, and with, the Buddha's teachings. Given that this is an ethical concern, Buddhist teachers and scholars reference Buddhist material such as the Buddha's teachings and Buddhist philosophy as justification for a particular approach to economics. Regarding individual activity within market economies, Buddhist laypersons are contemporarily guided to align economic participation with the Buddha's teaching of "right livelihood." Right livelihood is one of the limbs of the Eightfold Path taught by the Buddha for cultivating the path to nirvana. It incorporates ethical living, and as Sri Lankan monk Bhikkhu Basnagoda Rahula explains, it refers to how one should approach all aspects of life—including the acquisition of wealth. The Buddha offered guidance on how to retain prosperity and achieve long-term wealth, and his recommendations included achieving wealth through right effort and just means. What this means is that one should only acquire wealth through harmless actions (Rahula 2008: 34). Often in the West, Buddhism is viewed as a nonmaterial tradition focused solely on contemplating the mind through meditation (Winfield 2018), but many of the Buddha's teachings are concerned with this-worldly activities, including financial security and long-term prosperity. Rahula (and many other teachers) provide advice to their communities regarding how to attain financial stability while following key Buddhist tenets, and this advice makes up one form of "Buddhist economics."

Another component of Buddhist economics is guidance on how societies should ethically organize their economies. This interest has been the concern of Western scholars such as Schumacher who argued that a Buddhist view of an organized economy looks different than a modern Western one. He contended that Western economists view organized work from the standpoint of the employer. When doing so, the individual workers who give up their own leisure and comfort in sacrifice for labor are praised as ideal. But from a Buddhist standpoint, work must have three functions: enabling the worker the chance to utilize and develop faculties, the opportunity to overcome the individual's ego through connecting with others in a common task, and to bring forth goods and services required for existence (Schumacher 1973). From this perspective, work should not be organized in manners that render it meaningless for the worker, and the focus should be on the worker's well-being, not the goods produced. Work and leisure should not, therefore, be seen as oppositional but rather as complementary.

Schumacher was greatly influenced by Western views of Buddhism that see the tradition as meditative and nonmaterial, and this comes through in his argument that Buddhist economics is about purifying one's human character while Western economies emphasize multiplying one's desires. One can enjoy pleasurable things, but they should not be attached to them nor crave them: "The keynote of Buddhist economics, therefore, is simplicity and non-violence" (Schumacher 1973: 165).

Essentially, while modern economics might consider consumption the purpose of economic activity itself, a Buddhist approach to economics concentrates on the purpose of consumption—if it is to satisfy one's desires, it is irrational. But if consumption is to sustain life itself, it is worthwhile (166).

What can be gathered from Rahula and Schumacher is the main concern of Buddhist economics: participating in work, acquiring wealth, and consuming must all align with teachings of the Buddha. Thus, embedded within Buddhist economics is a concern for ethical living and following the Buddha's teaching of right livelihood. For Schumacher, the appropriate approach to economics is one that maximizes humanity's well-being by encouraging consumption that modestly satisfies individuals' needs. This means not over consuming, which thereby creates a scenario of violence over scarce resources. Rahula too proposes economic activity centered on moderate satisfaction of one's desires and turns to Buddhist teachings maintained in Pali sources for justification. But interestingly, he does not interpret the Buddha's teachings as being nonmaterial in emphasis, but rather he explains that the Buddha understood a renounced lifestyle as appropriate for some individuals while a non-monastic (lay) lifestyle focused on the acquisition of material goods as appropriate for others. Given that a lay community is necessary for the sustainment of the monastic lifestyle, lay individuals are entitled to wealth as long as it is earned ethically (without harming others).

The implications of these interpretations of Buddhist economics are great. For example, an approach to economic development from the standpoint of profit and production maximization might not distinguish between renewable and nonrenewable resources, but an approach from Schumacher's Buddhist economics does. Additionally, consumption based on the interpretations set forth by Schumacher and Rahula must necessarily question whether or not one's consumption enriches the lives of humans at large, and whether or not the achievement of wealth harms any living beings. The individual must consider the impact of their consumption beyond their own profit and wealth. Thus, making use of Buddhist teachings as a foundation for ethical consumption, the individual necessarily questions modern views of progress.

Buddhist economics has inspired scholars and practitioners to criticize Western economic systems based on Buddhist ethics, and to furthermore propose Buddhist economics as a morally superior approach. In 1988, Venerable Payutto, a Thai Buddhist monk and intellectual, wrote about the relationship between Buddhism and economics, and in doing so, questioned many attributes of Western approaches to economic activity. He criticized viewing economic activity in isolation, and explained that from a Buddhist perspective, economic activities cannot be separated as independent acts. To illustrate this, he explained that the act of advertising simply persuades people to buy things, and from a Buddhist perspective, this has an ethical significance. Images, symbols, and ideas transmitted through advertisements shape the mindsets of viewers. Thus while Western economic theories view advertising as a means to an end (the end being an increase in consumption), Buddhist teachings view the increase in materialism as harmful because they might contain inappropriate images or messages that disrupt public morality (Payutto 1992: 5).

Payutto sought to integrate Buddhist ethics into the study of economics, and to encourage an interdisciplinary approach to economic scholarship. And as an alternative to modern capitalism, he drew on Schumacher's work. He wrote that because the Buddhist way of life is a "middle-way" between the extremes of self-indulgence and asceticism, one can understand Buddhist economics as a middle-way economic theory as well. The Buddha's teaching of right livelihood from Schumacher focuses attention to a correct way of living, and Payutto expanded upon this to explain that right economic activity as a middle-way includes consuming the right amount based on paying attention to moderation and not consuming goods and services to fill individual wants and needs. "In the Buddhist view, when enhancement of true well-being is experienced through consumption, then that consumption is said to be successful. If consumption issues merely in feelings of satisfaction, and those feelings are indulged without any understanding of the nature of that consumption or its repercussions [...] it is incorrect" (Payutto 1992: 32). To summarize, his perspective of Western economics is that Western views value consuming for the *sake of* consumption, but Buddhist economic activity cautions that consuming without proper motivation has *harmful* effects on the individual.

Economic professor Clair Brown further clarifies this stance in her text *Buddhist Economics: An Enlightened Approach to the Dismal Science*. She explains that shopping and buying things to make us feel better does not in fact improve our levels of happiness. Instead, societies should aim to relieve pain by focusing on compassion and not desire. According to free market economics, human nature is self-centered, people care only for themselves, are eager to increase incomes and their own lifestyles. With this view in mind, buying and consuming will make people happy. However, this endless cycle of desire continuously leaves us wanting more, and we are never completely satisfied. Thus, free market economics is not helping us have meaningful lives, nor is it creating a healthy world. Instead, it is resulting in global wars, income inequality, and environmental threats (Brown 2017). Buddhist economics offers an alternative view—instead of trying to find happiness through consuming, practice compassion; and instead of focusing on maximizing one's social position, view everyone's well-being as interconnected.

These brief perspectives of Buddhist economics provide a variety of views that theorize the benefits of coordinating consumption and Buddhist morality of "right livelihood." And while the scholars and practitioners come from diverse cultural backgrounds and interpret the Buddha's teachings in slightly different ways, they are aligned in their concern that consumption must improve the individual and society's well-being. Moving from theories of Buddhist economics to applications of such theories, it is necessary to question the effectiveness of organizing a society's economic system based on these proposed theories. In Brown's theory of Buddhist economics, a nation's progress would be determined by the well-being of its ecosystem (its natural environment) plus the well-being of its residents (in terms of overall physical and psychological health). Gross domestic product (GDP) would not determine the nation's success. Currently, GDP is often used as the measure for whether or not an economy is "successful." This is particularly true of China's economy, and given that GDP refers to the total value of goods and services produced in a country during one year, China goes to great lengths to expand its sources of production (The World Bank 2020). If we were to adjust China's economy from one focused on GDP to one aligned with Buddhist economics based on Brown's theory, the nation would move away from general concerns of production and instead focus on supporting green production, providing living wages and suitable working conditions, regulating carbon consumption, keeping fossil fuel reserves in the ground, and sharing green technology around the world (Brown 2017: 133).

This proposition of implementing a Buddhist economic approach is ambitious. It not only intends to counteract climate change and income inequality, but also to provide environmental protection, social well-being, and a stable economy. At present, the most helpful example of a nation attempting to create an economy based on the values summarized by the theorists above is Bhutan. In 1972 King Jigme Singye Wangchuck promoted an alternative to GDP. Rather than measuring the nation's success based on the amount of goods produced over the year (the economy's GDP), the king proposed a "Gross National Happiness" (GNH) index. This GNH index includes nine domains: (1) living standards (material comfort measured by income, financial security, housing, and asset ownership), (2) health (physical and mental), (3) education (knowledge, values, and skills), (4) good government (how people perceive the government's functionality), (5) ecological diversity and resilience (peoples' perception of the environment), (6) time use (work–life balance), (7) psychological well-being (quality of life, satisfaction, and spirituality), (8) cultural diversity and resilience (cultural traditions and festivals), and (9) community vitality (relationships and interactions within the community, social cohesion, and volunteeerism). This index encourages policies that integrate spirituality and compassion into governance, and according to the 2015 index, happiness of Bhutanese citizens had indeed increased from 2010. In 2015, 43.4 percent of people reported being deeply happy and 91.2 percent said they had experienced happiness (Centre for Bhutan Studies and GNH Research 2016). Although GNH was not a policy created in correlation with the establishment of the scholarly theories of Buddhist economics, it is a way of governing and creating social policies that embody the ideals of Buddhist economics. With its emphasis on the nation's overall happiness, plus its understanding that other domains such as cultural and ecological diversity are as important as one's living standards, GNH is an approach arguably attaining the values Buddhist economics seeks to establish.

Conclusion

Overall, the study of Buddhism and economics considers approaches to economy from Buddhist ethics, plus relationships between Buddhists and surrounding socio-economic contexts. Historical examinations reveal that Buddhism's survival was often contingent upon imperial support, and in East Asian contexts, studies uncover

Buddhist monasteries as sites of economic exchange. Furthermore, activities such as pilgrimage and financial support of temples and monasteries have been connected to the religion's internal economy of exchange. Merit-making activities influenced Buddhist practices and helped establish sacred sites across Asia, and in recent settings, interconnected global economies have inspired governments to make use of such sacred sites as a means to create tourism. Buddhist sites are physical connections to a nation's history and heritage, and because of this governments market and advertise them as destinations to experience Buddhist spirituality while also encountering the nation's unique culture. Thus, in contemporary settings, Buddhist temples and monasteries continue to be locations for economic exchange. But what differentiates current settings from the past are the global markets and growing number of tourists influencing each site.

In addition to this intersection of Buddhism and economics, the two are furthermore connected in the theory of Buddhist economics that offers an alternative approach to Western models emphasizing ubiquitous consumption. Buddhist economics questions consumption as an ideal and source of happiness, and contends that because humans have endless desires, buying things to fulfill them will not generate satisfaction. Instead, consumption will simply lead to further consumption resulting in excess, waste, and the destruction of natural resources. Humans will not only fail to find the happiness they seek, they will perpetuate further suffering from human-created climate change, income inequality, and global conflict. Buddhist economics seeks to relieve these sufferings, and encourages individuals to consume with purposeful intentions (ones based on achieving a higher quality of life), view the suffering of others as their own, understand one's well-being as interdependent with nature and the well-being of all others, and wake up to the reality that an ideology valuing materialism will not lead to long-term satisfaction. It is therefore a "middle-way" economic viewpoint emphasizing moderation and the reduction of desires. Further, it is an approach to economics incorporating Buddhist ethics to inspire a right way of living for the well-being of all of humanity and not simply an elite few.

Further Reading and Online Resources

Bhikkhu, T. (2005), *Merit: A Study Guide*. Available online: https://www.accesstoinsight.org/lib/study/merit.html (accessed September 26, 2020).

Brown, C. (2017), *Buddhist Economics: An Enlightened Approach to the Dismal Science*, New York: Bloomsbury.

Payutto, P.B. (1992), *Buddhist Economics*, trans. J.B. Dhammavijaya, Bangkok: Buddhadhamma Foundation.

Schumacher Center for New Economics (2020). Available online: https://centerforneweconomics.org/ (accessed September 26, 2020).

Schumacher, E.F. (1973), *Small Is Beautiful: Economics as if People Mattered*, London: Blond and Briggs.

Zsolnai, L. (2007), "Western Economics versus Buddhist Economics," *Society and Economy*, 29 (2): 145–53.

References

Adamek, W. (2005), "The Impossibility of the Given: Representations of Merit and Emptiness in Medieval Chinese Buddhism," *History of Religions*, 45 (2): 135–80.

Brown, C. (2017), *Buddhist Economics: An Enlightened Approach to the Dismal Science*, New York: Bloomsbury.

Bruntz, C. and B. Schedneck, eds. (2020), *Buddhist Tourism in Asia*, Honolulu: University of Hawai'i Press.

Centre for Bhutan Studies and GNH Research (2016), *A Compass towards a Just and Harmonious Society: 2015 GNH Survey Report*. Available online: http://www.grossnationalhappiness.com/ (accessed August 8, 2019).

Collins, R. (1997), "An Asian Route to Capitalism: Religious Economy and the Origins of Self Transformation Growth in Japan," *American Sociological Review*, 62: 843–65.

Cultural Corps of Korean Buddhism (2016), "Templestay: Finding Your True Self." Available online: https://eng.templestay.com/ (accessed May 15, 2020).

Freiberger, O. (2000), "Profiling the Sangha: Institutional and Non-institutional Tendencies in Early Buddhist Teachings," *Marburg Journal of Religion*, 5 (1): 1–6.

Geary, D. (2020), "Peace and the Buddhist Imaginary in Bodh Gaya," in C. Bruntz and B. Schedneck (eds.), *Buddhist Tourism in Asia*, 27–43, Honolulu: University of Hawai'i Press.

Payutto, P.B. (1992), *Buddhist Economics*, trans. J.B. Dhammavijaya, Bangkok: Buddhadhamma Foundation.

Rahula, B.B. (2008), *The Buddha's Teachings on Prosperity: At Home, At Work, in the World*, Somerville, MA: Wisdom Publications.

Reader, I. (2005), *Making Pilgrimages: Meaning and Practice in Shikoku*, Honolulu: University of Hawai'i Press.

Schumacher, E.F. (1973), *Small Is Beautiful: Economics as if People Mattered*, London: Blond and Briggs.

Spiro, M.E. (1966), "Buddhism and Economic Action in Burma," *American Anthropologist*, 68: 1163–73.

UNESCO (n.d.), "World Heritage Journeys of Buddhist Heritage Sites." Available online: https://whc.unesco.org/en/activities/955/ (accessed May 15, 2020).

Walsh, M. (2007), "The Economics of Salvation: Toward a Theory of Exchange in Chines Buddhism," *Journal of the American Academy of Religion*, 75 (2): 353–82.

Winfield, P. (2018), "Why so Many Americans Think Buddhism Is Just a Philosophy," *The Conversation*, January 22. Available online: https://theconversation.com/why-so-many-americans-think-buddhism-is-just-a-philosophy-89488 (accessed May 15, 2020).

The World Bank (2020), "The World Bank in China." Available online: https://www.worldbank.org/en/country/china/overview (accessed May 15, 2020).

Yü, C. (1992), "P'u-t'o Shan: Pilgrimage and the Creation of the Chinese Potalaka," in S. Naquin and C. Yü (eds.), *Pilgrims and Sacred Sites in China*, 190–245, Berkeley: University of California Press.

Glossary Terms

Dana A term in both Pali and Sanskrit meaning "gift," "generosity," or "donation." Dana is an act of giving that is foundational in Buddhist practice. Any gift can serve as an act of *dana*, but frequently, non-ordained Buddhists (laypersons) donate robes, medicine, food, and shelter to the monastic community. Monks and nuns in turn provide sermons on the Dhamma, uphold rituals, and recite sutras for well-being. Dana provides an opportunity for practitioners to earn merit, and because of their vows, monks and nuns serve as a field of merit. Laypersons earn merit as a by-product of their generosity to the monastic community, but intentionality is important in this regard. One who gives selflessly is believed to accumulate endless merit as opposed to one who gives for self gain.

Mahayana A Sanskrit term meaning "great vehicle." It is a term used by practitioners who emphasize Sanskrit sutras that began to appear four centuries after the Buddha's death. Mahayana traditions are found in Tibet, China, South Korea, and Japan, and diverse schools make up the Mahayana branch of Buddhism. In addition to following the Pali canon, Mahayana practitioners emphasize wisdom from the Sanskrit sutras that focus on cultivating a bodhisattva path of compassion that leads toward full enlightenment and Buddhahood.

Stupa A circular structure, often including a dome-shaped structure (resembling a burial mound). Across Asia, the architecture of stupas alters because of differences in artistic representations, but in Buddhist contexts, they serve as shrines for relics. After death and cremation has occurred, if amongst someone's ashes there appears to be pearl, crystal, or bead-shaped objects, these are considered symbols of enlightenment and are housed in a stupa. Buddhists also hold on to relics such as the parts of the Buddha's body, and enshrine those in a stupa as well. Regarded as sacred sites and embodiments of enlightenment, stupas are significant locations for pilgrimage.

Theravada Literally meaning the "School of the Elders," Theravada is one of the major branches of Buddhism, tracing its history back to the third century BCE when the Indian Sthāviravāda school was established in Sri Lanka. In addition to Sri Lanka, Theravada Buddhism is prevalent in Thailand, Burma (Myanmar), Cambodia, and Laos. It emphasizes following the path of the Arhat—one who has renounced the afflictions causing rebirth and has instead cultivated the four-step path of enlightenment.

10

Socially Engaged Buddhism

Jim Deitrick

Introduction

Socially engaged Buddhism (or, simply, engaged Buddhism) came to prominence in the final decades of the twentieth century and has since come to be widely regarded as among the most significant movements in modern Buddhism. It is commonly portrayed, especially in North America, as expressive of a new, uniquely Western (or even American) form of Buddhism, a "New Vehicle" for the promulgation of Buddhism (Queen 2000: 22–6), unlocked by the "magical" or "auspicious" meeting of Buddhism and the religious and cultural traditions of the West (Gross 1993: 220). While the degree and significance of Western influence is debatable, it is impossible to conceive of engaged Buddhism without it. For this reason, the roots of socially engaged Buddhism may be traced to the nineteenth century, when Buddhist and Western religious and cultural traditions first began to make sustained contact with one another. As I will suggest below, engaged Buddhism is a product of this contact and continues to develop along lines established during this formative period.

We will work in this chapter first to place engaged Buddhism in historical perspective. We will then identify several of the people and organizations that have played prominent roles in shaping the movement. Finally, we will discuss a few of the movement's defining characteristics.

Socially Engaged Buddhism in Historical Perspective

The roots of present-day engaged Buddhism lie in the initial contacts between Asia and the West during the period of Western imperialism, especially from the nineteenth century onward. Max Weber, in his monumental *Religions of India* ([1916] 1958), was among the first scholars in the West to devote sustained effort to understanding the religious traditions of Asia and their impact on society (see Figure 10.1). His analysis of Buddhism was not only influential but also, in many ways, representative of his times. Weber's portrayal of Buddhism was not necessarily unflattering, but it did contain what amounted to an accusation, namely, that Buddhism is thoroughly "other-worldly" and hence lacks, and has lacked from its inception, the inclination to develop a social ethics. In other words, for Weber and many in the West who came after him, Buddhism is fundamentally about escaping this world, not about changing it, and thus has little relevance for life in society. According to historian Thomas A. Tweed (1992), this perception of Buddhism as lacking the kind of "activist" spirit that North Americans expect of religion was common among those who made initial contact with Buddhism during the Victorian era (1837–1901). Although some Americans were drawn to this "exotic" and "foreign" religion, most found it difficult to overcome their distaste for what they perceived as a religion lacking relevance for social life and Buddhism thus failed to make much of an impact on the lives of most Americans during these initial and subsequent years of contact.

FIGURE 10.1 *Max Weber.* Source: *Wikimedia Commons.*

Regardless of the rectitude of these early perceptions of Buddhism, it became clear by the latter part of the twentieth century that if Buddhism were to attract followers in North America, and perhaps throughout the world, it would have to address the challenge of rendering explicit its relevance for life in society and especially for large-scale social problems, such as war, poverty, oppression, and environmental degradation. It would have to show people, in other words, not only or even especially how to escape the world; it would have to show them how to respond effectively to the challenges of life in the world as well (see, e.g., Prebish 1979). While the historical roots of socially engaged Buddhism are more tangled and complex than I portray them here, the movement may, nevertheless, be usefully interpreted as so many responses to this challenge of articulating Buddhism's relevance for life in the modern world (for additional discussions of engaged Buddhism origins, see Queen 1996 and Main and Lai 2013. Main and Lai's discussion, which interprets engaged Buddhism as a response to secularism and secularization, is especially insightful).

In general, engaged Buddhism's responses to this challenge of rendering Buddhism relevant to the problems of social life have tended to fall along two lines (see Temprano 2013; Yarnall 2003). On the one hand are those, commonly from Asia, who take issue with the characterization of Buddhism as lacking social relevance. They insist that, to the contrary, Buddhism has never been as "other-worldly" as Weber paints it and has always, from its inception, been interested in applying its wisdom to the everyday affairs of this world. For them, there is nothing essentially new about today's engaged Buddhism; it is part of an ongoing tradition within Buddhism to address the suffering of the world. What is new is the way in which Buddhism is being applied specifically to the large-scale problems of life in today's world, which are themselves unprecedented. It might also be that Buddhism is learning from modern advances in science and technology to address social problems more insightfully or efficiently than before. Still, the application of Buddhism to social problems, from this perspective, is in itself nothing new. Westerners may have found it difficult to recognize the social significance of Buddhism in the past, but it has been socially significant (see Rahula 1974; Sivaraksa 1988). As Patricia Hunt-Perry and Lyn Fine (2000) put it, summarizing the teachings of Thich Nhat Hanh, "all Buddhism is engaged," and the movement thus represents nothing more than a modern iteration of an ongoing tradition of Buddhist concern for the suffering of the world.

On the other hand are those, commonly found in the West, who agree with Weber that Buddhism has historically lacked a social ethics, or at best has contained one only implicitly, and thus portray engaged Buddhist movements as novel forms of Buddhism inspired by the "auspicious" or "magical" meeting of Asian and Western cultures (Gross 1993: 220). Indeed, some have gone so far as to call engaged Buddhism "New Buddhism" (Brazier 2001) or a "Navayana" (Queen 2000), a novel and unprecedented form of Buddhism, sparked by the influence of Western ideals on Buddhism. What is new, for them, is the fact that Buddhism is now being interpreted by and made relevant to modern, Western cultures, cultures that, among other things, demand social relevance from their religions. This, in turn, is leading to novel interpretations and applications of Buddhism that are rendering the tradition explicitly relevant to social life for the first time in Buddhism's history. At best, it is argued, Buddhism has historically contained within it only an implicit social ethics; but this ethics has never (or only rarely) been fully developed or exploited in Asian contexts. Indeed, according to some proponents of this view, it is only in Western, and especially American, contexts—where freedom, justice, and equality are prized values—that these implicit teachings of Buddhism may finally be fully realized. This, it is contended, is what we see happening in socially engaged Buddhist movements in the twentieth and twenty-first centuries.

There is certainly something to both of these positions, but, unfortunately, little space to explore the implications of either here. It is not hard to see, on the one hand, how cultural biases have often prevented Western scholars from recognizing Buddhism's social relevance, which has clearly been understated by previous generations (a theme to which we will return below). On the other hand, Western influence on engaged Buddhism (even in the mere insistence on social relevance) is undeniable. If nothing else, it has led to an explicit articulation of ideas and practices that were previously invisible to Western eyes. Regardless of how new or old the application of Buddhism to social problems might be, what is clear is that the movement's explicit articulation of Buddhism's relevance for contemporary social problems and its efforts to enact this relevance in various forms of social activism are profoundly influencing the development of Buddhism in North America and around the world.

Influential Engaged Buddhist Figures and Movements

Socially engaged Buddhism consists of numerous individuals and organizations working at local, regional, national, and global levels to address social and ecological issues that likewise range from local to global significance. These individuals and movements influence one another and often work together through various organizations and networks; they are also linked together through the use of traditional media (e.g., books and periodicals) as well as more recent online communication technologies. A few of the more influential architects of engaged Buddhism and of the organizations that support its activities are identified here. Of course, this discussion is necessarily selective and important figures and movements will unavoidably be neglected.

Certainly no one has been more influential on engaged Buddhism in North America than Vietnamese **Zen** (*Thien*) Buddhist monk, Thich Nhat Hanh, who is credited with coining the term "engaged Buddhism" in the 1960s as he worked to address the turmoil ravaging his country (see Figure 10.2). Nhat Hanh was, of course, indelibly influenced by his experiences in Vietnam during the war and his efforts have focused ever since on achieving peace, in ourselves and the world, through Buddhist **mindfulness** practices. He is the founder of the Order of Interbeing, a new "engaged" Buddhist order comprised of both lay and monastic practitioners. He has also established monastic communities and dharma centers in France and various parts of the United States, including California, New York, and Mississippi. Nhat Hanh's influence is perhaps felt most profoundly, however, through the dozens of books he has published on engaged Buddhism that have been positively received by millions of readers worldwide. Indeed, Parallax Press, founded by Nhat Hanh in 1986 to disseminate his ideas, is among the most significant publishers of engaged Buddhist writings in the world. Significantly, Nhat Hanh is also credited with having influenced Martin Luther King Jr. to oppose the war in Vietnam, who, in turn, nominated Nhat Hanh for the Nobel Peace Prize in 1967.

FIGURE 10.2 *Thich Nhat Hanh*. Source: *Duc via Wikimedia Commons.*

At least equally influential, not only on engaged Buddhism but on Buddhism more generally, and not only in North America but also around the world, Tenzin Gyatso, the fourteenth Dalai Lama, leader of the Tibetan Gelugpa Buddhist sect and widely recognized leader of the Tibetan people in exile (see Figure 10.3). Like Nhat Hanh, the Dalai Lama has spent most of his life in exile where he has also worked to address the suffering of the Tibetan people, and others around the world, from a Buddhist perspective. Also, like Nhat Hanh, he has influenced countless millions with his many speeches, appearances, and publications through which he articulates a vision of nonviolence that most engaged Buddhists take as axiomatic (see, e.g., Dalai Lama 2001, 2011). And, once more, like Nhat Hanh, he was nominated for the Nobel Peace Prize, an award that he then went on to receive in 1989.

FIGURE 10.3 *Tenzin Gyatso, the fourteenth Dalai Lama.* Source: *Christopher via Wikimedia Commons.*

Other influential global figures and movements include A.T. Ariyaratne, founder of the Sri Lankan Sarvodaya community development movement, which has served as a model of engaged Buddhist community development programs around the world; Sulak Sivaraksa, founder of the International Network of Engaged Buddhists (INEB), one of the key global networks of engaged Buddhists; Daisaku Ikeda, President of Soka Gakkai International, which under Ikeda's leadership has become increasingly defined by its commitment of engaged Buddhism and, like the INEB, serves as one of the key networks linking engaged Buddhists on a global scale; and Cheng Yen, Taiwanese Buddhist nun and founder of the Tzu Chi Foundation, yet another of the key organizations that link engaged Buddhists and their activities globally (see Figure 10.4). The writings of the UK's Ken Jones (1989, 1994, and 2003) have also exerted significant influence, as has the Buddhist-inspired *Small Is Beautiful* economics of the German-born economist E.F. Schumacher (1975). Others could be mentioned, as well, and we would be remiss if we did not make explicit mention of Mohandas K. Gandhi's vision of nonviolent social change, the influence of which on so many of these and other engaged Buddhist figures and movements is incalculable. Suffice it to say that the global influences on engaged Buddhism in North America are many and diverse.

In North America, several figures and organizations stand out as significant in their influence. Pride of place probably should go to Robert and Anne Aitken, Nelson Foster, and the others who gathered with them in 1978 to found the Buddhist Peace Fellowship

FIGURE 10.4 *Volunteers from the Tzu Chi Foundation help flood victims in New Jersey.* Source: *FEMA photo library via Wikimedia Commons.*

(BPF), the oldest engaged Buddhist organization in the United States. Robert Aitken's writings have been influential on American Buddhism generally (see, especially, Aitken 1984) and the BPF serves as one of the most important organizations linking engaged Buddhists in North America. While the initial aim of the BPF was simply "to bring a Buddhist perspective to the peace movement, and to bring the peace movement to the Buddhist community" (Rothberg 1998: 270), its concerns have since expanded to include environmental and social justice concerns, as well. Perhaps its most important role over the years has been in linking people together and disseminating the ideas of engaged Buddhism through its various publications.

Joanna Macy's "Work That Reconnects" workshops (aka "Despair and Empowerment," "Deep Ecology," and "Active Hope" workshops) use Buddhist meditative techniques to help participants transform the feelings of despair that arise in connection with the problems of life in today's world into "constructive, collaborative action" (Macy and Johnstone 2012: 271; see also Macy and Brown 2014). According to Macy's website, these workshops have "helped countless thousands of people around the globe find solidarity and courage to act despite rapidly worsening social and ecological conditions" (Macy n.d.). Macy, a charter member of the BPF, has also written a number of influential books that have helped provide a theoretical basis for engaged Buddhism and its activities (see, especially, 1983, 1991). Macy (1991) is also among those, for instance Judith Simmer-Brown (2002) and, especially, Rita M. Gross (1993, 1996, 2009), whose writings have helped to steer engaged Buddhism in North America toward issues of sex and gender and to make work for justice in this area one of North American engaged Buddhism's central concerns (see also Dresser 1996).

One of the most innovative architects of American engaged Buddhism is Zen Buddhist Bernard Tetsugen Glassman Roshi, who along with his wife, Sandra Jishu Holmes Roshi, founded, the Greyston Foundation (which began as the Greyston Bakery) in 1982 and the Zen Peacemakers (formerly, the Zen Peacemaker Order) in 1996 (see Figure 10.5). Both are complex organizations that link diverse, innovative projects and activities, including "street retreats" or "homeless *sesshins*" and pilgrimages to the Nazi death camp at Auschwitz-Birkenau. These and similar activities allow their participants to "bear witness" to the world's suffering and are seen by Glassman as a kind of *koan* practice in which participants are able to become one with the problems they are working to solve. Like the other influential architects of engaged Buddhism mentioned here, Glassman has published several books through which his ideas have been disseminated (Glassman 1998; Glassman and Fields 1996).

Other influential North Americans include scholar-practitioners Christopher S. Queen (Queen 1996, 2000; Queen and King 1996; Queen, Prebish, and Keown 2003), Kenneth Kraft (1988, 1992), Donald Rothberg (2006), Stephanie Kaza (2019a, b), and Sallie B. King (2005, 2009), whose writings have not only contributed to our knowledge about engaged Buddhism but have also helped to shape the movement, both through their efforts to define the movement and through their criticisms. As with Gandhi, the influence of Martin Luther King Jr. and his commitment to nonviolence is also ever-present. As above, we are reminded that the sources of engaged Buddhism are many

FIGURE 10.5 *Bernard Glassman.* Source: *Stephanie Young Merzel via Wikimedia Commons.*

and complex. For this reason, it can be difficult to talk about the movement in general terms. Nevertheless, this is the task to which we now turn as we work to understand what it is that defines engaged Buddhism, especially as it is developing in the North American context.

Defining Traits of Socially Engaged Buddhism

The theoretical backbone of engaged Buddhism is the notion that all things are "interrelated" or "interdependent." Engaged Buddhists give expression to this concept through their foundational appropriation of the Buddhist teaching of *pratitya samutpada* or dependent arising. For Macy, **interdependence** is "the central doctrine" of Buddhism and is "essential" for the elucidation of engaged Buddhist social principles (1991: 53; 1988: 170). Kraft likewise identifies the doctrine of interrelatedness as "the touchstone" of engaged Buddhism, "a vision of interdependence, in which the universe is experienced as an organic whole, every 'part' affecting every other 'part'" (1988: xiii).

Aptly, the movement's other teachings and practices relate to and derive from this cardinal notion. Among the most important of these is a rejection of "dualistic" ways of thinking, which issues in, among other things, a thoroughly this-worldly focus. As Queen notes, "the most distinctive shift of thinking in socially engaged Buddhism [in contrast to more traditional forms of Asian Buddhism] is from a transmundane (lokuttara) to a mundane (*lokiya*) definition of liberation" (1996: 11). In other words, the traditional Buddhist goal of liberation from suffering is reinterpreted by engaged Buddhists as a this-worldly liberation from this-worldly suffering. As Queen notes, this represents a significant reinterpretation of Buddhist suffering and liberation, occasioned, as he sees it, by Buddhism's encounter with the West (20).

In keeping with these notions of interrelatedness and **nondualism**, engaged Buddhists commonly assert that we humans are related to the world in such an intimate way that it is appropriate to regard it as an extension of ourselves. Macy refers to this extended, universal self as the "eco-self." According to Macy, as a "nondualistic spirituality," Buddhism "undermines categorical distinctions between self and other and belies the concept of a continuous, self-existent entity. It then goes farther [...] in showing the pathogenic character of any reifications of the self [...]. What the Buddha woke up to under the Bodhi tree was the *paticca samuppada*, the co-arising of phenomena, in which you cannot isolate a separate, continuous self" (1990: 60). In short, for engaged Buddhists, self and world comprise together an ever evolving and organic whole wherein what affects the one, ipso facto affects the other.

From the notion of the interrelatedness of self and world, engaged Buddhists have construed several styles of social activism that are often regarded as distinguishing the movement from other religious and secular social activist movements. This distinctiveness is seen as rooted in the conviction that "social work entails inner work, that social change and inner change are inseparable" (Kraft 1992: 12). For Queen, work directed toward outer as well as inner peace is the most distinguishing characteristic of the movement (1996: 5).

Exactly what it means to say that social change and inner change are inseparable is debated among engaged Buddhists and there is not space here to consider in detail the various ways in which engaged Buddhists interpret this idea. In general, the movement is torn between those who regard personal, "spiritual" work as enough to bring about desired social change—as the effects of personal betterment ripple outward to the rest of society—and those who believe that spiritual work must be coupled with overt social and/or political activism of some sort. Patricia Marx Ellsberg, for instance, responding to her experiences at a retreat with Thich Nhat Hanh, complains that she found herself "uncomfortable with what [she] perceived to be an underlying premise of the retreat: that if enough individuals change, society will change." For Ellsberg and others in the movement, "society is not merely an aggregate of individuals. It is also shaped by social structures and concentrations of power" (1996: 240). It is not enough, therefore, according to these practitioners, to better oneself; one must also work overtly in the world to transform the social and political structures that lead to suffering.

Whether one chooses to work toward personal betterment alone as a means of transforming society or in conjunction with social service and/or political activism, there is almost unanimous agreement among engaged Buddhists that it must be pursued nonviolently. Indeed, for King, "engaged Buddhism is by definition nonviolent" (2009: 3). Again, the grounds for **nonviolence** are the belief that all things are interrelated, that means cannot be separated from ends. Nonviolence is also rooted in the self-interested notion that in harming others, one is literally harming oneself as others are interrelated extensions of the self.

Similarly, engaged Buddhists commonly argue that we are all "co-responsible" for the goods, as well as the evils, of social life. According to Kraft, "awareness of interconnectedness fosters a sense of universal responsibility" (1988: xvi). In like manner, Robert Aitken argues that we must "take responsibility for all beings and all things" (1988: 89). This theme is also elaborated upon by Rothberg who suggests that "understandings of interdependence and the interconnection inner and outer" leads to an assumption of "coresponsibility with others for the state of things, recognizing in particular that problems cannot simply be attributed to others, to scapegoats or to those who are somehow 'bad' or 'evil'" (1998: 64). As we have already seen, many engaged Buddhists thus stress the corporate dynamics of social evils, and encourage everyone, not only to notice their own complicity in the structures of social and environmental oppression, but also to take responsibility for correcting them (see Figure 10.6).

Another crucial aspect of engaged Buddhism derived from its teaching of interrelatedness is the widespread notion, found throughout North American Buddhism, that the "hierarchical" and "dualistic" Buddhist social structures inherited from Asia are not appropriate for the American sangha. Gross explains,

> In terms of the formal, traditional distinction between monastic and lay Buddhists, most Western Buddhists are lay practitioners, in that we have not taken vows that imply celibacy and renunciation of family and occupation. However, that affiliation as lay Buddhist practitioners does not have the simplicity and finality for us American lay Buddhists as it does for most classical Asian patterns of Buddhism, nor does it limit us to the same peripheral role of supporting monastics as it does in most forms of Asian Buddhism. Most of us see ourselves as trying to engage in full-fledged Buddhist practice as lay people who also have some involvement in family and some responsibility in livelihood—an ideal that would seem preposterous in many forms of Asian Buddhism.
>
> (1996: 134)

Many North American engaged Buddhists see this drive to democratize their institutions as occurring under the influence of mainstream American values. Interestingly, others understand this tendency as arising not from inherited American values, but from the core of Buddhist philosophy itself. Several have argued, for instance, that the hierarchy of Asian Buddhist institutions derives not from Buddhism, but from the cultures in which Buddhism has traditionally flourished. These "hierarchical" and "patriarchal" cultures, it is argued, have effectively stifled Buddhism's inherent cosmological egalitarianism for 2,500 years, an egalitarianism that may now be instituted in the West with its commitment to equality and justice. For Gross, therefore, Buddhism's arrival in America marks an "auspicious" occasion in which Buddhism's inherent democratic ideal can finally be realized. Such ideas are, at the very least, debatable and may even be expressive of an ethnocentric bias that runs throughout North American Buddhism (see Mitchell 2016: ch. 10, for a helpful discussion of race and identity in North American Buddhism).

Other engaged Buddhists have gone even further than leveling distinctions between monastics and the laity. As noted above, engaged Buddhism's focus on the interrelatedness of all phenomena has led to an extension of the notion of the self and of self-interest to include the entirety of reality. This has led in some instances to a leveling of the distinctions between human and nonhuman life, and even between living and nonliving matter. Joan Halifax and Bill Devall, for example, have each argued that the Buddhist sangha ought to be expanded to include, among other things, "other species, plant and animal, as well as environmental features and unseen ancestors and spirits" (Halifax 1990: 22). This "ecocentric sangha," or what poet Gary Snyder poetically calls "Great Earth Sangha" (Barnhill 1998), must therefore take into account the "rights of other species" (Devall 1990: 158) and even inanimate objects. The sangha is not to be limited solely to monastics or even humans, or further, even to sentient beings; all of reality is the sangha and every identifiable aspect of that reality—be it animal, plant, ecosystem, planet, or solar system—has an equal place within that sangha, the universal Buddhist ecological community. As would be expected, these ideas are typically coupled with involvement in environmental preservation and activist movements.

Finally, some engaged Buddhists, such as the Dalai Lama, work to transcend even the distinctions between Buddhism and other religions, suggesting that it is not necessary to be a Buddhist per se, to practice the essential teachings of engaged Buddhism

FIGURE 10.6 *Engaged Buddhists gather for "Work That Reconnects" at the Buddhafield Festival.* Source: *Akuppa / Creative Commons.*

(Dalai Lama 2011). Engaged Buddhists are thus active in interfaith dialogue and other ecumenical movements. Indeed, a flourishing discussion has emerged during the early part of the twenty-first century among engaged Buddhists and proponents of Christian Liberation Theology, a movement that has much in common with engaged Buddhism (see, e.g., King 2016; Knitter 2016; Largen 2016; and Willis 2017). It is also worth noting that the Buddhist Peace Fellowship is an affiliate of the ecumenical, but predominantly Protestant, Fellowship of Reconciliation.

In summary, we might suggest that engaged Buddhism is best defined by its innovativeness, even as questions about the nature and extent of this innovativeness remain. Notably, these innovations sometimes lead critics to wonder how consistent the teachings and practices are with more traditional understandings of the religion (e.g., Blum 2009; Deitrick 2003; and Keown 2012). As we have already seen, engaged Buddhists insist on the legitimacy of their interpretations, often claiming to uncover the Buddha's "original intention" (Brazier 2001: back cover). Macy argues, for instance, that engaged Buddhism "represents not so much a departure from tradition as a return to the early teachings of its founder and a reclamation of their original meaning" (1983: 76). For Kraft, "qualities that were inhibited in pre-modern Asian settings [...] can now be actualized through Buddhism's exposure to the West, where ethical sensitivity, social activism, and egalitarianism are emphasized" (1988: xii–xiii).

As suggested above, the degree to which these qualities have been "inhibited" by premodern Asian cultures is debatable, as is the claim among engaged Buddhists to have recovered the Buddha's "original meaning." Indeed, Amod Lele's (2019) historically grounded defense of "disengaged Buddhism," namely, forms of Buddhism that deliberately remain aloof from politics and social engagement, should at least raise doubts, as should the many critiques of "Orientalist" influence on the discipline of Buddhist Studies to appear in recent decades (for a formative and influential presentation of such critiques, see Lopez 1995).

At the same time, we should be careful not to overstate engaged Buddhism's innovativeness. Questions about how new or old Buddhism is, as they have been addressed among engaged Buddhist scholars, often seem to have more to do with how "authentic" the tradition is and who has the authority to speak for it than with understanding it objectively. For some, as Yarnall suggests, "new" means improved and "old" is corrupt and outdated. For others, "new" means illegitimate and "old" is authoritative and true. In any event, these are not questions for us to decide, they belong to the Buddhists who comprise the tradition and thus define it. Our questions have to do instead with the particular ways in which engaged Buddhism is both new and old and thus represents a modern iteration of ancient religious tradition. Indeed, the key to understanding all new movements and their places in the histories of which they are a part is in understanding the particular ways in which they are both continuous with their pasts and transformed by their present circumstances. For students of engaged Buddhism, this remains the central question.

Conclusion

While the future is, of course, open, engaged Buddhism has already left an indelible impression on Buddhism, an impression that is sure to affect all subsequent developments. At this point, it would seem that the expectation of social relevance is becoming the norm in North American Buddhism, and perhaps also globally. While it may not be practically true that "all Buddhism is socially engaged," the explicit articulation of Buddhism's relevance for the social and ecological problems is becoming definitive of much of Buddhism as it is developing around the world. For this reason, however, we answer the questions raised above, engaged Buddhism's significance is hard to overestimate and the movement undoubtedly deserves the attention it has enjoyed among scholars and practitioners in the latter years of the twentieth and early years of the twenty-first centuries.

Further Reading and Online Resources

Chappell, D.W., ed. (1999), *Buddhist Peacework: Creating Cultures of Peace*, Boston: Wisdom Publications.

Kaza, S. and K. Kraft, eds. (2000), *Dharma Rain: Sources of Buddhist Environmentalism*, Boston: Shambala Publications.

King, S.B. (2009), *Socially Engaged Buddhism*, Honolulu: University of Hawaii Press.

Queen, C.S., ed. (2000), *Engaged Buddhism in the West*, Boston: Wisdom Publications.

Queen, C.S., C. Prebish, and D. Keown, eds. (2003), *Action Dharma: New Studies in Engaged Buddhism*, New York: Routledge Curzon.

References

Aitken, R. (1984), *The Mind of Clover: Essays in Zen Buddhist Ethics*, New York: North Point Press.

Aitken, R. (1988), "Gandhi, Dogen, and Deep Ecology," in F. Eppsteiner (ed.), *The Path of Compassion: Writings on Socially Engaged Buddhism*, 86–92, Berkeley, CA: Parallax Press.

Barnhill, D. (1998), "Great Earth Sangha: Gary Snyder's View of Nature as Community," in M.E. Tucker and D.R. Williams (eds.), *Buddhism and Ecology: The Interconnection of Dharma and Deeds*, 187–217, Cambridge, MA: Harvard University Press.

Blum, M. (2009), "The Transcendental Ghost in EcoBuddhism," in N. Bhushan, J.L. Garfield, and A. Zablocki (eds.), *TransBuddhism: Transmission, Translation, Transformation*, 209–38, Amherst: University of Massachusetts Press.

Brazier, D. (2001), *The New Buddhism*, New York: Palgrave.

Dalai, Lama (2001), *Ethics for a New Millennium*, New York: Riverhead Books.

Dalai, Lama (2011), *Beyond Religion: Ethics for a Whole World*, Boston: Houghton Mifflin Harcourt.

Deitrick, J.E. (2003), "Engaged Buddhist Ethics: Mistaking the Boat for the Shore," in Q.S. Queen, C. Prebish, and D. Keown (eds.), *Action Dharma: New Studies in Engaged Buddhism*, 252–69, New York: Routledge Curzon.

Devall, B. (1990), "Ecocentric Sangha," in A.H. Badiner (ed.), *Dharma Gaia: A Harvest of Essays in Buddhism and Ecology*, 155–64, Berkeley, CA: Parallax Press.
Dresser, M., ed. (1996), *Buddhist Women on the Edge: Contemporary Perspective's from the Western Frontier*, Berkeley, CA: North Atlantic Books.
Ellsberg, P.M. (1996), "The Five Precepts and Social Change," in A. Kotler (ed.), *Engaged Buddhist Reader: Ten Years of Engaged Buddhist Publishing*, 240–2, Berkeley, CA: Parallax Press.
Glassman, B. (1998), *Bearing Witness: A Zen Master's Lessons in Making Peace*, New York: Bell Tower.
Glassman, B. and R. Fields (1996), *Instructions to the Cook: A Zen Master's Lessons in Living a Life That Matters*, Boston: Shambala Publications.
Gross, R.M. (1993), *Buddhism after Patriarchy: A Feminist History, Analysis, and Reconstruction of Buddhism*, Albany: State University of New York Press.
Gross, R.M. (1996), "Community, Work, Relationship, and Family: Renunciation and Balance in American Buddhist Practice," in M. Dresser (ed.), *Buddhist Women on the Edge: Contemporary Perspective's from the Western Frontier*, 133–50, Berkeley, CA: North Atlantic Books.
Gross, R.M. (2009), *A Garland of Feminist Reflections: Forty Years of Religious Exploration*, Berkeley: University of California Press.
Halifax, J. (1990), "The Third Body: Buddhism, Shamanism, and Deep Ecology," in A.H. Badiner (ed.), *Dharma Gaia: A Harvest of Essays in Buddhism and Ecology*, 20–38, Berkeley, CA: Parallax Press.
Hunt-Perry, P. and L. Fine (2000), "All Buddhism Is Engaged: Thich Nhat Hanh and the Order of Interbeing," in C.S. Queen (ed.), *Engaged Buddhism in the West*, 35–66, Boston: Wisdom Publications.
Jones, K. (1989), *The Social Face of Buddhism: An Approach to Political and Social Activism*, Boston: Wisdom Publications.
Jones, K. (1994), *Beyond Optimism: A Buddhist Political Ecology*, Charlbury: Jon Carpenter Publishing.
Jones, K. (2003), *The New Social Face of Buddhism: A Call to Action*, Boston: Wisdom Publications.
Kaza, S. (2019a), *Conversations with Trees: An Intimate Ecology*, updated edn., Boston: Shambala Publications.
Kaza, S. (2019b), *Green Buddhism: Practice and Compassionate Action in Uncertain Times*, Boston: Shambala Publications.
Keown, D. (2012), "Buddhist Ethics: A Critique," in D.L. McMahan (ed.), *Buddhism in the Modern World*, 215–31, New York: Routledge.
King, S.B. (2005), *Being Benevolence: The Social Ethics of Engaged Buddhism*, Honolulu: University of Hawaii Press.
King, S.B. (2009), *Socially Engaged Buddhism*, Honolulu: University of Hawaii Press.
King, S.B. (2016), "Through the Eyes of Auschwitz and the Killing Fields: Mutual Learning between Engaged Buddhism and Liberation Theology," *Buddhist-Christian Studies*, 36: 55–67.
Knitter, P.F. (2016), "Liberation Theology and Engaged Buddhism: Challenging Each Other, Learning from Each Other," *Buddhist-Christian Studies*, 36: 97–108.
Kraft, K. (1988), "Engaged Buddhism: An Introduction," in F. Eppsteiner (ed.), *The Path of Compassion: Writings on Socially Engaged Buddhism*, xi–xviii, Berkeley, CA: Parallax Press.
Kraft, K. (1992), *Inner Peace, World Peace: Essays on Buddhism and Nonviolence*, Albany: State University of New York Press.

Largen, K.J. (2016), "Introduction to Liberation Theology and Engaged Buddhism," *Buddhist-Christian Studies*, 36: 51–3.

Lele, A. (2019), "Disengaged Buddhism," *Journal of Buddhist Ethics*, 26: 239–89.

Lopez, D.S., Jr., ed. (1995), *Curators of the Buddha: The Study of Buddhism under Colonialism*, Chicago: University of Chicago Press.

Macy, J. (1983), *Dharma and Development: Religion as Resource in the Sarvodaya Self-Help Movement*, West Hartford, CT: Kumarian Press.

Macy, J. (1988), "In Indra's Net: Sarvodaya and Our Mutual Efforts for Peace," in F. Eppsteiner (ed.), *The Path of Compassion: Writings on Socially Engaged Buddhism*, 170–81, Berkeley, CA: Parallax Press.

Macy, J. (1990), "The Greening of the Self," in A.H. Badiner (ed.), *Dharma Gaia: A Harvest of Essays in Buddhism and Ecology*, 53–63, Berkeley, CA: Parallax Press.

Macy, J. (1991), *World as Lover, World as Self*, Berkeley, CA: Parallax Press.

Macy, J. (n.d.), "Joanne Macy." Available online: https://www.joannamacy.net/ (accessed September 29, 2020).

Macy, J. and M.Y. Brown (2014), *Coming Back to Life: The Updated Guide to Work That Reconnects*, rev. edn., Gabriola Island, BC: New Society Publishers.

Macy, J. and C. Johnstone (2012), *Active Hope: How to Face the Mess We're in without Going Crazy*, Novato, CA: New World Library.

Main, J.L. and R. Lai (2013), "Reformulating 'Socially Engaged Buddhism' as an Analytical Category," *The Eastern Buddhist*, 44 (2): 1–34.

Mitchell S.A. (2016), *Buddhism in America: Global Religion, Local Contexts*, London: Bloombury Academic.

Prebish, C.S. (1979), *American Buddhism*, North Scituate, MA: Duxbury Press.

Queen, C.S. (1996), "Introduction: The Shapes and Sources of Engaged Buddhism," in C.S. Queen and S.B. King (eds.), *Engaged Buddhism: Buddhist Liberation Movements in Asia*, 1–44, Albany: State University of New York Press.

Queen, C.S. (2000), "Introduction: A New Buddhism," in C.S. Queen (ed.), *Engaged Buddhism in the West*, 1–31, Boston: Wisdom Publications.

Queen, C.S. and S.B. King, eds. (1996), *Engaged Buddhism: Buddhist Liberation Movements in Asia*, Albany: State University of New York Press.

Queen, C.S., C. Prebish, and D. Keown, eds. (2003), *Action Dharma: New Studies in Engaged Buddhism*, London: Routledge Curzon.

Rahula, W. (1974), *What the Buddha Taught*, New York: Grove Press.

Rothberg, D. (1998), "Responding to the Cries of the World: Socially Engaged Buddhism in North America," in C.S. Prebish and K.K. Tanaka (eds.), *The Faces of Buddhism in America*, 266–86, Berkeley: University of California Press.

Rothberg, D. (2006), *The Engaged Spiritual Life: A Buddhist Approach to Transforming Ourselves and the World*, Boston: Beacon Press.

Schumacher, E.F. (1975), *Small Is Beautiful: A Study of Economics As if People Mattered*, New York: Harper & Row.

Simmer-Brown, J. (2002), *Dakini's Warm Breath: The Feminine Principle in Tibetan Buddhism*, Boston: Shambala Publications.

Sivaraksas, S. (1988), "Buddhism in a World of Change," in F. Eppsteiner (ed.), *The Path of Compassion: Writings on Socially Engaged Buddhism*, 9–18, Berkeley, CA: Parallax Press.

Temprano, V.G. (2013), "Defining Engaged Buddhism: Traditionists, Modernists, and Scholastic Power," *Buddhist Studies Review*, 30 (2): 261–74.

Tweed, T.A. (1992), *The American Encounter with Buddhism: 1844–1912*, Bloomington: Indiana University Press.

Weber, M. ([1916] 1958), *The Religions of India*, Glencoe, IL: The Free Press.
Willis, G.R. (2017), "Abandon All Hope of Fruition: Critical Notes on Engaged Buddhism," *Buddhist-Christian Studies*, 37: 247–56.
Yarnall, T.F. (2003), "Engaged Buddhism: New and Improved? Made in the U.S. of Asian Materials," in Q.S. Queen, C. Prebish, and D. Keown (eds.), *Action Dharma: New Studies in Engaged Buddhism*, 286–344, New York: Routledge Curzon.

Glossary Terms

Interdependence One of the many ways in which the Buddhist teaching of *pratitya samutpada* is translated into English. For contemporary engaged Buddhists, the idea serves, along with the complementary idea of *shunaya*, or "emptiness," as the Buddha's most basic insight and the foundation of the movement's socially engaged ethics. The teaching implies the interrelatedness of all phenomena and, hence, the mutual dependence of the self on all the various aspects of the external world. Taken together, self and world comprise an ever evolving and organic whole wherein what affects the one, ipso facto affects the other. Insight into the interdependence of all phenomena thus leads, for engaged Buddhists, not only to awakened insight but also to compassionate behavior toward all the interdependent aspects of what Joanna Macy calls the "eco-self."

Mindfulness A form of meditation taught by the Buddha as leading to insight into the nature of suffering and its release. In Pali (*sati*) and Sanskrit (*smirti*), the word derives from the root "to remember," with the implication not of remembering the past but of concentrating or remembering to focus one's awareness on the present. As such, mindfulness meditation involves paying careful attention to mental and physical processes as they arise and cease so as to gain insight into the impermanence and interdependence of all things. Essential to the practice of mindfulness is not simply the act of paying attention but doing so nonjudgmentally, so as not to impose meaning on the world but, rather, to allow it to appear to consciousness as it is.

Nondualism Literally "not-two," is sometimes regarded as an implication of the Buddha's teaching of interdependence, at least as interpreted among many contemporary engaged Buddhists who are, in turn, influenced by certain strains of Mahayana Buddhist thought. On the one hand, this teaching is taken to mean that nirvana and samsara are identical, and thus, that the salvation taught by Buddhism is not to be had in some transcendent reality but here, in a world transformed by the Buddha's teachings. At the same time, the teaching is taken as referring to the identity of the self and world as interdependent aspects of a single, non-dual reality. Finally, the teaching may be seen as alluding to one's own identity with the Buddha and one's own potential for Buddhahood.

Nonviolence (ahimsa) Literally "not harming" or "nonviolence," is a key ethical concept for Indian religions, in general, and the first of Buddhism's Five Precepts or Basic Rules of Moral Conduct. Basically, the precept prohibits intentionally causing harm to any sentient being, namely, any being capable of experiencing suffering, including animals. Conversely, the precept is often taken positively to enjoin compassionate behavior toward all beings. Among contemporary engaged Buddhists, the precept is commonly seen as rooted in the Buddhist teaching of *pratitya samutpada* or interdependence where acting harmfully toward others is regarded, implicitly, as also acting harmfully toward oneself.

Zen A form of Mahayana Buddhism that originated in China, where it is known as Ch'an; from China, it spread first to Korea and Japan, and, by the beginning of the twenty-first century, around the world. The word itself derives from the Sanskrit "dhyana," which implies intense concentration and is most commonly translated into English as "trance" or "meditation." Accordingly, this form of Buddhism emphasizes the practice of meditation as a means for gaining direct experience of the truth of Buddhism and, hence, of one's own Buddha-nature. Zen is, so far, among the most popular forms of Buddhism to take root in North America.

Index